Ancient Greece

Ancient Greece

Volume 1

Achaean League — Dorian Invasion of Greece
1-338

Edited by
Thomas J. Sienkewicz
Monmouth College, Illinois

SALEM PRESS, INC.
Pasadena, California   Hackensack, New Jersey

Cover image: Michael Palis/Dreamstime.com

Some essays originally appeared in *Great Events from History: The Ancient World, Prehistory-476 C.E.* (2004), *Great Lives from History: The Ancient World, Prehistory-476 C.E.* (2004), *Cyclopedia of World Authors, Fourth Revised Edition* (2004), *Encyclopedia of the Ancient World* (2002), *Weapons and Warfare* (2002), and *Magill's Guide to Military History* (2001). New essays and other material have been added.

Library of Congress Cataloging-in-Publication Data

Ancient Greece / edited by Thomas J. Sienkewicz.
    p. cm. — (Magill's choice)
    Includes bibliographical references and index.
    ISBN-13: 978-1-58765-281-3 (set : alk. paper)
    ISBN-13: 978-1-58765-282-0 (vol. 1 : alk. paper)
    ISBN-10: 1-58765-281-1 (set : alk. paper)
    ISBN-10: 1-58765-282-X (vol. 1 : alk. paper)
    [etc.]
    1. Greece—History—To 146 B.C. 2. Greece—History—146 B.C.-323 A.D.
I. Sienkewicz, Thomas J. II. Series.

    DF214.A49 2007
    938.003—dc22

                                                        2006016525

PRINTED IN CANADA

Contents

CONTENTS

Publisher's Note

Ancient Greek civilization—the heroic tales of Homer and the philosophical musings of Plato, the bloody Peloponnesian Wars between Athens and Sparta and the vast empire of Alexander the Great—served as the touchstone for much of Western history that followed. *Ancient Greece* is a three-volume, A-Z survey of Greek history and culture from its earliest archaeological remains until the Battle of Actium in 31 B.C.E., when Greek civilization merged with Roman to become Greco-Roman civilization, that is sure to fascinate students and general readers of all ages.

The 315 essays in this work range in length from 1 to 8 pages. They include general overviews of such topics as art and architecture, daily life and customs, education and training, government and law, language and dialects, literature, medicine and health, mythology, the performing arts, philosophy, religion and ritual, science, sports and entertainment, warfare, and women's life. Biographical entries cover statesmen, military leaders, artists, writers, scientists, and philosophers. Descriptive entries examine types of literature, battles, and philosophical movements.

By design, Magill's Choice reference sets compile and update previously published material from Salem Press in order to produce affordable and useful works. *Ancient Greece* brings together relevant essays from six different sets: *Great Events from History: The Ancient World, Prehistory-476 C.E.* (2004), *Great Lives from History: The Ancient World, Prehistory-476 C.E.* (2004), *Cyclopedia of World Authors, Fourth Revised Edition* (2004), *Encyclopedia of the Ancient World* (2002), *Weapons and Warfare* (2002), and *Magill's Guide to Military History* (2001). For each of these essays, the bibliography was brought up to date with the latest sources. In addition, 29 essays were newly commissioned specifically for *Ancient Greece*, making the work the only comprehensive source on this subject matter from Salem Press.

Each biographical essay in the set identifies the figure's field of accomplishment, such as "Playwright" or "Statesman." Entries on rulers also provide locations and date ranges, such as "King of Seleucid Dynasty (r. 223-187 B.C.E.)." The best information about year and place of birth and death is provided; in some cases, only the century in when an individual flourished is known. Each topical essay begins with a brief summary and provides information on date and locale, where applicable. Every entry, both biographical and topical, then identifies one or more categories in which the essay belongs:

- agriculture
- art and architecture
- astronomy and cosmology
- cities and civilizations
- daily life
- economics
- education
- expansion and land acquisition
- geography
- government and politics
- historic sites
- historiography
- language
- law
- literature
- mathematics
- medicine
- military
- music
- oratory and rhetoric
- organizations and institutions
- philosophy
- poetry
- religion and mythology
- scholarship
- science and technology
- sports
- theater and drama
- trade and commerce
- treaties and diplomacy
- wars and battles
- women

The main text of each essay includes a phonetic rendering of the name of the profiled figure or topic on the first mention, such as (EHS-kih-neez) for Aeschines; a Key to Pronunciation is provided at the beginning of each volume. Biographical essays include subheadings called "Life" and "Influence." Most entries on topics offer the sections "Summary" and "Significance." Longer overviews use topical subheadings to guide readers through the text. All essays end with a "Further Reading" section of additional resources, an author byline, and "See also" cross-references directing readers to related entries within *Ancient Greece*.

At the beginning of all three volumes are a Complete List of Contents, the Key to Pronunciation, and three maps showing ancient Greece from different periods: the seventh century B.C.E., during the Archaic Age; the fifth century B.C.E., during the Classical Age; and 185 B.C.E., during the Hellenistic Age. At the end of volume 3 are six appendixes: a Time Line of important events from 2600 to 31 B.C.E.; a Glossary of more than 150 terms; a Bibliography of helpful sources; a list of Web Sites about ancient Greece; a list of Literary Works arranged by author; and an annotated list of Historic Sites, including Web sites.

Three indexes provide multiple access to the text: a Category Index, a Personages Index of people discussed in the entries, and a comprehensive Subject Index of concepts, names, titles, and places. In addition, the set is fully illustrated with more than 150 photographs, lists, tables, maps, and other useful sidebars to help bring ancient Greece to life.

We would like to thank our Editor, Thomas J. Sienkewicz, the Minnie Billings Capron Professor of Classics at Monmouth College, for his invaluable expertise. Our gratitude is also extended to the outstanding scholars who contributed material to this work; a list of their names and affiliations follows.

Contributors

Linda Perry Abrams
Bob Jones University

Amy Ackerberg-Hastings
Iowa State University

Patrick Adcock
Henderson State University

Richard Adler
University of Michigan-Dearborn

James A. Arieti
Hampden-Sydney College

O. Kimball Armayor
University of Alabama

Richard Badessa
University of Louisville

Rozmeri Basic
University of Oklahoma

Barbara C. Beattie
Independent Scholar

Evelyn E. Bell
San Jose State University

Milton Berman
University of Rochester

Richard M. Berthold
Independent Scholar

Nicholas Birns
New School University

Robert G. Blake
Elon University

Denvy A. Bowman
Coastal Carolina University

John Buckler
University of Illinois

Jeffrey L. Buller
Mary Baldwin College

Kenneth L. Burres
Central Methodist College

Joan B. Burton
Trinity University

Joseph P. Byrne
Belmont University

Richard C. Carrier
Columbia University

James T. Chambers
Texas Christian University

Craige B. Champion
Allegheny College

Paul J. Chara, Jr.
Northwestern College

Frederick B. Chary
Indiana University Northwest

Mark W. Chavalas
University of Wisconsin—La Crosse

Carl W. Conrad
Washington University

Patricia Cook
Emory University

M. Joseph Costelloe
Creighton University

Alan Cottrell
American International College

Robert D. Cromey
Virginia Commonwealth University

Janet B. Davis
Truman State University

Paul K. Davis
University of Texas at San Antonio

Frank Day
Clemson University

René M. Descartes
SUNY, Cobleskill

M. Casey Diana
*University of Illinois at Urbana-
    Champaign*

T. Keith Dix
University of Georgia

Sviatoslav Dmitriev
Harvard University

Margaret A. Dodson
Independent Scholar

Laura Rinaldi Dufresne
Winthrop University

John P. Dunn
Valdosta State University

William E. Dunstan
North Carolina State University

Jennifer Eastman
Clark University

Tammy Jo Eckhart
Indiana University, Bloomington

Wilton Eckley
Colorado School of Mines

Samuel K. Eddy
Syracuse University

Michael M. Eisman
Temple University

Todd William Ewing
William Baptist College

Jonathan Fenno
College of Charleston

Gary B. Ferngren
Oregon State University

Michael S. Fitzgerald
Pikeville College

Edwin D. Floyd
University of Pittsburgh

Robert J. Forman
St. John's University, New York

Donald R. Franceschetti
University of Memphis

Keith Garebian
Independent Scholar

CONTRIBUTORS

Nancy M. Gordon
Independent Scholar

William S. Greenwalt
Santa Clara University

Irwin Halfond
McKendree College

Robert Hannah
University of Otago

Wells S. Hansen
Milton Academy

Kenneth W. Harl
Tulane University

Robert W. Haynes
Texas A&M International University

Kevin Herbert
Washington University

Michael Hernon
University of Tennessee at Martin

Nicolle Hirschfeld
Trinity University

David B. Hollander
Iowa State University

John R. Holmes
Franciscan University of Steubenville

Leslie J. Hoppe
Catholic Theological Union

Randall S. Howarth
Mercyhurst College

Patrick Norman Hunt
Stanford University

Robert Jacobs
Central Washington University

Edward Johnson
University of New Orleans

Leah Johnson
Wayne State University

Robert R. Jones
Granite School District

Charles L. Kammer III
The College of Wooster

Gayla Koerting
University of South Dakota

Grove Koger
Boise Public Library

Donald G. Kyle
University of Texas at Arlington

David J. Ladouceur
University of Notre Dame

David H. J. Larmour
Texas Tech University

John W. I. Lee
*University of California, Santa
    Barbara*

John Lewis
Ashland University

Thomas T. Lewis
College of St. Scholastica

Elizabeth Johnston Lipscomb
Randolph-Macon Women's College

Janet M. Luehring
Independent Scholar

Eric v.d. Luft
SUNY, Upstate Medical University

Joseph M. McCarthy
Suffolk University

Sara MacDonald
St. Thomas University

Kelly A. MacFarlane
University of Alberta

Thomas McGeary
Independent Scholar

Paul Madden
Hardin-Simmons University

Wilfred E. Major
Louisiana State University

Chogollah Maroufi
*California State University,
   Los Angeles*

Hubert M. Martin, Jr.
University of Kentucky

Victor M. Martinez
*University of Illinois at Urbana-
   Champaign*

Marc Mastrangelo
Dickinson College

Frederick C. Matusiak
University of Southern Colorado

Diane P. Michelfelder
Utah State University

Martin C. J. Miller
Metropolitan State College of Denver

R. Scott Moore
University of Dayton

William V. Moore
College of Charleston

Trevor J. Morgan
Independent Scholar

Terry R. Morris
Shorter College

Hans-Friedrich Mueller
Florida State University

B. Keith Murphy
Fort Valley State University

Ann M. Nicgorski
Williamette University

John A. Nichols
Slippery Rock University

Eric Niderost
Chabot College

John Maxwell O'Brien
Queens College

Joseph R. O'Neill
University of Toronto

Zoe A. Pappas
Columbia University

Robert J. Paradowski
Rochester Institute of Technology

Michael C. Paul
University of Miami

CONTRIBUTORS

Mary L. B. Pendergraft
Wake Forest University

John Pepple
Kenyon College

George E. Pesely
Austin Peay State University

Nis Petersen
New Jersey City University

Alan P. Peterson
Gordon College

Darryl A. Phillips
College of Charleston

Hugh J. Phillips
Independent Scholar

Christopher Sean Planeaux
*Indiana University—Purdue University
    at Indianapolis*

George R. Plitnik
Frostburg State University

Oliver B. Pollak
University of Nebraska at Omaha

Frances Skoczylas Pownall
University of Alberta

William H. Race
University of North Carolina

F. E. Romer
University of Arizona

Michele Valerie Ronnick
Wayne State University

Shawn A. Ross
University of Washington

Robert Rousselle
Independent Scholar

Scott M. Rusch
University of Pennsylvania

Willard J. Rusch
University of Southern Maine

Brian Rutishauser
Fresno City College

Christina A. Salowey
Hollins University

D. Brent Sandy
Grace College

Daniel C. Scavone
University of Southern Indiana

Nancy Serwint
Arizona State University

Susan O. Shapiro
Xavier University

R. Baird Shuman
*University of Illinois at Urbana-
    Champaign*

James P. Sickinger
Florida State University

Thomas J. Sienkewicz
Monmouth College

Jeffrey Sikkenga
Ashland University

Michael J. Siler
California State University,
Los Angeles

Svetla Slaveva-Griffin
Florida State University

Roger Smith
Independent Scholar

Larry Smolucha
Joliet Junior College

Sonia Sorrell
Pepperdine University

August W. Staub
University of Georgia

Gaius Stern
University of California, Berkeley

Stephen A. Stertz
Seton Hall University

Leslie A. Stricker
Park University

Sally A. Struthers
Sinclair Community College

Glenn L. Swygart
Tennessee Temple University

Andrius Tamulis
Cardinal Stritch University

Donathan Taylor
Hardin-Simmons University

Gregory S. Taylor
Grambling State University

Carol G. Thomas
University of Washington

Jonathan L. Thorndike
Belmont University

Lee Ann Turner
Boise State University

Peter L. Viscusi
Central Missouri State University

Gilmar E. Visoni
Queensboro Community College,
CUNY

Albert T. Watanabe
Louisiana State University

Robert J. White
Hunter College, CUNY

John F. Wilson
University of Hawaii—Manoa

Joseph P. Wilson
University of Scranton

Michael Witkoski
University of South Carolina

Andrew Wolpert
University of Wisconsin, Madison

Ian Worthington
University of Missouri—Columbia

Lisa A. Wroble
Redford Township District Library

Complete List of Contents

Volume 1

Volume 2

Volume 3

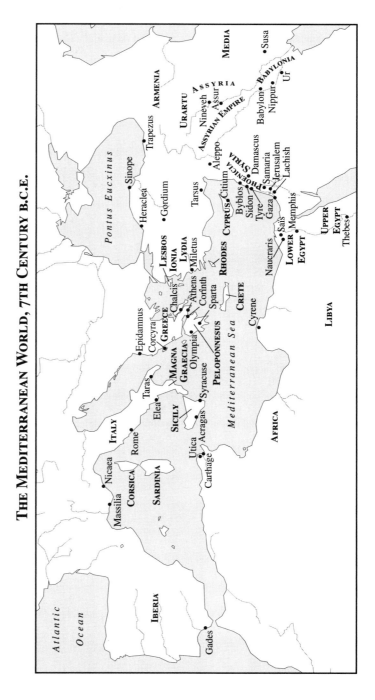

THE MEDITERRANEAN WORLD, 7TH CENTURY B.C.E.

CLASSICAL GREECE, 5TH CENTURY B.C.E.

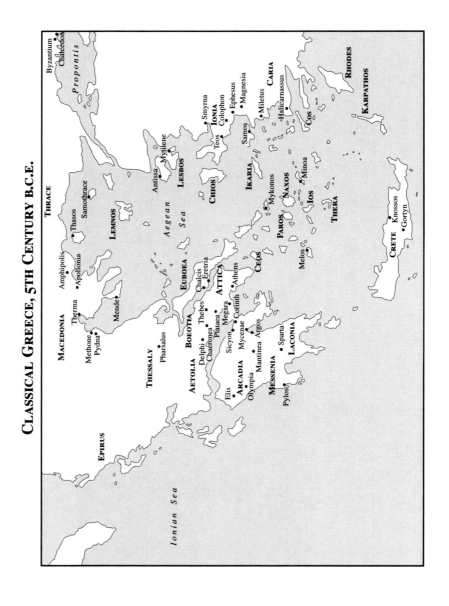

THE HELLENISTIC WORLD, 185 B.C.E.

Maracanda
(Samarqand)

Bactria

GRECO-BACTRIA

GEDROSIA

Pura

Aral
Sea

Hecatompylos

PARTHIA

Persepolis

Caspian Sea

SELEUCID
EMPIRE

Susa

Artaxata

MEDIA-
ATROPATENIA

Indian Ocean

Seleucia
on the
Tigris

Trapezus

ARMENIA

Pontus Euxinus

Karasi

Sinope

PONTUS

CAPPADOCIA

Edessa

Antioch

Seleucia

BITHYNIA

GALATIA

Byzantium

PERGAMUM

LYCIA

ILLYRA

MACEDONIA

Pella

GREECE

Athens

Sparta

Alexandria

PTOLEMAIC
EGYPT

Mediterranean Sea

ROME

Key to Pronunciation

Many of the names and topics profiled in *Ancient Greece* may be unfamiliar to students and general readers. For these names and terms, guides to pronunciation have been provided upon first mention in the text. These guidelines do not purport to achieve the subtleties of the languages in question but will offer readers a rough equivalent of how English speakers may approximate the proper pronunciation.

Vowel Sounds

Symbol	Spelled (Pronounced)
a	answer (AN-sur), laugh (laf), sample (SAM-puhl), that (that)
ah	father (FAH-thur), hospital (HAHS-pih-tuhl)
aw	awful (AW-fuhl), caught (kawt)
ay	blaze (blayz), fade (fayd), waiter (WAY-tur), weigh (way)
eh	bed (behd), head (hehd), said (sehd)
ee	believe (bee-LEEV), cedar (SEE-dur), leader (LEE-dur), liter (LEE-tur)
ew	boot (bewt), lose (lewz)
i	buy (bi), height (hit), lie (li), surprise (sur-PRIZ)
ih	bitter (BIH-tur), pill (pihl)
o	cotton (KO-tuhn), hot (hot)
oh	below (bee-LOH), coat (koht), note (noht), wholesome (HOHL-suhm)
oo	good (good), look (look)
ow	couch (kowch), how (how)
oy	boy (boy), coin (koyn)
uh	about (uh-BOWT), butter (BUH-tur), enough (ee-NUHF), other (UH-thur)

CONSONANT SOUNDS

Symbol	Spelled (Pronounced)
ch	beach (beech), chimp (chihmp)
g	beg (behg), disguise (dihs-GIZ), get (geht)
j	digit (DIH-juht), edge (ehj), jet (jeht)
k	cat (kat), kitten (KIH-tuhn), hex (hehks)
s	cellar (SEHL-ur), save (sayv), scent (sehnt)
sh	champagne (sham-PAYN), issue (IH-shew), shop (shop)
ur	birth (burth), disturb (dihs-TURB), earth (urth), letter (LEH-tur)
y	useful (YEWS-fuhl), young (yuhng)
z	business (BIHZ-nehs), zest (zehst)
zh	vision (VIH-zhuhn)

Achaean League

The Achaean League, a federation of Greek city-states, was the chief military power in Greece in the third and early second centuries B.C.E.

Date: Fourth century B.C.E.-c. 323 B.C.E. and 280 B.C.E.-146 B.C.E.
Category: Organizations and institutions; government and politics
Locale: Peloponnese, southern Greece

SUMMARY   A confederation of Achaean (ah-KEE-uhn) cities, located in the northern Peloponnese, existed during the fourth century B.C.E., but this league was dissolved after the Macedonian conquest. The league was revived in 280 B.C.E., and in 251 B.C.E., it extended membership to Sicyon (Sikyon), a non-Achaean city. Under the leadership of Aratus of Sicyon, the league grew, and by 228 B.C.E., it had expelled the Macedonians from the Peloponnese and become the chief power in southern Greece.

The Achaean League was governed by a federal assembly, but a council and several magistrates handled daily business. The chief league official was an annually elected general who could hold office only in alternate years. Member cities did not give up local autonomy and lived under their own laws.

SIGNIFICANCE   The resurgence of Sparta forced the Achaean League into alliance with Macedonia in 224 B.C.E., but Achaea joined Rome against Macedonia in 198 B.C.E. Relations with Rome soured, and in 167 B.C.E., the Romans took one thousand Achaeans, including the historian Polybius, to Rome as hostages. In 146 B.C.E., the Romans declared war on and defeated the Achaean League. The league was dissolved, ending the last vestige of Greek freedom.

FURTHER READING
Cartledge, Paul, and Antony Spawforth. *Hellenistic and Roman Sparta: A Tale of Two Cities*. 2d ed. London: Routledge, 2002.

1

Larsen, J. A. O. *Greek Federal States: Their Institutions and History*. Oxford, England: Clarendon Press, 1968.

Walbank, F. W. *The Hellenistic World*. Rev. ed. Cambridge, Mass.: Harvard University Press, 1993.

James P. Sickinger

See also: Achaean War; Hellenistic Greece; Polybius.

Achaean War

The Achaean War resulted in the defeat of the Achaean League, the last important and independent military force in Hellenistic Greece.

Date: 146 B.C.E.
Category: Wars and battles
Locale: Peloponnese, southern Greece

SUMMARY   In the second century, the Peloponnese housed two competing powers, Sparta and the Achaean (ah-KEE-uhn) League. After decades of disagreement, their quarreling provoked decisive Roman intervention.

At first, Rome attempted to arbitrate. Responsible for the Republic's foreign affairs, the Roman senate dispatched ambassadors in 147 B.C.E. However, its instructions to detach several cities from the league angered the Achaeans, who at Corinth threatened the ambassadors with violence. Although Rome sent another, more conciliatory embassy, the Achaeans obstructed negotiations and soon afterward declared war on Sparta.

In 146 B.C.E., Quintus Caecilius Metellus Macedonicus and a Roman army marched south from Macedonia, defeating Achaean troops in central Greece. Caecilius's successor, Lucius Mummius, crushed the league's remaining forces at the isthmus in late summer. After sacking Corinth, Mummius began organizing Greek affairs with the assistance of ten commissioners from Rome.

SIGNIFICANCE   While Corinth was razed to the ground, those communities that had fought against the Republic were attached to the Roman province in Macedonia. Kept under the watchful eye of a Roman governor, the entire Greek peninsula was eventually incorporated into Rome's overseas empire.

FURTHER READING

Cartledge, Paul, and Antony Spawforth. *Hellenistic and Roman Sparta: A Tale of Two Cities*. 2d ed. London: Routledge, 2002.

Green, Peter. *Alexander to Actium: The Historical Evolution of the Hellenistic Age*. Reprint. Berkeley: University of California Press, 1993.

Gruen, Erich S. "The Origins of the Achaean War." *Journal of Hellenic Studies* 96 (1976): 46-69.

Denvy A. Bowman

See also: Achaean League; Hellenistic Greece.

Achilles Painter

ARTIST

Flourished: c. 460-c. 430 B.C.E.; Athens, Greece
Category: Art and architecture

LIFE   Named after the figure of Achilles on an amphora, or wine jar, in the Vatican Museums, the Achilles Painter (uh-KIHL-EEZ PAYN-tuhr) was one of the finest Athenian vase painters of the Classical period. More than 230 vases of various shapes, large and small, have been attributed to him. A pupil of the Berlin Painter, the Achilles Painter worked mainly in the red-figure and white-ground techniques but occasionally in black-figure for Panathenaic amphoras. His most beautiful vases are white-ground *lekythoi*, or oil jugs, decorated in delicate colors on a white background, often with a mistress and maid or two mourners at a tomb.

The drawing style of the Achilles Painter is exceptionally fine, with a beautiful quality of line. His figures tend to be serene and noble, similar to the contemporary sculptures of the Parthenon. The artist favored a variety of figure types, including deities, heroes, and mortals. Once, on a *lekythos* in Lugano, he represented an exquisite scene of two Muses on Mount Helicon.

Apparently, the Achilles Painter's vases were prized commodities, for they have turned up not only in Athens and nearby Eretria, but as far afield as Etruria, Sicily, Egypt, and Turkey.

INFLUENCE   The Achilles Painter set the standard of excellence for white-ground *lekythoi*. His pupils, such as the Phiale Painter, continued his style into the later fifth century B.C.E.

FURTHER READING

Beazley, J. D. *Attic Red-Figure Vase-Painters*. Oxford, England: Clarendon Press, 1963.
_____. *Paralipomena*. Oxford, England: Clarendon Press, 1971.

Boardman, John. *Athenian Red Figure Vases: The Classical Period*. London: Thames and Hudson, 1989.
Kurtz, Donna Carol. *Athenian White Lekythoi: Patterns and Painters*. Oxford, England: Clarendon Press, 1975.

Evelyn E. Bell

See also: Art and Architecture; Classical Greece.

Battle of Actium

The Battle of Actium ended the era of the civil wars and made Octavian (later Augustus) master of the Roman world.

Date: September 2, 31 B.C.E.
Category: Wars and battles
Locale: Actium, a promontory at the mouth of the Gulf of Ambracia, on the western coast of Greece

SUMMARY   After the death of Julius Caesar in 44 B.C.E., the rivals Marc Antony and Octavian were reconciled and formed (with Marcus Aemilius Lepidus) the Second Triumvirate. In 32 B.C.E., the Triumvirate ceased and the two were again enemies. Octavian returned to Rome, gained power, and had war declared on Marc Antony and Cleopatra VII.

The Battle of Actium. (F. R. Niglutsch)

Marc Antony was camped at Actium (AK-shee-uhm) with 70,000 infantry and 500 ships. Octavian, advancing from the north with 80,000 infantry and 400 ships, blockaded Antony. Antony drew up his fleet outside the gulf, facing Octavian's fleet to the west, with Cleopatra's more than sixty galleys behind him in reserve. Both fleets tried to outflank each other to the north. With the sea battle going against Antony, Cleopatra (perhaps on Antony's orders) broke through the center and suddenly fled with her galleys; Antony fought through to the open sea with a few ships and followed her to Egypt. The battle continued until the rest of Antony's fleet was set on fire. Antony's land forces surrendered a week later.

SIGNIFICANCE   The battle was a decisive victory by Octavian over Antony and Cleopatra, who fled to Egypt, where they were pursued by Octavian.

FURTHER READING
Califf, David J. *The Battle of Actium*. Philadelphia: Chelsea House, 2004.
Carter, J. M. *The Battle of Actium: The Rise and Triumph of Augustus Caesar*. London: Hamish Hamilton, 1970.
Southern, P. *Augustus*. New York: Routledge, 1998.

Thomas McGeary

See also: Cleopatra VII; Ptolemaic Egypt.

Battle of Aegospotami

Sparta captured approximately 170 Athenian ships and executed more than three thousand Athenian soldiers, thus sealing its victory over Athens in the Peloponnesian War.

Date: September, 405 B.C.E.
Category: Wars and battles
Locale: Aegospotami, in the Chersonese on the shore of the Hellespont (Dardanelles)

SUMMARY   In the last stage of the Peloponnesian War (431-404 B.C.E.), Sparta built a fleet, thanks to Persian support, and carried out operations along the coast of Asia Minor, but with only moderate success.

To block the route of grain ships heading from the Black Sea to Athens, Lysander of Sparta entered the Hellespont with the Peloponnesian fleet and seized Lampsacus by force. The Athenian generals stationed their ships on the opposite shore at Aegospotami (ee-guh-SPAH-tuh-mi), but they could not lure Lysander into battle. Then, according to historian Xenophon, Lysander attacked the Athenians while they were searching for food and captured nearly the entire fleet. Only nine ships escaped.

SIGNIFICANCE   After this battle, Sparta besieged Athens by land and by sea. Lacking the resources to rebuild its fleet, Athens could not withstand the siege and was forced to surrender to Sparta in (probably late March) 404 B.C.E. Terms included the destruction of defensive walls and fortifications, reduction of the fleet to twelve ships, surrender of foreign lands, and an alliance with Sparta.

FURTHER READING

Hanson, Victor Davis. *A War Like No Other: How the Athenians and Spartans Fought the Peloponnesian War*. New York: Random House, 2005.

Kagan, Donald. *The Fall of the Athenian Empire*. Ithaca, N.Y.: Cornell University Press, 1987.

⸻. *The Peloponnesian War*. New York: Viking, 2003.

Strauss, Barry. "Aegospotami Reexamined." *American Journal of Philology* 104 (1983): 24-35.

Andrew Wolpert

See also: Lysander of Sparta; Peloponnesian Wars.

Aeschines

ORATOR

Born: 390 B.C.E.; probably Athens, Greece
Died: c. 315 B.C.E.; possibly Samos, Greece
Category: Oratory and rhetoric; theater and drama

LIFE Originally a civil official and then an actor, Aeschines (EHS-kih-neez) seems to have entered political life at a relatively advanced age. In 348 B.C.E., when Philip II of Macedonia was threatening the Chalcidice, Aeschines was sent as an ambassador to rouse the Greek states against him. He was a member of the boule, or council, in 347/346 B.C.E. and served on embassies to Philip in connection with the Peace of Philocrates, as did Demosthenes, in 346 B.C.E. Aeschines believed that the only peace attainable was a so-called Common Peace, and this, together with his more conservative policy and conciliatory attitude to Philip, clashed with Demosthenes. This was the start of a long personal enmity between Aeschines and Demosthenes, seen in the famous court battles in 343 B.C.E., when Demosthenes prosecuted Aeschines for misconduct on the embassies and narrowly lost, and in 330 B.C.E., when Aeschines prosecuted Ctesiphon, who had proposed a crown in 336 B.C.E. for Demosthenes' great services to the state, and overwhelmingly lost.

Between 343 and 330 B.C.E., Demosthenes' political influence rose; however, Aeschines seems to have played a passive role in politics. He was prominent at a meeting of the Amphictyonic Council in 339 B.C.E., but in persuading that council to vote for the Sacred War on Amphissa, he opened the door for Philip's further involvement in Greece. After the Greeks' defeat at Chaeronea in 338 B.C.E., Aeschines served as ambassador to Philip to discuss peace terms. In 336 B.C.E., he impeached Ctesiphon for making an illegal motion to crown Demosthenes, but the case did not come to court until 330. The impeachment was an attack on Demosthenes; hence, it was Demosthenes who delivered the official defense speech. Misjudging the political situation, not to mention Demosthenes' influence, Aeschines failed to win one-fifth of the votes and went into self-imposed exile. According to tradition, he opened a school of rhetoric on Rhodes and later moved to Samos, where he died.

Only three speeches by Aeschines have survived. They are marred by personal attacks, emotional arguments, and too great a tendency to quote from poetry; he is at his best in the narrative sections of his speeches, where his vocabulary is simple and effective. However, his oratorical ability was enough for him to be included in the canon of the ten Attic orators.

INFLUENCE   Aeschines' speeches from the false embassy and Ctesiphon/ Demosthenes trials survive, as do those of Demosthenes; although the speeches of both orators are riddled with bias and embellishment, they are vital source material for the history of this period.

FURTHER READING

Aeschines. *Aeschines*. Translated by Chris Carey. Austin: University of Texas Press, 2000.

Harris, E. *Aeschines and Athenian Politics*. New York: Oxford University Press, 1995.

Kennedy, G. *The Art of Persuasion in Greece*. Princeton, N.J.: Princeton University Press, 1963.

Worman, Nancy. "Insults and Oral Excess in the Disputes Between Aeschines and Demosthenes." *American Journal of Philology* 125, no. 1 (Spring, 2004): 1-25.

Ian Worthington

See also: Demosthenes; Oratory; Philip II of Macedonia.

Aeschylus

PLAYWRIGHT

Born: 525-524 B.C.E.; Eleusis, Greece
Died: 456-455 B.C.E.; Gela, Sicily
Category: Theater and drama

LIFE   Aeschylus (EHS-kuh-luhs), the earliest of the great tragic poets
and dramatists of Athens, was the son of Euphorion, a well-born landowner
of Eleusis, the city of the mysteries of Demeter. He fought in the Battle of
Marathon, 490 B.C.E., and possibly at Salamis. He won fame at Athens
because of his tragedies and more than once visited Hiero, the king of Syracuse, to produce tragedies there. One tragedy, *Women of Aetna*, he produced to celebrate Hiero's refoundation of Etna, which had been destroyed
in the volcanic eruption of Mount Etna in 475 B.C.E. He died at Gela about
455, during his last visit to Sicily.

Aeschylus's predecessors had developed, from choral songs in honor of
gods, a primitive drama with one actor taking the part of all characters in
the myth narrated in the song. He spoke to the chorus to carry on the story.
This form became popular and was established as a regular part of the festival of Dionysus at Athens. Poets competed for prizes; they submitted three
poems each, as well as a farcical after-piece called a satyr play.

Aeschylus entered this competition first around 499 B.C.E. with an unknown trilogy. His first prize was won in 484, again with unknown works.
The entrance of Aeschylus into competition was a great event in literary
history. He transformed tragedy completely. Aristotle tells of two technical
innovations Aeschylus made that had a profound effect. He reduced the
number of chorus members from fifty to twelve, and he began using a second actor. This latter change made possible a more flexible drama; two persons of the play could now appear together and converse. The former
change signalized the shift to an emphasis on dramatic interplay. Aeschylus also invented the trilogy of plays on one theme.

More important, however, than technical improvements was Aeschylus's change of the tone of tragedy. Partly because of the greater dramatic

possibilities that his improvements allowed, Aeschylus fashioned a means of using the old myths to express fundamental questions of human life. He had the imagination to present these themes through characters of grandeur and power, and he possessed the poetic gifts to dress them in language of dignity and grace. His powers needed greater scope than a single play provided. Therefore he usually presented true trilogies, three plays based on the same myth.

The seven of his plays that have been preserved give a good view of his development as a dramatist and the range of his imagination. *Hiketides* (c. 463 B.C.E.; *The Suppliants*, 1777) tells the story of the fifty daughters of Danaus who flee with their father from the land of the Nile to Argos, home of their ancestor, Io, to escape unwanted marriage with their fifty cousins, the sons of Danaus's brother, Aegyptus. With hesitation, and after consulting the citizens, the king of Argos agrees to take the suppliants under his protection. The herald of Aegyptus arrives, makes melodramatic threats to persuade the girls to return with him, tries to use force, and is finally driven away by the king of Argos. The story is an old and naïve folktale, and the dramatic action is slight. Except for a few scenes there is but a single actor on the stage at any one time, yet the work's pathos—and the lovely verse of the choral odes, with their rich tapestry of mythological allusion—show the hand of a major poet.

Patriotism dominates *Persai* (472 B.C.E.; *The Persians*, 1777). This play is unique among extant tragedies in having a plot drawn not from myth but from recent history, the glorious victory of the Persian War. It is also un-

---

Principal Works of Aeschylus

Of the more than 80 known plays of Aeschylus, only 7 tragedies survive in more or less complete form:

Persai, 472 B.C.E. (*The Persians*, 1777)
Hepta epi Thēbas, 467 B.C.E. (*Seven Against Thebes*, 1777)
Hiketides, 463 B.C.E.? (*The Suppliants*, 1777)
Oresteia, 458 B.C.E. (English translation, 1777; includes *Agamemnōn* [*Agamemnon*], *Choēphoroi* [*Libation Bearers*], and *Eumenides*)
Prometheus desmōtēs, date unknown (*Prometheus Bound*, 1777)

Aeschylus. (Library of Congress)

usual among Aeschylus's works in not being part of a trilogy but complete in itself. Aeschylus achieves the detachment necessary for tragedy by setting the scene in Persia and having the chorus and all the characters be Persians: Atossa, the mother of Xerxes; the ghost of Darius, her husband; the unfortunate Xerxes himself; and the chorus of Persian elders. Beginning with their forebodings, the play moves on to reveal in grand verse the catastrophes that befall the invincible army. Through the lamentations of their enemies, the Athenian audience relives their god-favored victory. For once in tragedy, the spectacle of hubris bringing the downfall of the mighty is seen without fear, though Aeschylus achieves the tremendous feat of infusing a sense of pity for the fallen, enemies though they are.

Hepta epi Thēbas (467 B.C.E.; *Seven Against Thebes*, 1777) tells the story of the battle for the throne of Thebes between the two sons of Oedipus, Polynices and Eteocles, who perish in single combat, while the six other Theban champions defeat and kill the Argive leaders who joined Polynices in his attempt to regain the throne. The great stories of Oedipus and Antigone are recalled and foreshadowed, but the play concentrates on the pageantry of the battle. The play is archaic and static: One sees groupings rather than movement. However, the hold of the Theban story on the imagination of Greeks shines upon it, and one senses the patriotic feelings that made the Greek polis so vital a culture.

Aeschylus's imagination grew more powerful as he progressed in his art. In *Prometheus desmōtēs* (n.d.; *Prometheus Bound*, 1777) he raised tragedy to a cosmic level. The old legend of the god who stole fire from Olympus to give to humankind and thus save humankind from extinction becomes in Aeschylus's treatment a complex drama of guilt and punishment in which, because the persons of the play are immortal, the mitigating power of death is absent. It portrays the Greek legend as analogous to the Christian doctrine of original sin and atonement. The latter theme is the subject of the lost *Prometheus Unbound*, which followed the extant play in the trilogy. The setting, the chorus, and the action all emphasize the stark aloneness of Prometheus, defying the ineluctable power of Zeus. The one human character, Io, portrays the misery of the human condition, with only a hint of the relief to follow in the fullness of time. In this play the essence of tragedy, abstracted from all human complexities, is most clearly revealed.

The last surviving work of Aeschylus, produced in 458 B.C.E., two years before his death, is the trilogy *Oresteia* (458 B.C.E.; English translation, 1777), consisting of *Agamemnōn* (*Agamemnon*), *Choēphoroi* (*Libation Bearers*), and *Eumenides*. It is the only trilogy preserved and shows the master's ability to develop a theme through three separate dramas, each complete in itself. In bare outline, *Agamemnon* enacts the murder of the conqueror of Troy by his faithless wife, Clytemnestra, and her paramour, Aegisthus; *Libation Bearers*, the murder of the two by Orestes, the son of Agamemnon and Clytemnestra, impelled by the old law of vengeance; and *Eumenides*, the justification of Orestes' deed against the claims of vengeance for matricide. *Agamemnon* is poetically the richest, with its brooding odes dwelling on the cycles of guilt of the house of Atreus, giving a magnificent portrait of the man-hearted queen and the prophetic Cassandra. The second play portrays the agony of Orestes, caught in the contradictory rules of ancient blood-feud. The third play raises the action to the level of the gods, who must find a solution that will reestablish justice for humankind on the basis of a rational order that finds its expression in the polis and brings humankind from barbarism to civilization.

These final plays show Aeschylus influenced by Sophocles in their greater variety of characters and complexity of scenes. On the other hand, they remain true to Aeschylus's bold simplicity of imagination. His characters are larger and simpler than life. They are moved to what they do by external forces and yet act of their own wills.

INFLUENCE   Aeschylus was the predecessor of Euripides and Sophocles. He was the first dramatist whose tragedies (seven out of some eighty to ninety) have been preserved.

FURTHER READING

Bloom, Harold, ed. *Aeschylus: Comprehensive Research and Study Guide.* Broomall, Pa.: Chelsea House, 2002.

Goldhill, Simon. *Aeschylus: "Oresteia."* New York: Cambridge University Press, 1992.

Heath, John. *The Talking Greeks: Speech, Animals, and the Other in Homer, Aeschylus, and Plato.* New York: Cambridge University Press, 2005.

Herington, John. *Aeschylus.* New Haven, Conn.: Yale University Press, 1986.

Rosenmeyer, Thomas G. *The Art of Aeschylus.* Berkeley: University of California Press, 1982.

Smethurst, Mae J. *The Artistry of Aeschylus and Zeami: A Comparative Study of Greek Tragedy and No.* Princeton, N.J.: Princeton University Press, 1989.

Spatz, Lois. *Aeschylus.* Boston: Twayne, 1982.

Vellacott, Philip. *The Logic of Tragedy: Morals and Integrity in Aeschylus' "Oresteia."* Durham, N.C.: Duke University Press, 1984.

Jonathan L. Thorndike

See also: Aristophanes; Euripides; Literature; Performing Arts; Sophocles; Sports and Entertainment.

Aesop

FABULIST

Born: c. 620 B.C.E.; possibly Thrace, Greece
Died: c. 560 B.C.E.; possibly Delphi, Greece
Category: Poetry; literature

LIFE   Although many Greek cities claim to be the birthplace of Aesop (EE-sahp), most scholars believe he never existed. In a marble figure on the Villa Albani, Paris, he is depicted as a dwarf, deformed and ugly, perhaps to symbolize his near approach to the so-called lower animals and his peculiar sympathy for their habits. Yet history contains a reference to a "noble statue" of him by Lysippus in Athens. Diego Velasquez's painting presents him as a sturdy figure in a brown cloak.

Many fables, supposedly by Aesop, have been traced to earlier Indian or

Aesop relates his fables. (F. R. Niglutsch)

Aesop. (Library of Congress)

fourteenth century B.C.E. Egyptian versions. Somebody, however, wrote them down, and this may have been the legendary sixth century B.C.E. slave of Iadmon of Samos. Tradition tells of his travels to Lydia, to meet Solon at the court of Croesus, and to Periander in Corinth. While visiting Athens, to keep its citizens from deposing Pisistratus, legend has him recounting to them the fable of the frogs who asked for a king.

Phaedrus, a Macedonian freedman of Augustus, translated the fables in

19

five volumes of Latin verse. Babrius versified them two centuries later, and Planudes Maximus, a learned thirteenth century Byzantine monk, compiled a collection in prose, prefaced by his account of Aesop's life.

INFLUENCE   Children and people of all ages and all ranges of sophistication have enjoyed Aesop's fables throughout the ages. Jean de La Fontaine gave them their most polished and sophisticated form in his *Fables* (1668-1694).

FURTHER READING

Aesop. *Treasury of Aesop's Fables*. Illustrated by Thomas Bewick. 1941. Reprint. New York: Avenal Books, 1973.

Perry, B. E. *Studies in the Text History of the Life and Fables of Aesop*. 1936. Reprint. Chico, Calif.: Scholars Press, 1981.

Wheatley, Edward. *Mastering Aesop: Medieval Education, Chaucer, and His Followers*. Gainesville: University Press of Florida, 2000.

Trevor J. Morgan

See also: Literature; Performing Arts.

Aetolian League

The Aetolian League was a confederation of small towns and villages drawn together by the desire for mutual defense and financial gain.

Date: Fifth-first centuries B.C.E.
Category: Organizations and institutions; government and politics
Locale: West-central Greece

SUMMARY   Because of the ruggedness of their homeland, the Aetolians long remained on the periphery of Hellenic history. However, their development of a federal state led to aggressive expansion in the third century B.C.E. The Aetolian (eh-TOH-lee-yen) League saved Delphi from Gallic destruction in 279 B.C.E., then drove across central Greece and acquired influence in Thessaly and the western Peloponnese. The Aetolians, hostile to Macedonia's Antigonid kings, became allies of Rome against Philip V and engaged in widespread piracy and brigandage.

An annually elected general served as chief magistrate of the Aetolian League. A primary assembly, consisting of all men of military age, decided issues of foreign policy and met at least twice a year, in spring and autumn. A representative council, elected from constituent cities in proportion to population, governed between these meetings, following the direction of an important committee, the *apokletoi*.

SIGNIFICANCE   Aetolia eventually quarreled with the Roman Republic and sought the support of Syria's ruler, Antiochus the Great. War against Rome concluded with a negotiated peace in 189 B.C.E. Although the league survived, its importance and influence withered. By the late first century B.C.E., Aetolia was depopulated.

FURTHER READING

Cartledge, Paul, and Antony Spawforth. *Hellenistic and Roman Sparta: A Tale of Two Cities*. 2d ed. London: Routledge, 2002.

Larsen, J. A. O. *Greek Federal States*. London: Oxford University Press, 1968.

Scholten, Joseph B. *The Politics of Plunder: Aitolians and Their Koinon in the Early Hellenistic Era, 279-217 B.C.E.* Berkeley: University of California Press, 2000.

Denvy A. Bowman

See also: Antiochus the Great; Classical Greece; Delphi; Hellenistic Greece; Philip V.

Agariste

NOBLEWOMAN

Born: c. 590 B.C.E.; place unknown
Died: c. 500 B.C.E.; place unknown
Category: Government and politics; women

LIFE   The only details known about the life of Agariste (ag-uh-RIS-teh) concern her wedding to Megacles of Athens. When she reached marriageable age, her father, Cleisthenes, tyrant of Sicyon (Sikyon), conducted a yearlong contest to determine who would marry her. Thirteen suitors, the best men of Greece, competed both in the gymnasium and in discussions at dinner until Cleisthenes made his decision. At the end of the year, he threw a banquet, at which he intended to announce his choice of Hippocleides of Athens. As the night wore on, Hippocleides had too much to drink, until he began dancing on a table. Each dance became more outrageous until he stood on his head and rhythmically flailed his legs in the air. At this point, Cleisthenes told Hippocleides that he had danced away his marriage. His response became an Athenian proverb: "It's all the same to Hippocleides." Agariste and Megacles were then married according to the Athenian rites.

The story illustrates the political function of aristocratic marriage in the Archaic period, to foster alliances with important families in other cities. It also contains the earliest historical description of the Athenian marriage rite. Agariste's interest in the proceedings is never mentioned, as her most important functions were to unite the two families through marriage and to bear children for her husband.

INFLUENCE   Agariste's primary influence was in the birth of her children, one of whom was Cleisthenes of Athens, a statesman famous for his democratic reforms. Her name became a popular one among her descendants, and her granddaughter Agariste was the mother of Pericles.

FURTHER READING

Herodotus. *The Histories*. Translated by Robin Waterfield. New York: Oxford University Press, 1998.

Lightman, Marjorie, and Benjamin Lightman. *Biographical Dictionary of Ancient Greek and Roman Women: Notable Women from Sappho to Helena*. New York: Facts On File, 2000.

Robert Rousselle

See also: Cleisthenes of Athens; Cleisthenes of Sicyon; Daily Life and Customs; Women's Life.

Agathon

PLAYWRIGHT

Born: c. 445 B.C.E.; place unknown
Died: c. 400 B.C.E.; Macedonia
Category: Theater and drama

LIFE   Although none of the works of Agathon (AG-uh-thahn) are extant, he is described by Plato, Aristotle, and Aristophanes as a tragic playwright. Plato's *Symposion* (388-368 B.C.E.; *Symposium*, 1701) depicts a celebration that takes place in Athens after the victory of one of Agathon's plays in 416 B.C.E. Plato portrays Agathon as a gentleman, well versed in the duties of hospitality. In this dialogue, Agathon joins his guests in eulogizing the god Eros. In a speech that Socrates compares to those of the Sophist

The politician Alcibiades (left) interrupts the banquet of Agathon (right), as related in Plato's Symposium. (F. R. Niglutsch)

25

Gorgias, Agathon initially describes Eros as both the most beautiful and the most virtuous among gods. However, like many of Socrates' interlocutors, after speaking with Socrates, Agathon admits to knowing nothing definite about the topic. In *De poetica* (c. 335-323 B.C.E.; *Poetics*, 1705), Aristotle says that Agathon's tragedies are among the first to be composed of fictitious characters and events. He also attributes to Agathon the inclusion of choral songs that are not connected to the plots of his plays. In Aristophanes' *Thesmophoriazousai* (411 B.C.E.; *Thesmophoriazusae*, 1837), Agathon is comedically depicted as delicate and effeminate. However, in Aristophanes' *Batrachoi* (405 B.C.E.; *The Frogs*, 1780), Dionysus describes him as a decent poet who, in death, is lamented by his friends.

INFLUENCE   Because none of his works survives, it is difficult to attribute to Agathon any lasting influence. However, Aristotle's descriptions of his works suggest that he had an impact on the poetry of ancient Greece.

FURTHER READING

Aristotle. *Poetics*. Translated by S. H. Butcher. New York: Hill & Wang, 1989.

Plato. "Symposium." In *The Dialogues of Plato*. New York: Bantam Classics, 1986.

Storey, Ian Christopher, and Arlene Allan. *A Guide to Ancient Greek Drama*. Malden, Mass.: Blackwell, 2005.

Sara MacDonald

See also: Aristophanes; Aristotle; Literature; Performing Arts; Plato; Socrates; Sports and Entertainment.

Agesilaus II of Sparta

STATESMAN AND MILITARY LEADER

Born: c. 444 B.C.E.; Sparta, Greece
Died: c. 360 B.C.E.; Cyrene, Cyrenaica (now in Libya)
Category: Military; government and politics

LIFE   Agesilaus (uh-jehs-uh-LAY-uhs) II of Sparta was the younger son of Archidamus II, a Eurypontid king of Sparta, and his second wife, Eupolia. Because he was not expected to become king, Agesilaus underwent the rigorous Spartan system of military training, known as the *agogē*. However, he did become a ruler in 400 B.C.E., when the Spartan general Lysander of Sparta persuaded the Spartans that Agesilaus's nephew, the heir-apparent, was actually the son of the Athenian Alcibiades.

Agesilaus ascended the throne at a time when Sparta and its allies dominated the Greek world following the defeat of Athens in the Peloponnesian War (431-404 B.C.E.). In 396-394 B.C.E., he campaigned successfully against the Persians in Asia Minor in support of the independence of Greek cities there. He was soon recalled home, however, to defend Sparta against an alliance of Athens, Thebes, Corinth, and Argos. Agesilaus defeated the allies at Coronea in 394 B.C.E., and Spartan hegemony over Greece was confirmed in the King's Peace (386 B.C.E.; also known as the Peace of Antalcidas).

Agesilaus spent the next decade and a half warding off several challenges to Sparta's power. Although he was an inspiring battlefield leader, Agesilaus failed to prepare the Spartan army for the military innovations of the fourth century B.C.E. Using a wider and deeper phalanx and an oblique battle line, the Thebans destroyed the Spartan army, led by King Cleombrotus (Sparta had a dual monarchy), at Leuctra (371 B.C.E.). Agesilaus was able to prevent a Theban seizure of Sparta by hard campaigning in 370-369 B.C.E., but Spartan supremacy in Greece was effectively ended. He died while leading a mercenary expedition to Egypt.

Agesilaus II of Sparta.
(Library of Congress)

INFLUENCE   Sparta's inability to maintain its power was mainly caused by the fact that its institutions were unsuited to empire building and by a progressive decline in the numbers of Spartan citizens. Agesilaus contributed to his city's decline by alienating Sparta's allies through frequent interference in their internal affairs.

FURTHER READING

Cartledge, Paul. *The Spartans: The World of the Warrior Heroes of Ancient Greece, from Utopia to Crisis and Collapse.* Woodstock, N.Y.: Overlook Press, 2003.

Cartledge, Paul, and Antony Spawforth. *Hellenistic and Roman Sparta: A Tale of Two Cities.* 2d ed. London: Routledge, 2002.

Hamilton, Charles D. *Agesilaus and the Failure of Spartan Hegemony.*

Ithaca, N.Y.: Cornell University Press, 1991.

Plutarch. *The Age of Alexander: Nine Greek Lives*. Translated by Ian Scott-Kilvert. New York: Penguin Books, 1973.

Shipley, D. R. *A Commentary on Plutarch's Life of Agesilaos*. Oxford, England: Clarendon Press, 1997.

Michael S. Fitzgerald

See also: Archidamus II of Sparta; King's Peace; Leuctra, Battle of.

Agriculture and Animal Husbandry

Employing a rudimentary technology upon a highly variable landscape, the ancient Greeks created a sophisticated agrarian base which aided the evolution of complex social and political systems.

Date: From the eighth millennium B.C.E. to 31 B.C.E.
Category: Agriculture

EVIDENCE FOR AGRARIAN ACTIVITY   Archaeological evidence, including representations on ceramic vessels, food processing equipment, and paleobotanical information, is the primary channel for establishing the sequence of agricultural development in Greece, including the islands in the Aegean and Mediterranean Seas. Literary sources from the Dark Ages of Greece through the Classical Age (from c. 1150 B.C.E. to the fourth century B.C.E.), for example Homer, Xenophon, Hesiod, and Theophrastus, are valuable, particularly for specific topics such as cattle husbandry.

ORIGINS OF AGRICULTURE IN GREECE   Franchthi Cave above the Gulf of Argos in the Peloponnese documents the transition from a Mesolithic hunting-and-foraging lifestyle to a Neolithic food-producing lifestyle. Dating to the eighth millennium B.C.E., the human population hunted red deer and wild pigs and collected a variety of vegetal foods, including lentils, oats, wild barley, and pistachio nuts. After 6000 B.C.E., an economic shift is apparent. Large-seeded lentils and domesticated wheat and barley were produced, and cattle, pigs, sheep, and goats were domesticated. Pottery, an essential component of farming communities, appears during this period. Stone remained the primary material for tool manufacture, with the sickle blades used in grain harvesting becoming more prevalent in the archaeological record.

A range of sites mirrors the developments at early Neolithic Franchthi: Argissa in Thessaly (c. 6000 B.C.E.), Nea Nicomedia in Macedonia (6230 B.C.E.), and Neolithic Knossos on Crete (c. late seventh millennium B.C.E.).

These communities ranged in size from fifty to three hundred individuals residing in wattle and daub huts, made of woven rods and twigs plastered with clay. Cultivated organisms included emmer and einkorn wheat, peas, lentils, barley, and the livestock complex noted above. Human power in tilling the soil was probably the rule in these early Neolithic settlements. Human diets continued to be supplemented through hunting and collecting wild vegetal foods, a strategy which would offset nutritional stress brought about through crop failure. Cattle and pigs were indigenous to Greece and were probably domesticated locally, while sheep and goats undoubtedly diffused from sites farther east in Asia. Barley, oats, and lentils were indigenous. The wheats, important throughout the entire culture history of ancient Greece, were diffused from Southwest Asia.

AGRARIAN COMPLEX IS ESTABLISHED   The environmental variability of Greece and the islands—specifically altitude, soil fertility, and moisture availability—influenced early agricultural decision making and subsequent practices. Upland regions, notorious for poor, thin soils, became adapted to pastorialism, with herds moving into prolific pastures during summer months. Dry heat was characteristic of summers, while wet winters predominated.

During the Neolithic period (c. 6000 B.C.E. to the third or early first millennium B.C.E., depending upon environmental conditions), an agricultural village economy became established which emphasized a mixed farming strategy. The subsequent pattern of cereals, grapes, olives, and domesticated livestock was established by Mycenaean times (c. 1575 to 1200 B.C.E.). The natural terrain dictated the form of village adaptation and agrarian enterprise: cattle husbandry and grain cultivation in northern Greece, while in the southern regions extensive cultivation of grapes and olives. Dry farming predominated, irrigation being minimal and used in orchards and gardens. The earliest evidence of olives (c. 3900 B.C.E.) comes from Crete. Wild grapes were indigenous over much of northern Greece; however, the history of Greek winemaking is imperfectly understood. By Mycenaean times winemaking was well developed, and trade in wine, in addition to olives, was central to the Mycenaean economy.

Two patterns emerged: expansion of agrarian enterprise for the production of trade commodities and small-scale mixed subsistence farming. Kinship-integrated cooperative households were the basic unit of small-scale production and consumption. Farm size varied during the Classical period from twelve to sixty-four acres, depending upon the owner's wealth and the topography. Farms comprised of thousands of acres were possible but rare. By Hellenistic and Roman times (the fourth to first centuries B.C.E.), much larger productive units were found. Primary crops of peasant households in the first century B.C.E. included cereals, beans, peas, and a variety of fruits and vegetables, including cabbage, onions, beets, and apples. Cattle were primarily used for tilling and transport. Sheep and goats provided milk for cheese, wool, and hides. Pigs, chickens, and bees were part of a farmstead's subsistence program. While Greece was not primarily a meat-consuming culture, the sacrifice of any livestock usually destined the meat for human consumption. Beginning in the first century B.C.E., food for livestock consisted of grasses, millet, and alfalfa, which were harvested and stored for winter use. Horses were used primarily for riding by

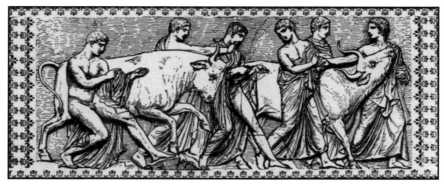

Cattle were an important part of ancient Greek society and were used for both farming and transportation. (F. R. Niglutsch)

individuals who could afford their upkeep.

CULTIVATION AND TECHNOLOGY   Variability in field cultivation was a constant in ancient Greece. If additional land was needed in a mountainous region, then terraces were cut into the hillsides. Terraces functioned not only to increase arable acreage but also to prevent erosion and conserve moisture. Artificial drainage and small-scale irrigation projects might be developed depending on local conditions. The value of manure in elevating soil fertility was recognized, and both animal and human wastes were applied to orchards and gardens. Fallowing arable land to recoup nutritional losses was a common practice. The value of nitrogen-fixing legumes was recognized from Mycenaean times, and, by the fourth century B.C.E., legumes were advocated in lieu of conventional fallowing.

Agricultural implements such as plows, hoes, and sickles were constructed of wood, stone, or metal. The plow, or ard, scratched the topsoil to destroy weeds and conserve moisture. The point of the oxen-drawn plow was made of bronze or iron. Devices that processed foodstuffs, stone presses, and mills for wine and oil were more complex and by Hellenistic and Roman times became increasingly sophisticated. The antiquity of these machines in Greece remains unknown.

Crop yields were low; however, the scarcity of information prevents any overall assessment of production throughout the Greek world. The local environment, specific cultural practices such as the use of manure, and the availability of land and labor greatly influenced yields. It is noteworthy, however, that from this simple yet adaptive productive system, the Greeks laid the foundation for the Western civilizational experience.

FURTHER READING

Burford, Alison. *Land and Labor in the Greek World.* Baltimore: Johns Hopkins University Press, 1993.

Gallant, Thomas A. *Risk and Survival in Ancient Greece: Reconstructing the Rural Domestic Economy.* Stanford, Calif.: Stanford University Press, 1991.

Hanson, Victor Davis. *The Other Greeks: The Family Farm and the Agrarian Roots of Western Civilization.* 2d ed. Berkeley: University of California Press, 1999.

Harris, David R., ed. *The Origins and Spread of Agriculture and Pastoralism in Eurasia.* Washington, D.C.: Smithsonian Institution Press, 1996.

René M. Descartes

See also: Archaic Greece; Classical Greece; Daily Life and Customs; Hellenistic Greece; Mycenaean Greece; Science; Settlements and Social Structure; Technology.

Alcaeus of Lesbos

POET

Born: c. 625 B.C.E.; Mytilene, Lesbos
Died: c. 575 B.C.E.; place unknown
Also known as: Alkaios
Category: Poetry; literature

LIFE   Alcaeus of Lesbos (al-SEE-uhs of LEHZ-bahs) was born into an aristocratic family of Mytilene, the most important city-state on the Aegean island of Lesbos. His contemporary, the poet Sappho, belonged to the same social class in Mytilene. Alcaeus and his brothers were energetically involved in the bitter rivalries that characterized the political affairs of Mytilene during his lifetime, and his poetry is replete with political references and partisan invective.

None of Alcaeus's poems has survived complete. The extant verses and any knowledge of lost poems are derived from a combination of mutilated papyrus copies and quotations and descriptions by later Greek and Roman writers. The poems were lyric, in the strict sense of the word, and monodic: Namely, they were composed to be sung by one person, originally Alcaeus, who accompanied himself on the lyre. Common themes were wine, warfare, politics, and pederastic love, although some were short hymns to individual Olympian gods. Among the surviving verses are portions of two allegorical poems in which Alcaeus's party is represented as a storm-tossed ship.

INFLUENCE   Alcaeus was greatly admired throughout antiquity, and the scholars at Alexandria placed him in the canon of nine Greek lyric poets. He exercised a profound influence on the *Odes* (23 B.C.E., 13 B.C.E.; English translation, 1621) of the Roman poet Horace in matters of form, theme, image, and versification.

FURTHER READING

Burnett, Anne Pippin. *Three Archaic Poets: Archilochus, Alcaeus, Sappho.*
    London: Bristol Classical Press, 1998.

Greene, Ellen, ed. *Women Poets in Ancient Greece and Rome*. Norman: University of Oklahoma Press, 2005.

Hutchinson, G. O. *Greek Lyric Poetry: A Commentary on Selected Larger Pieces*. New York: Oxford University Press, 2001.

Lattimore, R., trans. *Greek Lyrics*. Chicago: University of Chicago Press, 1960.

Martin, H. *Alcaeus*. New York: Twayne, 1972.

Schmidt, Michael. *The First Poets: Lives of the Ancient Greek Poets*. New York: Knopf, 2005.

Walker, Jeffrey. *Rhetoric and Poetics in Antiquity*. New York: Oxford University Press, 2000.

Hubert M. Martin, Jr.

See also: Literature; Lyric Poetry; Sappho.

Alcibiades of Athens

STATESMAN AND MILITARY LEADER

Born: c. 450 B.C.E.; Athens?, Greece
Died: 404 B.C.E.; Phrygia, Asia Minor (now in Turkey)
Also known as: Alkibiades; Son of Cleinias (or Kleinias)
Category: Military; government and politics

LIFE   A controversial, flamboyant general and an ambitious leading politician, Alcibiades (al-suh-BI-uh-deez) of Athens came from an ancient noble family that had diplomatic relations with Sparta. He received an excellent education and was a favorite pupil of the philosopher Socrates. He was an able speaker, and his physical beauty and charm were renowned.

Alcibiades competed with the demagogues who followed the generation of his uncle Pericles, but Alcibiades' chief opponent was the elder statesman Nicias of Athens. Alcibiades sought to expand Athenian influence, reversing the defensive strategy of the Peloponnesian War (431-404 B.C.E.). He engineered two military expeditions, Mantinea (418 B.C.E.) and Sicily (415 B.C.E.), but both ended in defeat. The Athenians banished Alcibiades following numerous accusations of sacrilege against important cults. He aided Sparta and Persia during this exile but lost their confidence. Upon returning to Athens in 407 B.C.E., he led a successful military campaign but withdrew again after a blunder. At war's end (404 B.C.E.), Alcibiades was murdered under mysterious circumstances.

INFLUENCE   A master of intrigue, Alcibiades was known as both a gifted and a brilliant leader. Though admired, he was often feared. His personal excesses and recklessness aroused deep suspicions.

FURTHER READING

Ellis, W. *Alcibiades*. New York: Routledge, 1989.
Forde, S. *Ambition to Rule: Alcibiades and the Politics of Imperialism in Thucydides*. Ithaca, N.Y.: Cornell University Press, 1989.

The philosopher Socrates (left) instructs a young Alcibiades. (F. R. Niglutsch)

Gribble, D. *Alcibiades and Athens: A Study in Literary Presentation.* Oxford, England: Clarendon Press, 1999.

Hanson, Victor Davis. *A War Like No Other: How the Athenians and Spartans Fought the Peloponnesian War.* New York: Random House, 2005.

Kagan, Donald. *The Peloponnesian War.* New York: Viking, 2003.

Christopher Sean Planeaux

See also: Athenian Invasion of Sicily; Athens; Mantinea, Battles of; Military History of Athens; Nicias of Athens; Peloponnesian Wars; Pericles; Socrates.

Alcmaeon

Philosopher and Scientist

Born: c. 510 B.C.E.; Croton, Magna Graecia (now in southern Italy)
Died: c. 430 B.C.E.; place unknown
Also known as: Alkmaeon
Category: Medicine

Life   Almost nothing is known about the early life of Alcmaeon (alk-MEE-uhn) other than that his father's name was Peirithous and that he was a native of Croton (Greek Crotona), a coastal town inside the "toe" of Italy. Diogenes Laertius reports that Alcmaeon wrote mostly on medicine, and it has been inferred from this statement that he was a physician. Given Croton's reputation as a medical center, it is not unlikely. He wrote on physics and astronomy as well, however, and in this respect he resembles the Ionian philosophers, some of whom were interested in medicine. He was certainly a natural philosopher, interested in science and medicine; he may or may not have been a physician.

Alcmaeon lived in the pre-Socratic period, when the study of physiology was merely a part of philosophy. Only later did Hippocrates separate medicine from philosophy. Greek medical theory, in fact, grew out of philosophical speculation rather than the practice of medicine. Alcmaeon's contributions include both cosmological conjecture and anatomical research. He was credited in antiquity with having written the first treatise on natural philosophy. The book is no longer extant, but some idea of its contents can be gleaned from portions that were summarized by later writers. In the opening sentence of the work, Alcmaeon declared that the gods alone have certain knowledge, while for humans only inference from things seen is possible. Thus, he eschewed all-encompassing, oversimplified hypotheses in favor of careful observation as the basis of understanding nature.

Nevertheless, Alcmaeon shared with the Ionian philosophers an interest in natural speculation. Thus, he posited a microcosmic-macrocosmic relationship between humans and the universe. He believed that the human soul was immortal because it was continuously in motion, like the heavenly

Alcmaeon.
(Library of Congress)

bodies, which he thought divine and immortal because they moved continuously and eternally in circles. While the heavenly bodies are immortal, however, humans perish because "they cannot join the beginning to the end." Alcmaeon seems to mean by this that human life is not circular but linear and thus is not eternally renewed but runs down and dies when its motion ceases. Alcmaeon developed a theory of opposites, according to which human beings have within them pairs of opposing forces, such as black and white, bitter and sweet, good and bad, large and small. He may well have been indebted to the Pythagoreans, who posited pairs of contrary qualities on mathematical lines (or they may have borrowed the notion from him). Alcmaeon, however, applied his theory particularly to health and disease.

Alcmaeon defined health as a balance or equilibrium (*isonomia*) of opposing forces in the body. He explained disease as the excess or predominance (*monarchia*) of one of these qualities or pairs of opposites that upsets the balance. This predominance could be caused by an excess or deficiency of food or by such external factors as climate, locality, fatigue, or exertion.

39

Of all Alcmaeon's theories, this concept of opposites was to be the most influential in later Greek thought. The Hippocratic treatise *Peri archaies ietrikes* (c. 430-400 B.C.E.; *On Ancient Medicine*, 1849) defends and elaborates on this explanation. Alcmaeon's theoretical speculation was balanced by a notable empirical tendency. It is this mixture of theory and observation that gives his work a distinctive and even pioneering nature.

Alcmaeon was interested in physiology, and he appears to have been the first to test his theories by examination of the body. In a celebrated case, he cut out the eye of an animal (whether dead or alive is uncertain). He was apparently interested in observing the substances of which the eye was composed. Whether he dissected the eye is not known. He also discovered (or inferred the existence of) the channels that connect the eye to the brain (probably the optic nerves). There is no evidence that Alcmaeon ever dissected human corpses, and it is unlikely that he did so. He believed that the eye contained fire (which could be seen when the eye was lit) and water (which dissection revealed to have come from the brain). He concluded that there were similar passages connecting the other sense organs to the brain, and he described the passages connecting the brain to the mouth, nose, and ears (and quite possibly was the first to discover the Eustachian tubes). He thought that these channels were hollow and carried *pneuma* (air). Alcmaeon concluded that the brain provided the sensations of sight, hearing, smell, and taste, for he noticed that when a concussion occurred, the senses were affected. Similarly, when the passages were blocked, communication between the brain and the sense organs was cut off. Plato followed Alcmaeon in holding that the brain is the central organ of thought and feeling, but Aristotle and many other philosophers continued to attribute that function to the heart.

Alcmaeon also differed from most contemporary philosophers in distinguishing between sensation and thought. He observed that sensation is common to all animals, while only humans possess intelligence. According to Alcmaeon, whether the body was awake or asleep had to do with the amount of blood in the veins. Sleep was caused by the blood retiring to the larger blood vessels, while waking was the result of the blood being rediffused throughout the body.

Alcmaeon was also interested in embryology, and he opened birds' eggs and examined the development of the embryos. He believed that the head, not the heart, was the first to develop. He resorted to speculation rather than observation in holding that human semen has its origin in the brain. He explained the sterility of mules by the theory that the seed produced by the male was too fine and cold, while the womb of the female did not open, and hence conception was prevented.

INFLUENCE   Alcmaeon exercised considerable influence on subsequent Greek writers in the fields of medicine and biology. His idea that health is a balance of opposing forces in the body, although later modified, was accepted for many hundreds of years. His anatomical investigations and his recognition that the senses are connected to the brain established Alcmaeon as a genuine pioneer in the development of Greek medical science.

FURTHER READING

Beare, John I. *Greek Theories of Elementary Cognition: From Alcmaeon to Aristotle*. Mansfield Centre, Conn.: Martino, 2004.

Codellas, P. S. "Alcmaeon of Croton: His Life, Work, and Fragments." *Proceedings of the Royal Society of Medicine* 25 (1931/1932): 1041-1046.

Gross, Charles G. *Brain, Vision, Memory: Tales in the History of Neuroscience*. Cambridge: Massachusetts Institute of Technology Press, 1998.

Guthrie, W. K. C. *A History of Greek Philosophy*. Vol. 1. New York: Cambridge University Press, 1978-1990.

Jones, W. H. S. *Philosophy and Medicine in Ancient Greece*. 1946. Reprint. New York: Arno Press, 1979.

Lloyd, Geoffrey. "Alcmaeon and the Early History of Dissection." *Sudhoffs Archiv* 59 (1975): 113-147.

Sigerist, Henry E., ed. *Early Greek, Hindu, and Persian Medicine*. Vol. 2 in *A History of Medicine*. New York: Oxford University Press, 1987.

Gary B. Ferngren

See also: Hippocrates; Medicine and Health; Philosophy; Pre-Socratic Philosophers; Science.

Alcman

POET

Born: Seventh century B.C.E.; Asia Minor
Died: Early sixth century B.C.E.; Greece
Also known as: Alkman
Category: Poetry; literature

LIFE   Traditional accounts claim that Alcman (ALK-muhn) was originally a slave in the Lydian city of Sardis before being sold and taken to Sparta. He earned fame as a choral writer for various public festivals. Of his reported six books of poetry, one work, *Partheneion* (n.d.; English translation, 1936), a choral piece that includes both mythical narrative and dialogue for a chorus of young women, survives intact along with various fragments. Alcman's work covered a wide range of topics: marriage, love, religion, nature, and myths.

INFLUENCE   A style of lyric meter was named after Alcman by ancients who considered his poetry difficult to understand because of his style and subject matter. Modern scholars cite his works as the earliest example of Greek choral poetry and as examples of the prevailing theme of eros, women as both object and subject of love poetry, and the high culture of Archaic Sparta.

FURTHER READING

Bing, Peter, and Rip Cohen. *Games of Venus*. New York: Routledge, 1991.
Calame, Claude. *The Poetics of Eros in Ancient Greece*. Translated by Janet Lloyd. Princeton, N.J.: Princeton University Press, 1999.
Davenport, Guy. *Archilochos, Sappho, Alkman: Three Lyric Poets of the Late Bronze Age*. Berkeley: University of California Press, 1980.
Hutchinson, G. O. *Greek Lyric Poetry: A Commentary on Selected Larger Pieces*. New York: Oxford University Press, 2001.

Robbins, Emmet. "Public Poetry: Alcman." In *The Companion to the Greek Lyric Poets*, edited by Douglas E. Gerber. Leiden, Netherlands: E. J. Brill, 1997.

Tammy Jo Eckhart

See also: Literature; Lyric Poetry.

Alexander the Great

KING OF MACEDONIA (R. 336-323 B.C.E.) AND EMPIRE BUILDER

Born: 356 B.C.E.; Pella, Macedonia (now in Greece)
Died: June 10 or 13, 323 B.C.E.; Babylon (now in Iraq)
Also known as: Alexander III of Macedonia
Category: Military; government and politics

LIFE Alexander the Great was the son of King Philip II of Macedonia and Olympias, an Epirote princess. From age thirteen to sixteen, he studied under Aristotle, who inspired his interest in science, medicine, philosophy, and literature. At age sixteen, Alexander served as regent for his father, and at age eighteen, he led the decisive cavalry charge at the Battle of Chaeronea. A rift between father and son occurred in 337 B.C.E., but the two were reconciled within a year. Philip was assassinated in 336 B.C.E., and Alexander was acclaimed as king of Macedonia. Alexander's swift and forceful actions enabled him to succeed his father as hegemon, or leader, of the League of Corinth and to command the invasion of the Persian Empire. In 335 B.C.E., Alexander secured Macedonia's northern borders and destroyed the city of Thebes, thus crushing Greek resistance to Macedonian overlordship.

In early 334 B.C.E., Alexander crossed the Hellespont with an invasion force of more than 37,000 men, joined by advance troops in Asia. His first great victory came at the Granicus River in 334 B.C.E., which opened Asia Minor to conquest. In 333 B.C.E., Darius III, the Persian king, met the invaders at Issus, where Alexander outmaneuvered his adversary and forced him to flee from the battlefield. Campaigning in a southwesterly direction, Alexander established his control over the Levant and was recognized as the Egyptian pharaoh in 332 B.C.E. Returning eastward, he defeated a formidable force under Darius III at Gaugamela in 331 B.C.E. Alexander marched south and then east, occupying Babylon, Susa, and Persepolis. Subsequently, he established himself as Persian king. In 327 B.C.E., Alexander invaded India (modern Pakistan) and a year later defeated Porus, the raja of Pauravas, at the Hydaspes (Jhelum) River. Alexander's troops re-

Alexander the Great. (Library of Congress)

fused to cross the Hyphasis (Beas) River, and he campaigned southward until he reached Ocean (the Arabian Sea) in 325 B.C.E. Alexander returned to Babylon in 323 B.C.E. and died there at the age of thirty-two from poisoning, a mysterious illness, or excessive drinking.

INFLUENCE Alexander's military genius, iron will, and boundless ambition produced an empire touching on three continents and encompassing two million square miles (more than five million square kilometers). His conquests, founding of new cities (seventy according to historian Plutarch), creation of a uniform currency, and circulation of vast amounts of

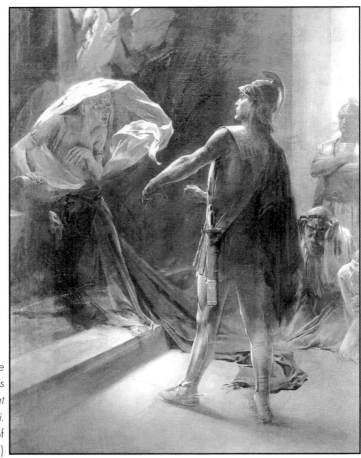

Alexander the Great consults the oracle at Delphi. (Library of Congress)

money contributed to the diffusion of Greek culture and helped usher in the Hellenistic era. Alexander has been portrayed as a philosopher in arms, an apostle of Hellenic culture, and a cosmopolitan visionary. He has also been depicted as a ruthless despot, a brutish despoiler, and a narcissistic drunkard. Nonetheless, Alexander continues to be the subject of impassioned debate more than twenty-three hundred years after his death and has thus achieved the everlasting fame he sought.

FURTHER READING

Adams, Winthrop Lindsay. *Alexander the Great: Legacy of a Conqueror.* New York: Pearson/Longman, 2005.

Bosworth, A. B. *Conquest and Empire: The Reign of Alexander the Great.* Cambridge, England: Cambridge University Press, 1988.

Cantor, Norman F., with Dee Ranieri. *Alexander the Great: Journey to the End of the Earth.* New York: HarperCollins, 2005.

Hammond, N. G. L., and F. W. Walbank. *A History of Macedonia.* Vol. 3. Oxford, England: Oxford University Press, 1988.

O'Brien, J. M. *Alexander the Great: The Invisible Enemy.* London: Routledge, 1994.

John Maxwell O'Brien

See also: Alexander the Great's Empire; Aristotle; Chaeronea, Battle of; Gaugamela, Battle of; Granicus, Battle of; Hellenistic Greece; Hydaspes, Battle of; Issus, Battle of; Olympias; Philip II of Macedonia; Ptolemaic Egypt.

Alexander the Great's Empire

Following the assassination of his father, Alexander the Great was proclaimed king of Macedonia, setting the stage for his military campaigns that would extend from Egypt to India and create the foundation of a vast empire.

Date: 336-323 B.C.E.
Category: Expansion and land acquisition; wars and battles; government and politics
Locale: Macedonian capital of Aegae (now Verghina, Greece)

SUMMARY Philip II, during his reign of more than twenty years (359-336 B.C.E.), consolidated the Macedonian kingdom and achieved hegemony over the Greek city-states of Europe, thus making possible the famous exploits of his son, Alexander the Great (356-323 B.C.E., r. 336-323). Philip's success was due in part to his skillful diplomacy, but even more important was his reorganization of the army into an effective killing machine. Rather than amateurs, Philip's soldiers were well-paid and well-trained professionals. Fighting in phalanx formations of eight to sixteen rows, they were armed with the sarisa, a 15-foot-long (4.5-meter-long) wooden spear with a metal tip. Philip supplemented the phalanx with many archers and a large cavalry. When these components worked together as intended, Philip's army was almost invincible.

After defeating Athens and Thebes in the Battle of Chaeronea in 338, Philip was the recognized master of all Greece. The following year, to preserve peace, he established the League of Corinth, which included all the Greek states except Sparta. As president of the league's council of representatives, Philip influenced the decisions of its representatives and had the authority to execute their orders. Not long before Philip's death, the council approved a joint invasion of Asia Minor (now Turkey) to drive out the Persians and further expand Macedonian hegemony.

Philip did much to prepare Alexander for future political and military leadership. Alexander's first teacher was Leonidas, a strict disciplinarian

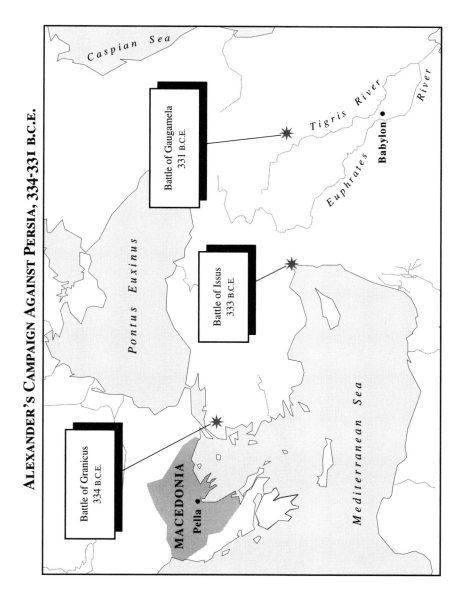

ALEXANDER'S CAMPAIGN AGAINST PERSIA, 334-331 B.C.E.

Caspian Sea

Tigris River

Euphrates River

Battle of Gaugamela
331 B.C.E.

Babylon

Pontus Euxinus

Battle of Issus
333 B.C.E.

Battle of Granicus
334 B.C.E.

Mediterranean Sea

MACEDONIA
Pella

Milestones in Alexander's Conquests, 334-323 B.C.E.

Date	Action
April, 334	Crosses into Asia in order to conquer Persia
May, 334	Meets and defeats Persian army at the River Granicus; liberates Miletus and other Greek coastal cities of Asia Minor
September-November, 334	Takes coastal city of Halicarnassus after a siege
Winter, 334-August, 333	Captures coastal cities of Phrygia, Gordium, and Cappadocia
September, 333	Seizes vital pass at Cilician Gates
November, 333	Decisively defeats Persian army along Pinarus River near Issus, capturing family of Emperor Darius IV
January-August, 332	Besieges then destroys Phoenician seaport of Tyre; takes control of Phoenicia; refuses peace offer from Darius
September-October, 332	Besieges, then storms and sacks Gaza
November, 332-April, 331	Occupies Egypt; founds city of Alexandria
April-September, 331	Marches into northern Mesopotamia through Tyre in pursuit of Darius; refuses second peace offer
October, 331	Defeats Persian army under Darius at Arbela/Gaugamela; occupies Babylon
November-December, 331	Occupies Susa; captures Persian Gates
December, 331-March, 330	Occupies, destroys Persepolis; continues pursuit of Darius

May, 330	Occupies Ecbatana
July, 330	Finds Darius murdered by Persian nobles; becomes ruler of Persian Empire
July-October, 330	Conquers tribes on southern shore of Caspian sea; subdues Parthia and Aria
January-May, 329	Invades Arachosia, then Bactria
August-October, 329	Defeats Scythians near Oxus River
February-August, 328	Puts down revolt in Sogdiana
January-February, 327	Captures fortresses at Sogdian and Chiorenes Rocks
July-September, 327	Invades India by the Khyber Pass and other passes north of the Kabul Valley
March-April, 326	Besieges and storms citadel of Aornas; crosses Indus River
May, 326	Defeats and captures King Porus at Hydaspes
July, 326	Decides to return to Persia after army mutinies
August, 326-July, 325	Travels down Indus River to the sea, subduing Mallians
September-November, 325	Leads grueling march through Gedrosian desert on way to Persepolis
July, 324	Tries to reunite empire by melding Greek and Persian cultures
Spring, 323	Arrives in Babylon
June, 323	Dies of a fever in Babylon

51

who helped develop his ascetic nature. From the age of thirteen, his personal tutor was the famous philosopher Aristotle. In 340 B.C.E., when Philip led a campaign against Byzantium, he authorized his sixteen-year-old son to rule over Macedonia as regent in his absence. While regent, Alexander led the army to suppress a tribal revolt in northern Macedonia. Two years later, he commanded a decisive cavalry charge at Chaeronea, thus acquiring the reputation of a fearless warrior. These political and military experiences developed the young man's leadership skills, and they also made him extremely popular among the soldiers, who exercised significant influence in governmental affairs.

Alexander was very close to his ambitious mother, Olympias (c. 375-316 B.C.E.), but he did not get along with Philip, who had seven wives and many concubines. In 337 B.C.E., a wedding between Philip and Cleopatra, the daughter of a Macedonian nobleman, was especially painful for Alexander and his mother. At a drinking party to celebrate the event, Cleopatra's uncle and protector, Attalus, asked those present to pray for a legitimate heir to the throne, referring indirectly to the fact that Philip's other wives, including Olympias, were of foreign birth. Alexander was so angry that he hurled his cup at Attalus. This act enraged Philip. However, when the intoxicated king tried to strike his son, he stumbled and fell on his face. Alexander then publicly ridiculed him. Within a few months, however, Alexander was reconciled with his father and was scheduled to be a commander in the invasion of Asia Minor.

As Philip was preparing for the campaign, he held a large celebration for his daughter's marriage to Olympias's brother. Delegations from most of the Greek states were gathered at Aegae for the occasion. When Philip was leaving the palace to go to the theater, he was fatally stabbed by Pausanius, a disgruntled young Macedonian nobleman (rumored to be Philip's lover) who was furious about a personal injustice that Philip had ignored. Soldiers immediately killed Pausanius, which made it impossible to gain accurate information about a possible conspiracy. Because Alexander and Olympias had the most to gain from Philip's death, some writers have suspected that one or both of them might have been involved, even though it appears unlikely that either would have risked cooperation with a person such as Pausanius.

The assassination of Philip created a condition of turmoil and uncertainty for the next several days. Alexander, only twenty years old, was not the only pretender to the vacant throne, but once the army recognized him as the legitimate successor, he quickly obtained the support of the most

Dynasties That Emerged from Alexander the Great's Empire

Dynasty	Founder	Reign (B.C.E.)
Antigonid Dynasty	Antigonus I Monophthalmos	306-301
Ptolemaic Dynasty	Ptolemy Soter	305-285
Seleucid Dynasty	Seleucus I Nicator	305-281

powerful noblemen of the country. Ancient historians, unfortunately, did not provide many details about the process and ceremonies for installing a Macedonian king. They did report that within a few weeks, Alexander promised the assembly at Aegae that he would continue the policies of his father.

Alexander's first official act was to punish all those who were suspected of involvement in Philip's murder. About a dozen alleged conspirators were quickly tried and executed before large crowds. The decision to execute these individuals publicly rather than secretly suggested that Alexander probably had no part in his father's death. After these acts of vengeance were completed, the body of Philip was cremated and interred in a large royal tomb (excavated by Manolis Andronikos in 1977).

Alexander further demonstrated his ruthlessness by eliminating all of his major rivals as well as the faction that opposed him. Attalus, who was in Asia Minor, desperately tried to reconcile with Alexander, but it was too late. Alexander ordered the assassination of both Attalus and his close relatives. However, Alexander limited the executions to those persons considered a threat to his rule. Philip's only other surviving son, Arrhidaeus, who was mentally disabled, was allowed to live. Olympias, however, was determined to get revenge. She personally engineered the death of Cleopatra and her infant daughter. Although Alexander expressed horror about their deaths, he took no action to protect them or to punish his mother.

After consolidating his power in Macedonia, Alexander then asserted his authority over the League of Corinth. The city-states of Thebes and Athens, not wanting to be ruled by a twenty-year-old youth, decided that the time was ripe to declare their independence. Without delay, Alexander marched to

Thebes with thirty thousand troops. When Thebes rejected his ultimatum, his soldiers stormed the city, killed about six thousand Thebans, burned most of the buildings, and sold thousands of the population into slavery. Faced with this cruel example, Athens wisely ceased its revolt. Shortly thereafter, the council of the league appointed Alexander commander (*hēgemōn*) of Greek forces for the anticipated war against Persia.

Alexander the Great was primarily a warrior, and during his thirteen-year reign, he achieved unprecedented military conquests that included much of the known world. Between 335 and 327 B.C.E., he established control over Asia Minor, Syria, Egypt, Mesopotamia (now Iraq), and Persia. During the next two years, he took control over much of Afghanistan and several small kingdoms of India. His commanders, however, forced him to return to Mesopotamia in 325. After Alexander died two years later, his kingdom was divided into several Hellenistic (or Greek-like) empires. For the next three hundred years, three of these empires achieved great accomplishments in science, technology, art, and literature.

SIGNIFICANCE   Historians disagree about whether Alexander's legacy was primarily good or bad. Those who admire Alexander argue that he was tolerant of different races and cultures and that he spread the blessings of Greek civilization, including government based on the rule of law, the practice of political representation, and Greek ideas of rationality and science. They insist that the Macedonian Empire promoted relative peace, stability, and prosperity. Critics of Alexander, on the other hand, tend to concentrate on the bloodshed and the cruel reprisals associated with his conquests. They maintain that almost none of the conquered peoples joined the Macedonian Empire voluntarily and that the Macedonians exploited the peoples with oppressive taxes. They further argue that the science and technology of the Hellenistic era was the result more of the impact of peaceful trade and cultural contact than of Alexander's military expansionism.

FURTHER READING

Adams, Winthrop Lindsay. *Alexander the Great: Legacy of a Conqueror.* New York: Pearson/Longman, 2005.

Bosworth, A. Brian. *Conquest and Empire: The Reign of Alexander the Great.* New York: Cambridge University Press, 1988.

Curtius, Quinntus. *History of Alexander.* New York: Penguin, 1984.

Fox, Robin Lane. *Alexander the Great.* New York: Viking Penguin, 1997.

Green, Peter. *Alexander of Macedon: A Historical Biography.* Berkeley: University of California Press, 1991.

Hammond, Nicholas. *Philip of Macedon.* Baltimore: Johns Hopkins University Press, 1994.

Lonsdale, David J. *Alexander the Great, Killer of Men: History's Greatest Conqueror and the Macedonian Art of War.* New York: Carroll & Graf, 2004.

Plutarch. "Alexander." In *Lives of Noble Grecians and Romans,* edited by Arthur Clough. New York: Modern Library, 1992.

Renault, Mary. *The Nature of Alexander.* New York: Pantheon Books, 1975.

Tarn, William. *Alexander the Great.* New York: Cambridge University Press, 1948.

Thomas T. Lewis

See also: Alexander the Great; Aristotle; Chaeronea, Battle of; Gaugamela, Battle of; Granicus, Battle of; Hellenistic Greece; Hydaspes, Battle of; Issus, Battle of; Olympias; Philip II of Macedonia; Ptolemaic Egypt.

Alexandrian Library

The Alexandrian library contained the greatest collection of Greek literature in the ancient world.

Date: c. 300 B.C.E.-before 700 C.E.
Category: Organizations and institutions; education; literature; scholarship
Locale: Alexandria, Egypt

SUMMARY   Much is in doubt about the Alexandrian library: its founder (Ptolemy Soter or his son, Ptolemy Philadelphus); its location (somewhere in the Royal Quarter); its relationship to the Alexandrian museum; the size, nature, and organization of its holdings; and its ultimate fate. The Peripatetic philosopher Demetrius Phalereus may have been "founding librarian," with Aristotle's library as his model. Subsequent librarians included Zenodotus of Ephesus, Aristophanes of Byzantium, and Aristarchus of Samothrace; all three produced editions of Homer and other poets, demonstrating the library's crucial role in preserving Greek literature for future generations.

Ancient anecdotes highlight dubious collecting methods. Every ship unloading at Alexandria was supposed to be searched, its books seized and copied, and the copies given to the original owners. Other Hellenistic rulers followed the Ptolemies' example in founding libraries, especially the Attalids in Pergamum. The library may have burned when Julius Caesar set fire to the Egyptian fleet in 48 B.C.E., but the library continued to exist during the Roman period.

SIGNIFICANCE   The library at Alexandria was the repository for the greatest collection of Greek literature in the world, serving a crucial role in preserving Greek literature for future generations. In later years, the bishop of Alexandria led an attack on the Serapeum (temple to Sarapis) in 391 C.E. and presumably destroyed the annex library that had been built there. ʿAmr

56

ibn al-ʿĀṣ, Arab conqueror of Egypt in 642 C.E., is said to have consigned the library's books to Alexandria's baths for fuel, but this story seems to have arisen only in the twelfth century C.E.

This engraving depicts the Alexandrian library at the time of the Ptolemies. (North Wind Picture Archives)

FURTHER READING

Abbadi, Mostafa el-. *The Life and Fate of the Ancient Library of Alexandria*. 2d ed. Paris: UNESCO, 1992.

"Alexandrian Library Opens at Last." *American Libraries* 33, no. 11 (December, 2002): 31.

Canfora, Luciano. *The Vanished Library*. Berkeley: University of California Press, 1990.

Frazer, Peter M. *Ptolemaic Alexandria*. Oxford, England: Clarendon Press, 1972.

MacLeod, Roy, ed. *The Library of Alexandria: Centre of Learning in the Ancient World*. New York: I. B. Tauris, 2000.

T. Keith Dix

See also: Apollonius Rhodius; Aristarchus of Samothrace; Demetrius Phalereus; Literature; Ptolemaic Dynasty; Ptolemaic Egypt; Ptolemy Soter; Strabo.

Amasis Painter

ARTIST

Born: c. 555 B.C.E.; place unknown
Died: c. 525 B.C.E.; place unknown
Category: Art and architecture

LIFE   "Amasis made me" is a signature found on many sixth century Greek vases. Eight vases so signed were also painted by the same artist, who is known to us today simply as the Amasis Painter (uh-MAY-suhs PAYN-tuhr). Today 132 vases are attributed to the Amasis Painter. This artist has a distinctive, sharp, flat, and meticulous black figure style. Black figure vase painters left the background of the vase "in reserve" (the natural color of the clay) and painted their subjects in black, with touches of white and red. Additionally, patterns in textiles and hair were incised through the paint to reveal the lighter color beneath. The Amasis Painter's figures are portrayed in silhouette, are muscular but sleek, and represent gods, nobles, and heroes. These elegant scenes exhibit exquisite detailing in hair, dress, and decorative bands of petals and spirals. The Amasis Painter preferred to paint on amphorae, vases with two handles used for storage, and is known for creating designs harmonious with the vases' shape.

INFLUENCE   One of the Amasis Painter's best known amphorae illustrates Dionysus and the Maenads on the front panel and Athena and Poseidon on its obverse. The Amasis Painter is known for the use of uncommon shapes, variations of standard scenes, and a refined, elegant style, often influencing other Attic painters, among them Exekias.

FURTHER READING
Boardman, John. *Athenian Black Figure Vases*. Reprint. New York: Thames and Hudson, 1991.
Isler-Kerényi, Cornelia. *Civilizing Violence: Satyrs on Sixth-Century Greek*

Vases. Translated from the Italian by Eric Charles de Sena. Fribourg, Switzerland: Academic Press Fribourg, 2004.

Neer, Richard T. *Style and Politics in Athenian Vase-Painting: The Craft of Democracy, ca. 530-460 B.C.E.* New York: Cambridge University Press, 2002.

Von Bothmer, Dietrich. *The Amasis Painter and His World: Vase Painting in Sixth-Century B.C.* Athens. New York: Thames and Hudson, 1985.

Laura Rinaldi Dufresne

See also: Archaic Greece; Art and Architecture.

Amazons

The Amazons were a race of female warriors in Greek mythology who dwelled on the northern limits of the known world.

Date: Legendary from before 800 B.C.E.
Category: Women; cities and civilizations
Locale: Themiscyra (a town on the south coast of the Black Sea), on the Tanais (the river Don), by the Caspian Gates

SUMMARY   The Amazons (AM-uh-zawnz) were fierce warriors governed by a queen. They worshiped Ares, the god of war, and Artemis, the virgin goddess of the hunt. They engaged in hunting and fighting on horseback, with bows, crescent-shaped shields, axes, and spears. In order to perpetuate their race, the Amazons periodically mated with men of neighboring tribes, afterward killing, maiming, or returning the male infants and cutting off the right breasts of the female offspring so that they would be better able to use a bow. The tales of breast removal led to the belief that the word "Amazon" was derived from the Greek words *a*, "not," and *mazos*, "breast," even though, in most ancient works of art, Amazons are portrayed with two breasts.

SIGNIFICANCE   The Amazons figure in much epic and other Greek literature. In Homer's *Iliad* (c. 750 B.C.E., English translation, 1611), the Trojan king Priam claims to have once helped ward off an Amazon attack, although another mythic tradition asserts that the Amazons, led by their queen Penthesilea, came to Priam's rescue after the death of his son Hector. After fighting bravely, Penthesilea was killed by the Greek warrior Achilles, who was so moved by her military prowess and by the beauty of her dead body that he ordered the Greeks to build a monument to her. When Greek soldier Thersites ridiculed Achilles' compassion and accused the hero of being in love with Penthesilea, Achilles killed him in anger.

Heracles fought the Amazons in order to complete the ninth labor im-

Amazons hunting. (F. R. Niglutsch)

posed upon him by Eurystheus, king of Mycenae and Tiryns. He had to obtain the girdle of the Amazon queen Hippolyta. Although Hippolyta was willing to hand over her girdle to Heracles, the goddess Hera spread a false rumor among the Amazons that the hero intended to carry off the wearer of the girdle as well. The Amazons attacked, and, in the battle that ensued, Heracles killed Hippolyta and many of her followers.

In another account, Theseus attacked the Amazons after their encounter with Heracles and carried off their queen, Antiope (or Hippolyta, in some versions). She became the mother of Theseus's son Hippolytus, who would later devote himself to hunting and to worshiping the virgin goddess Artemis.

FURTHER READING

Anderson, Florence M. *Religious Cults Associated with the Amazons.* 1912. Reprint. New York: AMS Press, 1967.

Blok, Josine H. *The Early Amazons: Modern and Ancient Perspectives on a Persistent Myth.* Religions in the Graeco-Roman World 120. Boston: Brill Academic, 1994.

Davis-Kimball, Jeannine, with Mona Behan. *Warrior Women: An Archaeologist's Search for History's Hidden Heroines*. New York: Warner Books, 2002.

Tyrrell, William B. *Amazons: A Study in Athenian Mythmaking*. Baltimore: Johns Hopkins University Press, 1984.

Wheelwright, Julie. *Amazons and Military Maids: Women Who Dressed as Men in Pursuit of Life, Liberty, and Happiness*. New York: New York University Press, 1990.

Wilde, Lyn Webster. *On the Trial of the Women Warriors: The Amazons in Myth and History*. New York: Thomas Dunne Books, 2000.

Robert J. White

See also: Mythology; Women's Life.

Anacreon

POET

Born: c. 571 B.C.E.; Teos, Ionia, Asia Minor (now Sigacik, Turkey)
Died: c. 490 B.C.E.; Athens, Greece
Category: Poetry; literature

LIFE Little is known of the early life of Anacreon (uh-NAK-ree-uhn). His father was Scythinus, about whom nothing has been recorded regarding his profession or his rank in society. Certain themes in Anacreon's poetry—especially love, drinking, and the refined pleasures of life—suggest that he had an aristocratic background, yet Anacreon's poetry may not have been autobiographical. Authors of early Greek lyrics composed works on standard themes, including drinking songs, erotic poems to both women and boys, funerary inscriptions, and battle hymns. As a result, Anacreon's poetry may reflect personal experience or may simply embody well-established themes.

The era of Anacreon's birth was that of the first Greek tragedies and the earliest speculations by the pre-Socratic philosophers. Thales (c. 625-546 B.C.E.), generally regarded as the founder of Greek philosophy, lived in Miletus, less than a hundred miles from Anacreon's native Teos. When Anacreon was a child, Greek cities in Asia Minor were threatened by the Persians under Cyrus the Great (c. 600-529 B.C.E.). In about 541 B.C.E., when Anacreon was still a young man, Teos fell to Cyrus's general, Harpagus. Along with other Teians, Anacreon sailed to Thrace on the shore of mainland Greece. There the city of Abdera was founded (or perhaps rebuilt). It was a major commercial center that would later produce the philosophers Protagoras (c. 480-411 B.C.E.) and Democritus (c. 460-370 B.C.E.).

In Abdera, Anacreon composed his earliest extant poetry. In addition to poems on drinking and love, he wrote works dealing with the wars that had so greatly affected his life. In one such poem, he speaks of a young friend who died fighting for Abdera. In another, he imitates Archilochus of Paros (c. 735-676 B.C.E.), who mentioned throwing away his shield in battle.

Other early poems by Anacreon are more humorous. In one, he speaks of a "filly" whom only a skillful "rider"—Anacreon himself—could tame. This poem contains the same mixture of symbolism and eroticism that recurs throughout Anacreon's later works.

After about ten years in Abdera, Anacreon was invited by the tyrant Polycrates (c. 570-522 B.C.E.) to live in Samos. Officially, Anacreon taught Polycrates' son music and poetry, but he also continued to write works of his own. The esteem in which Anacreon was held by Polycrates is suggested by Herodotus, who describes a herald's discovery of Polycrates relaxing with Anacreon in a banquet hall. A great patron of the arts, Polycrates also brought the poet Ibycus of Rhegium (c. 560-525 B.C.E.) to Samos. Ibycus, whose choral poems contained a rich imagery, influenced Anacreon in his mature period.

When Polycrates fell to the Persian king Darius in 522 B.C.E., Anacreon left Samos for Athens. As on Samos, in Athens Anacreon associated with the highest levels of society. One of his poems mentioned a young boy named Critias, an ancestor of a later Critias (c. 460-403 B.C.E.) who was Plato's uncle and one of the Thirty Tyrants ruling Athens after the Peloponnesian War (404-403 B.C.E.). Critias's household was extremely wealthy, and Anacreon praised it in a poem later remembered by Plato. So close were Anacreon's ties to the tyrant Hippias that, when the latter fell in 512 B.C.E., Anacreon took refuge in Thessaly. His exile was brief, however, and Anacreon soon returned to Athens for the rest of his life.

Late in his career, Anacreon wrote frequently about old age. In one work, he notes that his hair had gone white and that he had seen the horrors of the underworld. Anacreon lived into his eighties, long enough to influence the Greek playwright Aeschylus (525-456 B.C.E.), who adopted some of his meters. One unreliable tradition says that Anacreon died by choking on a grape seed. This story was almost certainly invented in a later age, when Anacreon had come to be regarded as a drunkard because of his numerous drinking songs. Another tradition reports that Anacreon was buried in Teos; this legend probably arose from a series of imaginary epitaphs composed by later poets. The site of his grave, now lost, was almost certainly in Athens, the city where he achieved his greatest fame.

INFLUENCE   A legend reports that when Anacreon sailed for Athens from Samos, he traveled in a penteconter, a fifty-oared ship that was one of the largest vessels found in Greece at that time. A column erected in Attica by

Hipparchus, the brother of the Athenian tyrant Hippias, contained lines composed by Anacreon, further suggesting the poet's high stature. On vases, Anacreon is often depicted playing a lyre before an audience of young aristocrats. A fragment of a later poem says that Anacreon drove women mad through the power of his music. Even in the second century C.E., the geographer Pausanias had seen a statue honoring Anacreon on the Athenian Acropolis.

FURTHER READING

Campbell, David A. *The Golden Lyre: The Themes of Greek Lyric Poets.* London: Duckworth, 1983.

Frankel, Hermann. *Early Greek Poetry and Philosophy.* Oxford, England: Basil Blackwell, 1975.

Hutchinson, G. O. *Greek Lyric Poetry: A Commentary on Selected Larger Pieces.* New York: Oxford University Press, 2001.

Kirkwood, G. M. *Early Greek Monody: The History of a Poetic Type.* Ithaca, N.Y.: Cornell University Press, 1974.

O'Brien, John. *Anacreon Redivivus: A Study of Anacreontic Translation in Mid-Sixteenth Century France.* Ann Arbor: University of Michigan Press, 1995.

Rosenmeyer, Patricia A. *The Poetics of Imitation: Anacreon and the Anacreontic Tradition.* Cambridge, England: Cambridge University Press, 1992.

Schmidt, Michael. *The First Poets: Lives of the Ancient Greek Poets.* New York: Knopf; distributed by Random House, 2005.

Jeffrey L. Buller

See also: Aeschylus; Archilochus of Paros; Critias of Athens; Ibycus; Literature; Lyric Poetry; Polycrates of Samos.

Anaxagoras

PHILOSOPHER AND SCIENTIST

Born: c. 500 B.C.E.; Clazomenae, Anatolia (now in Turkey)
Died: c. 428 B.C.E.; Lampsacus (now Lapseki, Turkey)
Category: Philosophy; science and technology

LIFE   Virtually nothing is known about the parents of Anaxagoras (an-aks-AG-ur-uhs) or about his childhood, adolescence, or education. Born into a wealthy family in an Ionian Greek city, he moved to Athens as a young man and became friends with the young Pericles, who apparently influenced him considerably.

Sometime in or shortly after 467 B.C.E. Anaxagoras published his only written work, apparently titled *Nature*. Of this work, only seventeen fragments totaling around twelve hundred words have survived, all recorded as quotations in the works of later generations of philosophers. Anaxagoras's book was an ambitious attempt to explain the origins and nature of the universe without recourse (or so it seemed to many of his contemporaries) to any supernatural agents. Other Ionian philosophers, notably Parmenides, had preceded Anaxagoras in this endeavor, but their systems were logically unable to explain the multiplicity of "things" in the universe or to explain physical and biological change in those things because they had postulated that all things are made from the same basic "stuff." Anaxagoras overcame the logical inconsistencies of this argument by postulating an infinite variety of substances that make up the whole of the universe.

Anaxagoras argued that there is something of everything in everything. By this he meant that, for example, water contains a part of every other thing in the universe, from blood to rock to air. The reason that it is perceived to be water is that most of its parts are water. In the beginning, according to the first fragment of Anaxagoras's book, infinitely small parts of everything in equal proportions were together in a sort of primal soup. In fragment 3, he proposes a primitive version of the law of the conservation of energy, by saying that anything, no matter how small, can be divided infinitely, because it is not possible for something to become nonexistent

Anaxagoras.

through dividing. This idea of infinite divisibility is unique to the Anaxagorean system; no philosopher before or since has proposed it.

This universal mixture of all things acquired form and substance, according to fragment 12, through the actions of *nous*, or "mind." Mind, Anaxagoras argues, is not part of everything (though it is a part of some things), nor is a part of everything found in mind (though parts of some things are found in mind). Mind set the primal soup into rotation, and the different things began to "separate off," thus forming the universe. The rotation of the primal mixture not only separated everything according to its kind (but not perfectly, as everything still contains parts of every other thing) but also supplied heat, through friction. Among other things, friction ignited the Sun and the stars. Considerable disagreement over the exact meaning Anaxagoras was trying to convey with the term "mind" has colored scholarly works on his book since Aristotle and continues to be a controversial issue.

Anaxagoras's system not only enabled him and his students to describe all existing objects, but it also permitted the explanation of physical and biological change. It was the introduction of the idea of mind and its action as a formative agent in the creation of the universe for which Anaxagoras became famous and that rejuvenated Socrates' interest and faith in philosophy.

One of Anaxagoras's most notable achievements during his stay in Athens was his postulation of the correct explanation for a solar eclipse. Anaxagoras was apparently the first to argue that an eclipse occurs when the Moon (which he said was a large mass of cold rocks) passes between the Earth and the Sun (which he said was a larger mass of hot rocks). He may have reached this conclusion after the fall of a large meteorite near Aegypotomi in 467 B.C.E., which excited wide discussion throughout the Hellenic world.

Sometime after 467, Anaxagoras was accused of and tried for impiety (denying the gods), after admitting that he thought the Sun was a huge mass of "hot rock," and Medism (sympathizing with the Persians). The actual date of his trial and subsequent banishment from Athens is still hotly debated among classical scholars. Several scholars have concluded that Anaxagoras's trial was engineered by Pericles' political rivals, in order to deprive Pericles of a trusted friend. Convicted of impiety Anaxagoras went into exile. Anaxagoras spent his remaining years as the head of a flourishing school at Lampsacus, where many young Greeks came to study with him before his death, probably in 428 B.C.E.

INFLUENCE   The thesis that Anaxagoras greatly influenced Socrates and Aristotle is easily proved by their elaborate discussions of his system in their own words. Through those two most influential of all Greek thinkers, he has had a profound impact on all subsequent generations of philosophers and natural scientists in the Western world. Some of Anaxagoras's critics, both ancient and modern, accuse him of merely substituting the word "mind" for "God" or "the gods." Thus, in their estimation, his philosophy becomes merely a humanistic religion. Other critics have dismissed Anaxagoras's teachings as simplistic and unworthy of serious consideration. His supporters, from Aristotle to the present, have defended him as a pioneering thinker who provided much of the inspiration for the flowering of post-Socratic philosophy during the Golden Age of Greece and the Hellenistic world.

FURTHER READING

Barnes, Jonathan. *The Presocratic Philosophers.* London: Routledge, 1999.

Brunschwig, Jacques, and G. E. R. Lloyd, eds. *Greek Thought: A Guide to*

Classical Knowledge. Cambridge, Mass.: Belknap Press of Harvard University Press, 2000.

Davison, J. A. "Protagoras, Democritus, and Anaxagoras." *Classical Quarterly* 3 (1953): 33-45.

Gershenson, Daniel E., and Daniel A. Greenberg. *Anaxagoras and the Birth of Physics*. New York: Blaisdell, 1964.

Guthrie, W. K. C. *A History of Greek Philosophy*. Vol. 2. Cambridge, England: Cambridge University Press, 1965.

Kirk, Geoffrey S., John E. Raven, and M. Schofield. *The Presocratic Philosophers*. 2d ed. New York: Cambridge University Press, 1983.

Mansfield, J. "The Chronology of Anaxagoras's Athenian Period and the Date of His Trial." *Mnemosyne* 33 (1980): 17-95.

Matthews, Gareth B. "On the Idea of There Being Something of Everything in Everything." *Analysis* 62, no. 1 (January, 2002): 1.

Mourelatos, Alexander P. D. *The Pre-Socratics: A Collection of Critical Essays*. Princeton, N.J.: Princeton University Press, 1993.

Schofield, Malcolm. *An Essay on Anaxagoras*. Cambridge, England: Cambridge University Press, 1980.

Paul Madden

See also: Cosmology; Pericles; Philosophy; Pre-Socratic Philosophers; Science; Socrates.

Anaximander

Philosopher, astronomer, and cartographer

Born: c. 610 B.C.E.; Miletus, Greek Asia Minor (now in Turkey)
Died: c. 547 B.C.E.; probably Miletus
Category: Philosophy; science and technology; geography; astronomy and cosmology

LIFE   Anaximander (uh-nak-suh-MAN-duhr) was a fellow citizen and student of Thales, the Milesian usually credited with having inaugurated Western philosophy. Thales, some forty years older than his protégé, put none of his philosophical thought in writing and maintained no formal pedagogical associations with pupils. However, Thales' cosmological views (as reconstructed by historians) doubtless inspired Anaximander, and Anaximander finally expanded on Thales' ideas with innovative leaps in conceptual abstraction.

Anaximander was known in his day for his practical achievements and his astronomical discoveries. He is said to have been chosen by the Milesians as the leader for a new colony in Apollonia on the Black Sea. He traveled widely and was the first Greek to publish a "geographical tablet," a map of the world. The map was circular, and it was centered on the city of Delphi, because Delphi was the location of the *omphalos*, or "navel" stone, that was thought to be the center of Earth. Anaximander is also said to have designed a celestial map and to have specified the proportions of stellar orbits.

In addition, he built a spherical model of the stars and planets, with Earth located at the center and represented as a disk or cylinder whose height was one third its diameter. The heavenly bodies were rings of hollow pipe of different sizes that were placed on circling wheels in ratios of three to six to nine, in proportion to the magnitude of Earth. This model was dynamic; the wheels could be moved at different speeds, making it possible to visualize patterns of planetary motion. Anaximander is also credited with inventing the gnomon (part of a sundial) and with having discovered the zodiac.

All these eclectic interests and discoveries illustrate Anaximander's rational view of the world. This approach received its fullest and most innovative expression in his philosophy of nature. It arose in part as a response to Thales' ideas on nature. Thales held that water was the nature of everything. This meant, in the light of the ancient idea of *physis* (a thing's origin or source, from which it is constantly renewed), that water was the origin of everything, a notion without any allegorical or mythical connotations. Anaximander agreed with Thales that the origin of the things of the world was some common stuff, but he thought that the stuff could not be some ordinary element. He rejected Thales' conception on purely logical grounds. How could any manifestly singular stuff ever give rise to qualities that pertained to things differently constituted, such as earth and fire? What is more, if water were the source of things, would not drying destroy them? Thus, reasoned Anaximander, the thing with which the world begins cannot be identical with any of the ordinary stuff with which humans are acquainted, but it must be capable of giving rise to the wide multiplicity of things and their pairs of contrary qualities. What therefore distinguishes the source from the world is that the source itself is "unbounded": It can have no definite shape or quality of its own but must be a reservoir from which every sort or characteristic in the world may be spawned.

Anaximander called the source of things this very name: *apeiron*, Boundlessness or the Boundless. The Boundless can have no beginning, nor can it pass away, for it can have no bounds, including temporal ones. This eternal source functions as a storehouse of the world's qualities. The qualities that constitute some present state of the world have been separated out of the stock, and when their contrary qualities become manifest, they will, in turn, be reabsorbed into the reservoir. When Earth is hot, heat will come forth from the Boundless; when Earth cools, cold will come forth and heat will go back. For Anaximander, this process continued in never-ending cycles. The cause of the alternating manifestations of contrary qualities is the subject of the single existing fragment of Anaximander's own words, the only remains of the first philosophy ever written. Out of the Boundless, Anaximander explains, the worlds arise, but from whatever things is the genesis of the things that are, into these they must pass away according to necessity; for they must pay the penalty and make atonement to one another for their injustice according to the ordering of Time.

History has produced no consensus of interpretation for this passage and its picturesque philosophical metaphor for the rationale of the world.

Anaximander was probably thinking of a courtroom image. Each existing thing is in a state of "having-too-much," so that during the time it exists it "commits injustice" against its opposite by preventing it from existing. In retribution, the existing thing must cede its overt existence for its opposite to enjoy and pay the penalty of returning to the submerged place in the great Boundless reservoir. This cycling, he added, is how time is ordered or measured. Time is the change, the alternating manifestation of opposites.

INFLUENCE   Anaximander, with his scientific curiosity and his genius for abstract insight, poised philosophical inquiry for new vistas of exploration; his new philosophical approach inaugurated penetrating, objective analysis. His principle of the eternal Boundless as the source of the world's multifarious qualities and change forms the conceptual backdrop against which twenty-five centuries of science and natural philosophy have developed.

Two particular innovations of Anaximander have never been abandoned. First, his extension of the concept of law from human society to the physical world continues to dictate the scientific worldview. The received view in Anaximander's time—that nature was capricious and anarchic—has never again taken hold. Second, Anaximander's invention of the use of models and maps revolutionized science and navigation and continues to be indispensable, even in people's daily lives.

FURTHER READING

Brumbaugh, Robert S. *The Philosophers of Greece.* Albany: State University of New York Press, 1981.

Burnet, John. *Early Greek Philosophy.* 4th ed. New York: Meridian Books/ World, 1961.

Couprie, Dirk L., Robert Hahn, and Gerard Naddaf. *Anaximander in Context: New Studies in the Origins of Greek Philosophy.* Albany: State University of New York Press, 2002.

Guthrie, W. K. C. *The Earlier Presocratics and the Pythagoreans.* Vol. 1 in *A History of Greek Philosophy.* New York: Cambridge University Press, 1978-1990.

Hahn, Robert. *Anaximander and the Architects: The Contributions of Egyptian and Greek Architectural Technologies to the Origins of Greek Philosophy.* Albany: State University of New York Press, 2001.

Kahn, Charles H. *Anaximander and the Origins of Greek Cosmology*. Indianapolis, Ind.: Hackett, 1994.

Kirk, Geoffrey S., and John E. Raven. *The Presocratic Philosophers*. 2d ed. New York: Cambridge University Press, 1983.

Wheelwright, Philip, ed. *The Presocratics*. New York: Odyssey Press, 1966.

Patricia Cook

See also: Cosmology; Philosophy; Pre-Socratic Philosophers; Science; Thales of Miletus.

Anaximenes of Miletus

PHILOSOPHER

Born: Early sixth century B.C.E.; probably Miletus (now in Turkey)
Died: Second half of the sixth century B.C.E.; place unknown
Category: Philosophy

LIFE The writings of Anaximenes of Miletus (an-ak-SIHM-uh-neez of mi-LEE-tuhs) no longer exist. Thus, knowledge of him is based on a few statements made by Aristotle and later writers on the history of Greek philosophy, some of whom quote earlier writers whose work is now lost. A few of these earlier writers show that they had access to Anaximenes' writings, but it is difficult to determine the veracity of any of their statements. Thus, scholars have almost no reliable information about Anaximenes' life; not even his dates can be accurately ascertained, and only the most general of assumptions can be made. Anaximenes, Thales, and Anaximander were the most famous thinkers from Miletus, then the largest and most prosperous Greek city on the west coast of Asia Minor. While they are known only for their philosophical work, it is believed that all three were financially secure and that philosophical thought was for them an avocation. Apparently, Anaximenes was the youngest of the three. Some sources suggest that Anaximenes was the pupil of Anaximander, while others suggest that he was a fellow student and friend. Most scholars place the work of Anaximenes after the fall of Sardis to Cyrus the Great (c. 545 B.C.E.) and before the fall of Miletus (494 B.C.E.).

Anaximenes, like his two predecessors, challenged the mythological world of Homer and Hesiod by introducing free and rational speculation. The work of Anaximenes was summarized in a single book whose title is unknown. In the fourth century, Theophrastus, Aristotle's successor, is said to have noted its "simple and economical Ionic style." One supposes that this comment refers to the shift from writing in poetry to writing in prose. Clearly, Anaximenes was more concerned with content than with the conventions of poetical expression. Anaximenes wrote that "air" was the original substance of matter. Scholars of ancient history agree, how-

75

ever, that the exact meaning of this statement is unclear. To take the position that all other matter was derived from air, Anaximenes must have believed that air was a changeable substance that, by rarefaction and condensation, was able to take other forms. When rarefied, it became fire; when condensed, it became wind, clouds, water, earth, and finally stones. Thus, Anaximenes had modified Thales' idea that water was the original substance and contradicted Anaximander's thesis of unchanging infinity while still staying within the Milesian monist tradition.

Having determined the nature of air and its properties, Anaximenes apparently developed other ideas by extension. Topics that he addressed include the nature of hot and cold as expressions of rarefaction and condensation, the divine nature of air, the motion of air, cosmogony, and cosmological problems. Under the latter heading he seems to have commented on the nature of Earth, which he saw as flat and riding on a cushion of air, and the nature of heavenly bodies. In his consideration of meteorological phenomena, Anaximenes seems to have followed Anaximander rather closely.

Anaximenes also presented a challenge by writing in prose. Prior to this, poetry had been the preferred form for serious expression—not only in literature but also in politics. By writing in prose, the early philosophers moved, in part, from the world of the aristocrat to that of the new man of Greece: the hoplite, the merchant, the small, free farmer. While this new method of thought was not accepted by the average Greek (nor even, one suspects, the average Milesian), it did gain respect and placed philosophical speculation on an elevated footing.

For Anaximenes, unlike his predecessors, however, the differences that could be observed in matter were not qualitative but quantitative. Thus it is that he was the first to suggest a consistent picture of the world as a mechanism.

INFLUENCE Anaximenes' methods were far more influential than his specific theories on matter. Together with Thales and Anaximander, he was the first to free speculative thought from mythology and mythological terms. The methods of these three thinkers are the foundation for all modern scientific and philosophical thought. They began with intellectual curiosity about the nature of matter and combined this curiosity with keen observation of the world around them—with little regard to prior religious explanations.

At first glance, Anaximenes' ideas about air seem regressive. When, however, the idea is seen as a more general concept—as the first theory to explain a single substance capable of changing its form—its sophistication can be appreciated. Most ancient thinkers agreed that Anaximenes provided a better explanation of natural phenomena.

It is a small step from Anaximenes' ideas of rarefaction and condensation to Empedocles' definition of matter and the atomic theories of Heraclitus of Ephesus and Democritus. Clearly, no one in the modern world would take these ideas at face value, but with a small shift in the translation of Anaximeneian terms, one approaches the modern concepts of states of matter and the relationship between energy and matter. Thus, Anaximenes is an important figure in the development of Western philosophical and scientific thought.

FURTHER READING

Barnes, Jonathan. *The Presocratic Philosophers*. New York: Routledge, 1999.

Burnet, John. *Early Greek Philosophy*. 4th ed. New York: World, 1961.

Graham, Daniel W. "A Testimony of Anaximenes in Plato." *Classical Quarterly* 53, no. 2 (2003): 327-337.

Guthrie, W. K. C. *The Earlier Presocratics and the Pythagoreans*. Vol. 1 in *A History of Greek Philosophy*. New York: Cambridge University Press, 1978-1990.

Hurwit, Jeffrey M. *The Art and Culture of Early Greece, 1100-480 B.C.* Ithaca, N.Y.: Cornell University Press, 1985.

Kirk, G. S., and J. E. Raven. *The Presocratic Philosophers*. 2d ed. New York: Cambridge University Press, 1983.

Stokes, M. C. *The One and Many in Presocratic Philosophy*. Washington, D.C.: Center for Hellenic Studies with Harvard University Press, 1972.

Sweeney, Leo. *Infinity in the Presocratics: A Bibliographical and Philosophical Study*. The Hague, Netherlands: Martinus Nijhoff, 1972.

Michael M. Eisman

See also: Anaximander; Cosmology; Democritus; Empedocles; Heraclitus of Ephesus; Philosophy; Pre-Socratic Philosophers; Science; Thales of Miletus; Theophrastus.

Andocides

ORATOR, POLITICIAN, AND MERCHANT

Born: c. 440 B.C.E.; place unknown
Died: c. 391 B.C.E.; place unknown
Category: Oratory and rhetoric; government and politics

LIFE   Andocides (an-DAHS-uh-deez) came from an old family known as the Kerykes (Heralds), whose roots were in Eleusis. His life was, in scholar H. J. Rose's description, "one long series of adventures and disgraces." In 415 B.C.E. during the Peloponnesian War (431-404 B.C.E.), he was among those accused of mutilating the herms (statues of Hermes) the night before the Athenian fleet departed for Sicily. He saved his life by turning state's evidence. After punishment by loss of civic rights, he went into exile and became a successful trader. His attempts to regain full citizenship in 411 and 410 B.C.E. failed, but he returned under Athenian general Thrasybulus in 403 B.C.E. and victoriously defended himself against the charge of impiety. Then after a brief time among those envoys negotiating peace during the Corinthian War (395-386 B.C.E.), he went into exile again in 392/391 B.C.E. when their treaty was rejected in Athens and Callistratus began prosecution of the peace team. Nothing further is known about him.

INFLUENCE   The surviving orations pertain to Andocides' personal affairs. There is no evidence that he ever wrote for others. Their tone is fresh and eager, and their style is natural, without evidence of seasoned rhetoric. In addition to fragments from four speeches, four speeches are extant, one of which is thought to be a forgery.

FURTHER READING

Furley, William D. *Andocides and the Hermes: A Study of Crisis in Fifth Century Athenian Religion.* London: Institute of Classical Studies, 1996.

Missiou, Anna. *The Subversive Oratory of Andocides*. Cambridge, England: Cambridge University Press, 1992.

Michele Valerie Ronnick

See also: Corinthian War; Peloponnesian Wars.

Antigonid Dynasty

The Antigonid Dynasty was the last to oversee Macedonia before Rome made the region a province under Roman control.

Date: 306 to 168 B.C.E.
Category: Cities and civilizations
Locale: Macedonia

SUMMARY   After the death of Alexander the Great, his lieutenants proceeded to civil war and a division of the Macedonian Empire. A provincial governor, Antigonus I Monophthalmos, the "One-Eyed," acquired Asia Minor and, calling himself king, established the Antigonid (an-TIHG-uh-nihd) Dynasty in 306 B.C.E. He soon perished in battle against a coalition of his enemies. However, his son, Demetrius I Poliorcetes, "Besieger of Cities," survived, only to win and lose Macedonia.

Renewing the dynasty's fortune, Antigonus II Gonatas became king of Macedonia in 276 B.C.E. and, from Pella, created a secure foundation for the rule of his successors. Although Demetrius II quarreled with Aetolia, Antigonus III Doson established a broad Hellenic alliance and, as its leader, encouraged cooperation between Greece and Macedonia. Yet Philip V drew that alliance into a dangerous struggle by supporting Hannibal of Carthage against Rome in the Second Punic War (218-201 B.C.E.).

SIGNIFICANCE   After defeating the Carthaginian general, the Romans vanquished Philip at Cynoscephalae in 197 B.C.E. and his son Perseus at Pydna in 168 B.C.E. After abolishing the Antigonid monarchy, Rome established four independent Macedonian republics. Years later, when adventurers claiming descent from Perseus aroused revolt, Rome intervened and reorganized Macedonia as a Roman province.

Major Kings of the Antigonid Dynasty, 306-168 B.C.E.

King	Reign
Antigonus I Monophthalmos	306-301 B.C.E.
Demetrius I Poliorcetes	294-287
Antigonus II Gonatas	276-239
Demetrius II	239-229
Antigonus III Doson	229-221
Philip V	221-179
Perseus	179-168

FURTHER READING

Billows, Richard A. *Antigonos the One-Eyed and the Creation of the Hellenistic State*. Berkeley: University of California Press, 1990.

Erskine, Andrew, ed. *A Companion to the Hellenistic World*. Malden, Mass.: Blackwell, 2003.

Gabbert, Janice J. *Antigonus II Gonatas: A Political Biography*. New York: Routledge, 1997.

O'Neil, James L. "The Ethnic Origins of the Friends of the Antigonid Kings of Macedon." *Classical Quarterly* 53, no. 2 (2003): 510-522.

Denvy A. Bowman

See also: Alexander the Great; Alexander the Great's Empire; Cynoscephalae, Battle of; Demetrius Poliorcetes; Hellenistic Greece; Philip V.

Antiochus the Great

KING OF SELEUCID DYNASTY (R. 223-187 B.C.E.)

Born: c. 242 B.C.E.; probably Antioch (now Antakya, Turkey)
Died: 187 B.C.E.; Elymais, near Susa (now in Iran)
Also known as: Antiochus III
Category: Government and politics

LIFE   The youngest son of Seleucus II, Antiochus (an-TI-uh-kuhs) the Great succeeded his assassinated brother Seleucus III in 223 B.C.E. Having put down the revolts of satraps Molon in Media (222-221 B.C.E.) and Achaeus in western Anatolia (220/213 B.C.E.), Antiochus undertook a campaign into the upper satrapies (212/205 B.C.E.) and established control over Commagene, Armenia, Parthia, and Bactria as well as southern Syria, Phoenicia, and Judaea. For his role in restoring and expanding the Seleucid kingdom, he received his title "the Great."

After the Roman defeat of Philip V, Antiochus claimed western Anatolia and Thrace as his ancestral inheritance. Following unsuccessful negotiations, he was defeated by the Romans in the battles at Thermopylae in Greece (191 B.C.E.) and at Magnesia ad Sipylum in Asia Minor (189 B.C.E.). In accordance with the Peace of Apamea (188 B.C.E.), Antiochus vacated Anatolia to the west of the Taurus Mountains but retained his eastern possessions, which stretched up to central Asia. He died soon afterward, on campaign in Elymais.

INFLUENCE   The pinnacle of the Seleucid Dynasty, Antiochus's reign also reflected increasing Roman interference in Greek affairs. He is credited with the separation of military and fiscal administration and the introduction of the royal cult.

FURTHER READING

Grainger, John D. *The Roman War of Antichos the Great*. Boston: Brill, 2002.

Antiochus the Great.

Kincaid, C. A. *Successors of Alexander the Great.* Chicago: Argonaut, 1969.

Ma, John. *Antiochus II and the Cities of Western Asia Minor.* New York: Oxford University Press, 1999.

Sviatoslav Dmitriev

See also: Magnesia ad Sipylum, Battle of; Philip V; Seleucid Dynasty; Thermopylae, Battle of.

Antipater

MILITARY LEADER AND REGENT OF MACEDONIA AND GREECE
(334-322 B.C.E.)

Born: 397 B.C.E.; place unknown
Died: 319 B.C.E.; Macedonia
Category: Military; government and politics

LIFE   Antipater (an-TIHP-uht-ur) was one of the most able generals of
Philip II of Macedonia and Alexander the Great. In 346 B.C.E., he helped
negotiate the Peace of Philocrates between Philip and Athens, and in 338
B.C.E. with Alexander, then heir to the Macedonian throne, he returned the
bones of the Athenian dead from the Battle of Chaeronea.

Alexander appointed him "regent" of Greece and Macedonia and acting
hegemon of the League of Corinth when he left for Persia in 334 B.C.E. As
regent, Antipater kept Macedonia united and Greece passive, apart from
the war of Agis III of Sparta (331-330 B.C.E.), which he ended with league
assistance. In 323 B.C.E., Alexander's death caused a widespread revolt of
the Greek states, led by Athens (the Lamian War). Although hard-pressed
at first, Antipater ended it in 322 B.C.E. and imposed an oligarchy on Athens. The final years of his life were set against the struggles of Alexander's
generals for power. Antipater sided with a group against the Macedonian
general Perdiccas, on whose death in 321 B.C.E., Antipater's possession of
Macedonia and Greece was confirmed, and he became regent for the young
Alexander IV and Philip III. His death in 319 B.C.E. led to further struggles.

INFLUENCE   Antipater kept Greece free from revolt and the Macedonian
kingdom secure while Alexander was in Persia and further east and also
provided him with reinforcements when demanded.

FURTHER READING
Errington, M. *A History of Macedonia*. Berkeley: University of California
     Press, 1990.

Gunther, Martin. "Antipater After the Lamian War." *Classical Quarterly* 55, no. 1 (2005): 301-305.

Heckel, W. *The Marshals of Alexander's Empire.* London: Routledge, 1992.

Ian Worthington

See also: Alexander the Great; Alexander the Great's Empire; Chaeronea, Battle of; Hellenistic Greece; Philip II of Macedonia.

Antiphon

Orator, speechwriter, and politician

Born: c. 480 B.C.E.; Athens, Greece
Died: 411 B.C.E.; probably Athens, Greece
Category: Oratory and rhetoric; government and politics

Life   Antiphon (AN-tuh-fahn) was born in Athens to an aristocratic family of the deme (local territorial district) of Rhamnus. He became a leading intellectual, writer, and orator. In 411 B.C.E., in the wake of the Sicilian disaster, Antiphon led a coup to replace the democracy with an aristocracy. The revolution failed, and Antiphon was tried and executed for his participation. The historian Thucydides reports that Antiphon's defense speech was the best ever delivered, but unfortunately only a few lines of it survive.

Six speeches Antiphon wrote for others do survive. Three are tetralogies, sets of four speeches each presenting a generic homicide case to demonstrate examples of arguments to be used. In *Against the Stepmother* (430-411 B.C.E.; English translation, 1941), a young man accuses his stepmother of having conspired to poison his father. In *The Murder of Herodes* (430-411 B.C.E.; English translation, 1941), a man defends himself against a charge of murder. In *The Chorus Boy* (430-411 B.C.E.; English translation, 1941), a chorus producer (*chorīgos*) denies having accidentally killed a boy by giving him a potion to improve his voice. More philosophical tracts *Concord* (n.d.; English translation, 1941) and *Truth* (n.d.; English translation, 1941) survive only in fragments. Scholars since antiquity have debated whether a different man named Antiphon wrote them.

Influence   The speeches break ground in using arguments from probability and in developing Attic prose style.

Further Reading
Antiphon. *The Fragments: Antiphon the Sophist.* Edited with introduction,

translation, and commentary by Gerard J. Pendrick. New York: Cambridge University Press, 2002.

Gagarin, Michael. *Antiphon the Athenian: Oratory, Law, and Justice in the Age of the Sophists.* Austin: University of Texas Press, 2002.

———. *Antiphon: The Speeches.* Cambridge, England: Cambridge University Press, 1997.

Gagarin, Michael, and D. M. MacDowell, trans. *Antiphon and Andocides.* Austin: University of Texas Press, 1998.

Wilfred E. Major

See also: Government and Law; Oratory; Thucydides.

Antisthenes

Philosopher

Born: c. 444 B.C.E.; Athens, Greece
Died: c. 365 B.C.E.; Athens, Greece
Category: Philosophy

Life   Antisthenes (an-TIHS-thuh-neez) was the son of an Athenian citizen, also named Antisthenes; his mother was a Thracian slave. Because both parents were not Athenian citizens, Antisthenes was not entitled to citizenship under a law passed by Pericles in 451 B.C.E., and he could not take part in Athenian politics or hold public office. He probably attended the Cynosarges gymnasium, located outside the gates of Athens and reserved for children of illegitimate unions. Although not a citizen, Antisthenes served in the Athenian army.

The young Antisthenes attended Gorgias's lectures on rhetoric and logic and adopted his Sophist approach. After Antisthenes met Socrates, however, he followed his new mentor, joining in the dialogues through which Socrates taught. Plato records that Antisthenes was one of the close friends of Socrates who attended him during his execution in 399 B.C.E. Afterward, Antisthenes returned to teaching at the Cynosarges gymnasium and developed the philosophical approach that came to be known as classical Cynicism.

During his lifetime, Antisthenes reportedly produced sixty-two dialogues, orations, and essays that were collected in ten volumes; however, only brief fragments of these survive, mostly in quotations and paraphrases by later Greek and Roman authors, many of whom were critical of Antisthenes. The quotations were frequently chosen for their wit and reflect Antisthenes' liking for paradoxes that challenged accepted ideas and customs. As a result, the fragments are sufficiently ambiguous to support widely varying interpretations.

Even the origin of the name "Cynicism" is disputed. The word "cynic" derives directly from the Greek word *cunikos*, meaning "doglike." Some claim that it came from Antisthenes' Greek nickname (which translates as

"Absolute Dog"), given him derisively because of his desire to live life as a dog might, free of human restraints and conventions. This appellation was accepted by Antisthenes and his successors.

From Socrates, Antisthenes had learned that virtue was the only good worth striving for and that it could be taught; in contrast, wealth, fame, pleasure, and power were worthless. Antisthenes proceeded to expand and exaggerate these ideas and to illustrate his concepts through his manner of living. To demonstrate his self-sufficiency and contempt for materialism, he reduced his possessions to the bare minimum, walking about Athens supporting himself by a strong stick, his hair and beard uncombed, in what became the Cynic uniform: a threadbare cloak and a leather knapsack containing a few necessities.

For Antisthenes, pleasure was to be avoided; it produced the illusion of happiness, thus preventing realization of true contentment, which was obtainable only through the practice of virtue. Antisthenes constantly ridiculed and expressed his contempt for the democratic political ideas and practices of Athens. He told its citizens that they might as well vote to call donkeys "horses" as to believe that they could create leaders and generals using the ballot. Like many of Socrates' followers, he admired the disciplined lifestyle of Sparta, finding it a more rational way to produce leaders and followers than democratic practices. Yet even Sparta was far from perfect; the political world as a whole was irrational and undesirable. Nor did the speculations of the philosophers and scientists of his day please Antisthenes. He dismissed their theories as linguistic games that failed to meet the Socratic standard of absolute truthfulness.

Antisthenes' focus was on practical ethics; anything beyond that he considered an illusion. He was especially scornful of the Platonic theory that ideal forms had a concrete existence outside the world of sense perception and were the unchanging reality that lay behind the world of appearances. Antisthenes is reported to have told Plato that while his horse could be seen, "equinity" (the idea of a horse) could not be seen.

Antisthenes liked to interpret the story of Heracles allegorically, as an example of the moral virtues of hard work and perseverance, but did not consider the Greek epics to be serious religious tracts. At times, he came close to espousing monotheism, arguing that "according to custom there are many gods, but in nature there is only one." He rejected the anthropomorphic approach of Greek mythology, claiming that God resembled nothing and no one.

Antisthenes rejected the idea that Greeks were by nature superior to the rest of humankind. He deplored the extreme parochialism and nationalism that dominated Greek city-states and led to endless internecine warfare. He was scornful of the widely held notion that work was demeaning and that craftsmen were of lower value than intellectual workers. Instead, he viewed hard labor and perseverance as a means of achieving true virtue. Women were not necessarily inferior to men, he held; because virtue could be taught to both sexes, men and women were virtuous or vicious depending on how they had been educated. By rejecting the distinction between Greek and barbarian, Antisthenes challenged the Greek justification of slavery as a status befitting inferior human beings.

INFLUENCE   Antisthenes' ideas and practices were admired and adopted by a series of Cynics, of which his immediate successor, Diogenes of Sinope, was best known. Diogenes, adopting the Cynic uniform that Antisthenes had pioneered, went further, limiting his possessions to what he could carry in his leather knapsack and sleeping outdoors in a barrel. He was even more vitriolic than Antisthenes in his condemnation of custom and society. Diogenes' successor, Crates of Thebes, continued the practice of asceticism and the public flouting of human customs, while avoiding the sarcastic insults that Diogenes employed. Zeno of Citium, the founder of Stoicism, began as a Cynic follower of Crates but by 300 B.C.E. had begun to create his own school of philosophy. Zeno stressed the self-reliant and independent strain of Antisthenes' philosophy while eliminating its challenges to the status quo.

Of the three philosophical traditions descending from Socrates, the two deriving from Plato and Aristotle are more significant for their impact on the modern world than that pioneered by Antisthenes. In the ancient world, however, the two schools of practical morality derived from Antisthenes, classical Cynicism and Stoicism, were of major significance in teaching people how to criticize and yet live in an imperfect society.

FURTHER READING

Branham, R. Bracht, and Marie-Odile Goulet-Cazé, eds. *The Cynics: The Cynic Movement in Antiquity and Its Legacy.* Berkeley: University of California Press, 1996.

Dudley, Donald R. *A History of Cynicism: From Diogenes to the Sixth Century A.D.* 2d ed. London: Bristol Classical Press, 1998.

Guthrie, William Keith Chambers. *The Fifth-Century Enlightenment*. Vol. 3 in *A History of Greek Philosophy*. New York: Cambridge University Press, 1978-1990.

Navia, Luis E. *Antisthenes of Athens: Setting the World Aright*. Westport, Conn.: Greenwood Press, 2001.

_____. *Classical Cynicism: A Critical Study*. Westport, Conn.: Greenwood Press, 1996.

_____. *The Philosophy of Cynicism: An Annotated Bibliography*. Westport, Conn.: Greenwood Press, 1995.

Rankin, H. D. *Sophists, Socratics, and Cynics*. Totowa, N.J.: Barnes & Noble, 1983.

Milton Berman

See also: Cynicism; Diogenes; Gorgias; Philosophy; Socrates; Stoicism; Zeno of Citium.

Anyte of Tegea

POET

Flourished: Early third century B.C.E.; Tegea, Arcadia, Greece
Category: Poetry; literature; women

LIFE   Named by Antipater as one of "nine earthly Muses," Anyte of Tegea (ahn-EE-tay of TEE-jee-uh), located in southern mainland Greece, composed epigrams. Twenty-one surviving poems have been identified as hers, and three appear falsely attributed. She composed both traditional epigrams as tombstone dedications and epigrams as poems commenting on life. Her subjects included both people and pets and show a strong valuation of domestic life by using "heroic language."

INFLUENCE   Her work is perhaps the foundation of the very popular pastoral and animal epigrams of the Hellenistic period, and it was copied by later male writers. Her style and language has been both praised and criticized by modern scholars, who often cite her as one of only a few female poets of the ancient world whose works survive.

FURTHER READING

Balmer, Josephine. *Classical Woman Poets*. Newcastle-upon-Tyne, England: Bloodaxe Books, 1996.
Greene, Ellen, ed. *Women Poets in Ancient Greece and Rome*. Norman: University of Oklahoma Press, 2005.
Rayor, Diane. *Sappho's Lyre: Archaic Lyric Women Poets of Ancient Greece*. Berkeley: University of California Press, 1991.
Snyder, Jane McIntosh. *The Woman and the Lyre: Women Writers in Classical Greece and Rome*. Carbondale: Southern Illinois University Press, 1989.

Tammy Jo Eckhart

See also: Literature; Women's Life.

Apollodorus of Athens

ARTIST

Flourished: Fifth century B.C.E.; Athens, Greece
Also known as: Sciagraphos; Skiagraphos
Category: Art and architecture

LIFE   The particulars of the life of Apollodorus (uh-pahl-uh-DOHR-uhs) of Athens are unknown, and none of his work survives. However, he is known to have continued the advances toward realism in art developed by the earlier fifth century B.C.E. painters Micon, Polygnotus, and Agatharcus. Agatharcus, the first to paint a scene for a production of tragedy, wrote a treatise on the use of perspective for creating the illusion of theatrical distance. Apollodorus furthered the illusion of perspective, employing the use of light and shadow to convey spatial relationships, a technique known as chiaroscuro. Apollodorus came to be known as "Sciagraphos," or "Shadow-Painter," from the Greek for "shadow-drawing." Historian Pliny the Elder spoke of him as the first to paint things as they really appear and to give glory to the brush. Yet he seemed to have been surpassed in realism by painter Zeuxis of Heraclea, who added highlights to shading and whose paintings of grapes are said to have deceived birds.

INFLUENCE   Apollodorus contributed to realism in painting, a feature that helped form Western taste for most of its history. The general movement toward realism influenced fourth century philosophical discourse, especially that of Plato, who worried over the moral probity of illusion in art, where a two-dimensional medium gives the false impression of three dimensions. In the *Politeia* (c. 388-368 B.C.E.; *Republic*, 1701), Plato's Socrates observes that the painter is several times removed from the pure reality of the idea—even more removed than the craftsperson, who makes a three-dimensional object.

FURTHER READING

Bruno, V. J. *Form and Color in Greek Painting*. New York: W. W. Norton, 1977.

James A. Arieti

See also: Art and Architecture; Plato; Polygnotus; Zeuxis of Heraclea.

Apollodorus of Athens

SCHOLAR AND HISTORIAN

Born: c. 180 B.C.E.; Athens, Greece
Died: After 120 B.C.E.; Athens, Greece
Category: Historiography; scholarship

LIFE   Apollodorus (uh-pahl-uh-DOHR-uhs) of Athens began his studies in his native city but eventually moved to Alexandria, Egypt, where he studied with Aristarchus of Samothrace, the head of Alexandria's great library. Apollodorus and other scholars were expelled from Egypt in about 145 B.C.E.; Apollodorus may have gone to Pergamum but later returned to Athens.

Apollodorus was a prolific scholar with diverse interests. All of his works have been lost, but they included treatises on the Greek gods, Athenian comedy, and Homer. He was best known for his *Chronica* (after 120 B.C.E.; "chronicles"), an account of Greek history from the fall of Troy (1184 B.C.E.) to 145/144 B.C.E. Apollodorus later added a chapter covering the period to 120 B.C.E. The *Chronica* provided dates for many historical events, but Apollodorus also touched on the careers of philosophers and poets. Curiously, Apollodorus wrote the *Chronica* in verse, perhaps to make it easier to memorize.

INFLUENCE   The *Chronica* of Apollodorus quickly became the standard work on Greek chronology in the ancient world. Apollodorus's reputation as a scholar was so great that works were falsely attributed to him, including the *Library*, an encyclopedic account of Greek mythology that still exists.

FURTHER READING

Habicht, Christian. *Athens from Alexander to Antony*. Translated by Deborah Lucas Schneider. Cambridge, Mass.: Harvard University Press, 1999.

Mosshammer, Alden A. *The Chronicle of Eusebius and the Greek Chrono-graphic Tradition*. Lewisburg, Pa.: Bucknell University Press, 1979.

James P. Sickinger

See also: Alexandrian Library; Aristarchus of Samothrace; Historiography; Homer; Literature; Troy.

Apollonius of Perga

MATHEMATICIAN

Born: c. 262 B.C.E.; Perga, Pamphylia, Asia Minor (now Murtana, Turkey)
Died: c. 190 B.C.E.; Alexandria, Egypt
Also known as: The Great Geometer
Category: Mathematics

LIFE   Little is known about the life of Apollonius of Perga (ap-uh-LOH-nee-uhs of PUR-guh), apart from what is found in the preface to his best-known work, the *Konica* (n.d.; *Treatise on Conic Sections*, 1896; best known as *Conics*). In the preface, he says that he started planning the work in Alexandria at the request of Naucrates, a geometer about whom nothing else is known. Apollonius hastily put together the eight books of the *Conics* so that they would be ready in time for Naucrates' departure. Apollonius later revised the work. Of the eight books, the first four, which offer a basic introduction to the subject, survive in the Greek original. Books 5 through 7,

Apollonius of Perga.
(Library of Congress)

which contain extensions of these basic principles, are found only in Arabic translation. The last book has been lost. The only other work of Apollonius to survive is *Logou apotomē* (n.d.; *On Cutting Off a Ratio*, 1987), which exists in Arabic translation.

INFLUENCE   In *Conics*, Apollonius described the fundamentals of conic sections in such a systematic manner that it became the standard work on the subject in the ancient and medieval worlds. The work was also known in the Arabic world.

FURTHER READING

Apollonius of Perga. *Conics: Books I to III*. Translated by R. Catesby Taliaferro. Santa Fe, N.Mex.: Green Lion Press, 1998.
_____. *Conics: Books V to VII*. Edited and translated by G. J. Toomer. Berlin: Springer-Verlag, 1990.
Fried, Michael N., and Sabetai Unguru. *Apollonius of Perga's Conica: Text, Context, Subtext*. Boston: Brill, 2001.

Albert T. Watanabe

See also: Science.

Apollonius Rhodius

Poet and Librarian

Born: Between 295 and 260 B.C.E.; Alexandria or Naucratis, Egypt
Died: Late third century B.C.E.; Alexandria, Egypt
Also known as: Apollonius of Rhodes; Apollonii Rhodii
Category: Poetry; literature; scholarship

LIFE The Greek poet Apollonius Rhodius (ap-uh-LOH-nee-uhs ROH-dee-uhs) has traditionally been identified with the island of Rhodes—where he may have withdrawn because of a quarrel with his teacher Callimachus or because his poetry had been poorly received. In any case, Apollonius served as director of the famous library at Alexandria from about 260 to 246 B.C.E.

Apollonius's major work is the *Argonautica* (third century B.C.E.; English translation, 1780), a long poem in four sections describing the adventures of a band of Greek heroes aboard the ship *Argo*. The heroes have been given the quest of seizing the Golden Fleece from King Aeëtes of Colchis on the far shores of the Black Sea. The most famous section of the work describes the passion of King Aeëtes' daughter Medea for the expedition's leader Jason.

INFLUENCE Apollonius's *Argonautica* is the most important classical retelling of the myths involving the Golden Fleece. It has sometimes been compared unfavorably to such epic works as the *Odyssey* (c. 725 B.C.E.; English translation, 1614) of Homer, but it embodies a more psychologically sophisticated treatment of human character.

FURTHER READING

Apollonius Rhodius. *The Argonautika*. Translated with an introduction, commentary, and glossary by Peter Green. Berkeley: University of California Press, 1997.

Beye, Charles Rowan. *Epic and Romance in the Argonautica of Apollonius*. Carbondale: Southern Illinois University Press, 1982.

Byre, Calvin S. *A Reading of Apollonius Rhodius' "Argonautica": The Poetics of Uncertainty*. Lewiston, N.Y. : Edwin Mellen Press, 2002.

Clare, R. J. *The Path of the Argo: Language, Imagery, and Narrative in the "Argonautica" of Apollonius Rhodius*. New York: Cambridge University Press, 2002.

Hunter, R. L. *The Argonautica of Apollonius: Literary Studies*. New York: Cambridge University Press, 1993.

Schmidt, Michael. *The First Poets: Lives of the Ancient Greek Poets*. New York: Knopf; distributed by Random House, 2005.

Grove Koger

See also: Alexandrian Library; Homer; Literature; Mythology.

Aratus

POET

Born: c. 315 B.C.E.; Soli, Cilicia, Asia Minor (now in Turkey)
Died: c. 245 B.C.E.; Macedonia
Also known as: Aratus of Soli
Category: Poetry; literature

LIFE Aratus (uh-RAYT-uhs) was born in Soli in Cilicia, where his portrait appeared on later coins. Ancient accounts associate him with many philosophers and poets, most important the Stoics Zeno and Persaeus of Citium. Like Persaeus, he accepted the invitation to join the court of another student of Stoicism, Antigonus II Gonatas, king of Macedonia, probably in 277 or 276 B.C.E. The poet may have worked in Syria and died in Macedonia.

Aratus's *Phaenomena* (n.d.; English translation, 1893), the most important example of Hellenistic didactic poetry, is a rendering in hexameter verse of two prose works, Eudoxus's description of the celestial sphere and a Peripatetic treatise on weather signs. Its affinities to the earlier poems of Hesiod were noted in antiquity, and its emphasis on the predictability of the natural world as evidence of divine providence made it particularly popular within Stoicism and later Christianity. Of the large number of other works attributed to Aratus, only two short epigrams survive.

INFLUENCE *Phaenomena* was praised and echoed by Aratus's contemporaries, Theocritus of Syracuse and Apollonius Rhodius, and by Latin poets including Vergil and Ovid. Several translations into Latin survive in whole or part, as do many late handbooks, often illustrated, that use *Phaenomena* as an introduction to the study of astronomy.

FURTHER READING

Aratus. *Phaenomena*. Translated by Douglas Kidd. New York: Cambridge University Press, 1997.

Gee, Emma. *Ovid, Aratus, and Augustus: Astronomy in Ovid's "Fasti."* New York: Cambridge University Press, 2000.

Lewis, A. M. "The Popularity of the 'Phainomena' of Aratus: A Re-evaluation." In *Studies in Latin Literature and Roman History*, edited by C. Deroux. 9 vols. Brussels: Latomas, 1979-2000.

Possanza, D. Mark. *Translating the Heavens: Aratus, Germanicus, and the Poetics of Latin Translation.* New York: Peter Lang, 2004.

Mary L. B. Pendergraft

See also: Apollonius Rhodius; Eudoxus of Cnidus; Literature; Philosophy; Stoicism; Theocritus of Syracuse; Zeno of Citium.

Archaic Greece

*Between 800 and 500 B.C.E., Greece, which already had achieved a
remarkably advanced civilization, saw the city-state organization of its
society grow and adopted a more advanced economy that promoted
trade.*

Date: 800-500 B.C.E.
Category: Cities and civilizations
Locale: Greek peninsula, Crete, Cyprus, Cyclades

INTRODUCTION During Greece's Archaic (ahr-KAY-ihk) period, the
economy was transformed by the invention of coinage, which inevitably
led to an expansion of trade and commerce. As its population grew and
prospered, Greece, hungry for land, colonized Mediterranean areas and
moved into the territories surrounding the Black Sea. The relatively unso-
phisticated economy of the ancient Greek villages was much disturbed by
this expansion. Land wars were common.

HISTORY The ancient Greeks called themselves Hellenes, but the Roman name for the area in southern Italy to which thousands of Hellenes mi-
grated in the period of great colonization between 750 and 500 B.C.E. was
Magna Graecia, from which the words "Greek," "Greece," and "Grecian"
are derived. During the Archaic period, which began around 800 B.C.E. and
continued until the Golden Age of Athens shortly after 500 B.C.E., there
was considerable emigration from the Greek islands and the Peloponnese.

Population growth, combined with a growing shortage of land, led many
of the country's citizens to colonize areas ranging from southern Spain to
the Black Sea, North Africa, and the Near East. In the first half of the eighth
century alone, the population of Attica quadrupled. In the next half century,
it doubled.

The only city-states that did not engage in colonization were Athens and
Sparta. During the early Archaic period, Athens had sufficient fertile land

to support its population, so it did not establish external colonies. When Sparta needed land to accommodate its swelling population, it used military might to overcome Messenia to its west (725 and 668 B.C.E.) and Arcadia to its north (560 and 550 B.C.E.), making colonization unnecessary.

The historian Herodotus recounts how famine struck the island of Thera, causing the Therans to exile some of their number. When these exiles failed to find a suitable place in which to begin a new colony, they returned to Thera, only to be rebuffed by arrows that prevented their landing, forcing them to depart hastily.

Archaic Greece had scores of city-states. The topography of the area lent itself to the establishment of isolated enclaves that originally were tribal but, by the beginning of the Archaic period, were centered around the polis, or city. The population in the outlying areas were also considered part of the political unit that was called the city-state. High mountain ranges separated many of the city-states from one another. Others grew on the islands of the Aegean and Mediterranean Seas.

Most of the cities around which the city-states formed were small. Sparta, geographically the largest of the city-states with an area of 3,360 square miles (8,712 square kilometers), had fewer than five thousand residents. Athens, during its Golden Age, with an area of 1,060 square miles (2,749 square kilometers), claimed an adult male population of forty-three thousand. Small villages existed outside the major cities. Their inhabitants were citizens of the city-state. Boeotia, whose major city was Thebes, had twelve villages in its outlying areas, each with an average size of 52 square miles (135 square kilometers).

Even though conflicts arose and border wars were fought among the city-states, an underlying unity existed, particularly as colonization in far-off venues became more common. A major unifying thread was Greek mythology, the basis for the religion of most Greeks regardless of their citizenship in individual city-states. The temple of Apollo at Delphi became a center to whose oracle most Greeks turned for advice.

Four major Panhellenic religious festivals united the citizens of disparate areas. Festivals and games held at Olympia and Nemea honored Zeus, the father of the gods. Corinth regularly honored Poseidon, god of the sea. Apollo was similarly honored at Delphi. The Olympic, Nemean, Isthmian, and Pythian Games were Panhellenic events during which any warring factions observed an inviolable truce. The Greeks measured time by Olympiads, using 776 B.C.E., the date of the first Olympic Games, as a starting point.

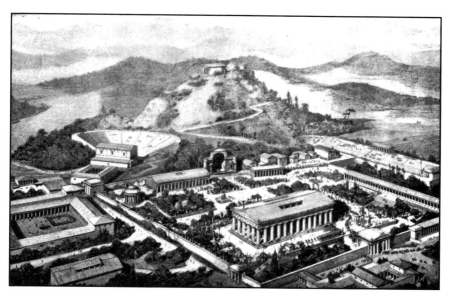

Festivals and games were held at Olympia during the Archaic Age. (F. R. Niglutsch)

Archaic Greece provided the blueprint for Western civilization. In approximately three hundred years, the country moved from a collection of tribes to federations of city-states. During this period, governments were formed, laws were codified, a simplified alphabet was adopted, enabling large numbers of Greeks to gain literacy, money was coined for the first time, and education became available to increasing numbers of citizens.

The art of the period moved from the stiff, geometrical art of the preceding period to a more fluid art that reflected Asian influences. Intellectual Greeks studied rhetoric and oratory, developing skills that enabled them to pose searching questions concerned with the position of humans in the universe and to articulate complex ideas according to the rules of formal logic.

Government became stratified according to class during this period. Initially ruled monarchically by kings, in time, the government became oligarchic, ruled by a wealthy, landed aristocracy that ruled autocratically, much as the kings had. They denied political power to those who did not own land. Following 680 B.C.E., when the first coinage of money took place, commerce developed, and the economy changed, creating new groups of landless but affluent people, a rising middle class, who, beginning around 650 B.C.E., grasped political power.

From among these citizens, mostly engaged in trades, crafts, and agriculture, emerged tyrants who wrested control from the aristocrats. These tyrants usually had the support of the slaves and the serfs. Among the city-states, only Sparta continued to be controlled by aristocrats. Many of the early tyrants were shrewd rulers. They spearheaded significant social improvement and offered hope to the serfs and the slaves who supported them. In time, however, many of them became autocratic and isolated from their constituencies, only to be overthrown by the lower classes on whom their power depended. After 500 B.C.E., no tyrants remained in the Greek city-states.

GOVERNMENT AND LAW   In the early Archaic period, the Greek city-states, originally ruled by monarchs who inherited their kingships, often became oligarchies, ruled by a landed gentry that excluded from the power structure those who did not own land and were not, therefore, aristocratic. As commerce grew during the mid-seventh century, a middle class of merchants, tradesmen, and farmers began to gain power. Supported by serfs and slaves seeking to improve their bleak lives, tyrants emerged as the rulers.

Although the tyrants initially were usually well-qualified men who engineered desirable change, many of them eventually became as autocratic as their aristocratic and monarchical predecessors had been. As they lost touch with the people, they were usually overthrown.

As early as the ninth century B.C.E., Lycurgus of Sparta, a lawgiver, had created a representative form of government that became a model for many city-states. This government consisted of a bicameral body. Its upper house, the *gerousia*, had twenty-eight elders, each over sixty years old. The lower house, the *apella*, was composed of citizens who were qualified to serve if they were more than thirty years old. Two kings ruled, but five powerful magistrates, called ephors, supervised and controlled these kings, whose tenure was in their hands.

The lawgivers in the city-states had almost unlimited power. The citizens chose them and trusted them, abiding by their judgment. The most renowned lawgiver, Solon, served Athens at the beginning of the sixth century B.C.E., a critical time in its existence. The Athenians had suffered a severe drought and an ensuing famine. Many Athenians who had borrowed money were unable to pay their debts and were enslaved by fellow citizens.

Solon resolved this dilemma through the controversial expedient of canceling all debts, thereby restoring some order to a society in crisis. He also mandated that no Athenian could incur further indebtedness but that any who did so and failed to repay his debts could be enslaved. Any son whose father failed to teach him a trade or profession was absolved from having to support that father in his old age. Solon also prohibited the export of all agricultural products except olive oil, of which Athens had an abundance. Under Solon, an assembly of citizens met regularly and a court of appeals was established to limit the power of magistrates. Solon's laws represent the most significant steps Athens took toward establishing a democracy.

RELIGION AND RITUAL Throughout the Greek city-states of the Archaic period, religion was a major unifying force. The mythology that had been imparted in oral form from a time when Greek society was largely tribal is recorded in the Homeric epics, the *Iliad* (c. 750 B.C.E.; English translation, 1611) and *Odyssey* (c. 725 B.C.E.; English translation, 1614). In these epics, the hierarchy of the ancient gods of the sea, of fertility, of war, and of various other elements of human existence was established, with Zeus, the king or father of the gods, holding the preeminent position.

Even into the fifth century B.C.E., when Euripides' dramas were mocking the gods as they were presented in the Homeric epics, polytheism flourished. One could mock the gods much as modern comedians mock prominent political figures, but it was unthinkable to deny them.

SETTLEMENTS AND SOCIAL STRUCTURE As Greece's city-states grew during the eighth century B.C.E., land became scarce and people had limited means of earning their livelihoods. As a result, hundreds of citizens from every city-state except Athens and Sparta were forced to leave their homes to colonize other places that offered them greater opportunities and less crowded conditions. Considerable numbers sailed west to Sicily and southern Italy, where numerous Greek colonies were established. Others traveled east to the shores of the Black Sea and the Sea of Mamara.

Each new colony maintained a sentimental and usually a commercial connection with the original city-state, often carrying a sacred flame from the mother city to the new colony. Nevertheless, these colonies were independent and, unlike Roman colonies, were not connected politically to the city-state from which they came.

Usually about two hundred men from an overcrowded city-state would set out to establish a colony elsewhere. Once they had set down some roots, they would bring their women—mothers, wives, daughters, sweethearts—to the new colony.

ECONOMICS   Unlike the economies of many ancient societies, the Archaic Greek economy was not wholly agricultural, although agriculture played an important role in it. Manufacturing, which flourished during the Bronze Age and the Iron Age, was a major economic factor in many Greek city-states. A turning point in commerce came with the first coinage of silver in the mid-seventh century B.C.E.

During this century, small villages grew into cities as manufactured goods such as pottery, textiles, metal utensils, and weapons found ready markets throughout the areas that bordered the Mediterranean and Black Seas. The rise in manufacturing created jobs for many who had previously been unemployed and in a number of city-states reduced considerably the pressure to colonize. Some exiles from the colonies were also able to return to their native homes to work in manufacturing.

PHILOSOPHY   Until the sixth century B.C.E., Greeks explained natural and social phenomena in terms of the myths that had been handed down through the ages. During the sixth century B.C.E., however, thinking Greeks began to seek deeper explanations for phenomena they could not easily understand. The pre-Socratic philosophers, notable among them Heraclitus, Thales of Miletus, Pythagoras, Anaximenes, and Anaximander, pondered such questions as the source and meaning of life. They sought the "world-stuff," or basis of all the material world. Heraclitus, considered the founder of metaphysics, postulated the philosophy that everything changes, that nothing ever remains the same.

Essentially, the early Greek philosophers had a pessimistic view of life. During the sixth century B.C.E., despite the notable strides they had made, most of the philosophers were still steeped in the myths with which they had been brought up and found it difficult to assess the world in other than the mythical terms that were so familiar to them.

WOMEN'S LIVES   Although many city-states bestowed citizenship on their female residents, Greece was largely a male-dominated society. Women generally did not serve in public office. Colonizing was done by males, who usually established their colonies and then sent for their women. Women's activities were usually domestic in nature, although some notable women, such as Sappho in the sixth century B.C.E., gained recognition as poets. Women were unable in most city-states to vote. Most married early because they required men in their lives as protectors.

WRITING SYSTEMS   In the ancient Greek script, now designated Linear B, each sign represented a single syllable. This script, recorded on clay tablets by using sharp instruments, died out around 1200 B.C.E. Greece was essentially illiterate for the next four hundred years. At the beginning of the Archaic period, however, the Greeks began to trade with the Phoenicians, from whom they adapted a sixteen-letter alphabet to which they added seven vowel sounds. The earliest extant examples of the Greek alphabet date to about 740 B.C.E.

WAR AND WEAPONS   With its vast coastline, Greece was vulnerable to naval attack. As a result, various city-states that bordered the sea had substantial navies manned partly by citizens who were given land and money in return for their services and partly by mercenaries. Such was also true of the armies formed for the protection of individual city-states, the strongest of which was Sparta.

Sparta, being inland, had more need for foot soldiers and cavalry than for a strong navy. Its soldiers were armed mostly with spears, clubs, and bows and arrows. Many mercenaries came to Greece to fight for various city-states. They accounted for the first coinage of money in Greece, but the currency minted for them was in denominations too large to be of much use to ordinary citizens. Within a short time, however, silver coins had become trading vehicles.

Although Athens is not renowned for its army or navy, it will be forever remembered for its victory at the Battle of Marathon in 490 B.C.E. Vastly outnumbered by a fierce contingent of Persian troops, the Athenians, aided by only a small contingent from Plataea, a nearby polis, scored an incredible victory. The Persians lost more than 6,400 men; the Athenians suffered 192 casualties.

FURTHER READING
Boardman, John. *Early Greek Vase Painting, Eleventh-Sixth Centuries B.C.: A Handbook.* New York: Thames and Hudson, 1998.

Cartledge, Paul. *The Greeks: Crucible of Civilization*. New York: TV Books, 2000.

Coldstream, J. N. *Geometric Greece, 900-700 B.C.* 2d ed. New York: Routledge, 2003.

Durando, Furio. *Ancient Greece: The Dawn of the Western World*. New York: Stewart, Tabori, and Chang, 1997.

Garland, Robert. *Daily Life of the Ancient Greeks*. Westport, Conn.: Greenwood Press, 1998.

Osborne, Robin. *Archaic and Classical Greek Art*. New York: Oxford University Press, 1998.

Pomeroy, Sarah B., Stanley M. Burstein, Walter Donlan, and Jennifer Tolbert Roberts. *Ancient Greece: A Political, Social, and Cultural History*. New York: Oxford University Press, 1999.

Sansson, David. *Ancient Greek Civilization*. Oxford, England: Blackwell, 2004.

Shanks, Michael. *Art and the Greek City State: An Interpretive Archaeology*. New York: Cambridge University Press, 1999.

R. Baird Shuman

See also: Art and Architecture; Athens; Classical Greece; Coins; Daily Life and Customs; Delphi; Government and Law; Hellenistic Greece; Homer; Homeric Hymns; Inscriptions; Language and Dialects; Linear B; Literature; Lycurgus of Sparta; Magna Graecia; Marathon, Battle of; Military History of Athens; Mycenaean Greece; Mythology; Olympic Games; Oratory; Philosophy; Pre-Socratic Philosophers; Religion and Ritual; Settlements and Social Structure; Solon; Solon's Code; Sports and Entertainment; Technology; Thera; Trade, Commerce, and Colonization; Warfare Before Alexander; Women's Life; Writing Systems.

Archidamian War

As part of the Peloponnesian War (431-404 B.C.E.), this conflict contributed to the destruction of the Athenian Empire and helped lead to the endless warfare that would ruin Greece in the fourth century B.C.E.

Date: May, 431-March, 421 B.C.E.
Category: Wars and battles
Locale: Greece

SUMMARY   The growth of Athenian power in the fifty years since the Greco-Persian Wars (499-449 B.C.E.) led to war between the Athenian Empire and Sparta's Peloponnesian League.

The Archidamian (ahr-kuh-day-MEE-uhn) War, named after the Spartan king Archidamus II, began as a defensive war on the part of Athens, but when Pericles died of the plague in 429 B.C.E., his plan for sheltering in the Athenian-Piraeus fortress while conducting naval raids on the Peloponnesians died with him. Led on by hawkish demagogues such as Cleon of Athens, the Athenians soon began conducting offensive operations and in 425 B.C.E. established a base at Pylos in the Peloponnese, capturing 120 Spartans in the process. Buoyed by their success, the Athenians refused a Spartan peace offer, but a year later, Brasidas of Sparta captured the vital city of Amphipolis. In 422 B.C.E., both Cleon and Brasidas, the main obstacles to peace, were killed in a failed Athenian attempt to recapture Amphipolis, and in March, 421 B.C.E., the ultimately ineffective Peace of Nicias was signed, bringing a temporary halt to hostilities.

SIGNIFICANCE   The war produced dangerous divisions in the democracy and a new aggressive imperialism that would ultimately lead to Athens's defeat in the next two decades.

FURTHER READING

De Souza, Philip. *The Peloponnesian War, 431-404 B.C.* New York: Routledge, 2003.

Hanson, Victor Davis. *A War Like No Other: How the Athenians and Spartans Fought the Peloponnesian War.* New York: Random House, 2005.

Kagan, Donald. *The Archidamian War.* Ithaca, N.Y.: Cornell University Press, 1974.

_____. *The Peloponnesian War.* New York: Viking, 2003.

Thucydides. "History of the Peloponnesian War." In *The Landmark Thucydides: A Comprehensive Guide to the Peloponnesian War*, edited by Robert B. Strassler. New York: Free Press, 1996.

Richard M. Berthold

See also: Archidamus II of Sparta; Athens; Brasidas of Sparta; Cleon of Athens; Peloponnesian Wars; Pericles.

Archidamus II of Sparta

KING OF SPARTA (R. C. 469-427 B.C.E.)

Born: Early fifth century B.C.E.; Sparta
Died: 427 B.C.E.; Sparta
Also known as: Arkhidamos, son of Zeuxidamos
Category: Military; government and politics

LIFE   A member of the Eurypontid royal line, Archidamus II (ahr-kuh-DAY-muhs) of Sparta probably became king in 469 B.C.E. When a great earthquake leveled the city of Sparta five years later, igniting a revolt by Sparta's helots (state-owned serfs), Archidamus rallied the surviving Spartans and defeated the rebels after a lengthy struggle.

When tensions with Athens mounted in 432 B.C.E., Archidamus unsuccessfully urged a delay in declaring war until Sparta was better prepared. He led the first three invasions of Attica in 431, 430, and 428 B.C.E. during the Peloponnesian War (431-404 B.C.E.), doing considerable damage to the Athenian countryside. This strategy proved ineffective, as he had feared, and he could neither lure the Athenian army into battle nor storm Athens's walls. His unsuccessful assaults of Oenoe (431 B.C.E.) and Plataea (429 B.C.E.) demonstrated Sparta's lack of skill in siege warfare. His strategy of seeking Persian assistance and preparing a fleet eventually proved successful but failed to achieve anything before, or long after, his death.

INFLUENCE   Archidamus preserved Spartan power but failed to defeat Athens, though he showed the way to ultimate success in the Peloponnesian War. His name became attached to the first part of that conflict, called the Archidamian War.

FURTHER READING

Hanson, Victor Davis. *A War Like No Other: How the Athenians and Spartans Fought the Peloponnesian War.* New York: Random House, 2005.
Kagan, Donald. *The Peloponnesian War.* New York: Viking, 2003.

Powell, Anton. *Athens and Sparta*. New York: Routledge, 1996.

Thucydides. "History of the Peloponnesian War." In *The Landmark Thucydides: A Comprehensive Guide to the Peloponnesian War*, edited by Robert B. Strassler. New York: Free Press, 1996.

Scott M. Rusch

See also: Archidamian War; Peloponnesian Wars; Plataea, Battle of.

Archidamus III of Sparta

KING OF SPARTA (R. 359-338 B.C.E.)

Born: c. 400 B.C.E.; Sparta
Died: 338 B.C.E.; Manduria, Calabria (in modern Italy)
Category: Government and politics

LIFE   Son of Agesilaus II of Sparta, Archidamus III (ahr-kuh-DAY-muhs) of Sparta led an unimpressive career in the twilight of Spartan greatness. He commanded the relief force that escorted the defeated Spartans back from Leuctra (371 B.C.E.). He successfully led Spartan forces against Arcadia in 368 and 365 B.C.E. The height of his success was his victory over Arcadia and Argos in the "Tearless Battle," in which he routed the enemy without loss to his own forces. When Epaminondas attacked Sparta in 362 B.C.E., Archidamus led a counterattack that saved the city. The Athenian orator Isocrates wrote two open appeals to him to recapture Messenia, which Sparta had lost in 369 B.C.E., and to continue the war against Thebes. Archidamus officially ascended the throne only in 359 B.C.E.

During the Third Sacred War (355-346 B.C.E.), Archidamus officially supported the Phocians, who had seized and plundered Apollo's sanctuary at Delphi. In the Peloponnese, he unsuccessfully attacked Megalopolis. At the end of the Sacred War, he attempted to take control of Thermopylae to thwart Philip II of Macedonia but failed.

After the Sacred War, Archidamus served as a mercenary to earn money for Sparta. In 346 B.C.E., he won a small victory in Crete before sailing to Tarentum (Taranto). There he defended the Spartan colony against the Lucanians but was killed in action. Many Greeks felt that he deserved his fate because of his aid to sacrilegious Phocis.

INFLUENCE   Archidamus III, though a Spartan king, was insignificant. Like his state, he stood in the shadow of greater events.

FURTHER READING

Cartledge, Paul. *Agesilaos and the Crisis of Sparta*. Baltimore: Johns Hopkins University Press, 1987.

Cartledge, Paul, and Antony Spawforth. *Hellenistic and Roman Sparta: A Tale of Two Cities*. 2d ed. London: Routledge, 2002.

John Buckler

See also: Agesilaus II of Sparta; Epaminondas; Isocrates; Leuctra, Battle of; Philip II of Macedonia; Sacred Wars; Sparta.

Archilochus of Paros

POET

Born: c. 680 B.C.E.; Paros, Greece
Died: c. 640 B.C.E.; Paros(?), Greece
Also known as: Archilochus of Paros; Archilochos
Category: Poetry; literature

LIFE The life of Archilochus of Paros (ahr-KIHL-uh-kuhs of PAR-ahs) is revealed in the few remaining fragments of his poetry and by references to him in the works of later writers. The illegitimate son of Telesicles, he left Paros following the surprising end of his engagement to Neoboule. Her father, Lycambes, first approved of and then forbade the marriage, perhaps because Archilochus publicly revealed his illegitimacy. It is said that the satiric verses that Archilochus wrote in revenge were so powerful that the father and daughter hanged themselves. After he left Paros, Archilochus lived as a mercenary, spending much time in the colonial outpost of Thásos. He died in battle after he had established a new form in poetry, the iambus, in which a short syllable followed by a long one defines the meter.

INFLUENCE Songs of triumph written by Archilochus were sung at the Olympic Games, and he composed elegiac epigrams for social occasions. According to Plutarch, a Greek biographer and historian, Archilochus was a major innovator. The Roman poet Horace claimed to have been the first to introduce Parian (Archolochean) iambuses into Latin. Archilochus is considered a founder of the Western literary tradition.

FURTHER READING
Burnett, Anne Pippin. *Three Archaic Poets: Archilochus, Alcaeus, Sappho.* London: Bristol Classical Press, 1998.
Clay, Diskin. *Archilochos Heros: The Cult of Poets in the Greek Polis.* Cambridge, Mass.: Harvard University Press, 2004.

Davies, Malcolm. "The Temptress Throughout the Ages: Further Versions of Heracles at the Crossroads." *Classical Quarterly* 54, no. 2 (2004): 606-610.
Rankin, H. D. *Archilochus of Paros*. Park Ridge, N.J.: Noyes, 1977.
Will, Frederic. *Archilochus*. New York: Twayne, 1969.

Margaret A. Dodson

See also: Iambic Poetry; Literature; Olympic Games.

Archimedes

MATHEMATICIAN, PHYSICIST, AND INVENTOR

Born: c. 287 B.C.E.; Syracuse, Sicily (now in Italy)
Died: 212 B.C.E.; Syracuse, Sicily (now in Italy)
Category: Mathematics; science and technology

LIFE   Historians know more about Archimedes (ahr-kuh-MEED-eez) than any other ancient mathematician, although they remain unable to determine the chronology of his discoveries and writings. Archimedes spent most of his life in Syracuse, but he may have also studied with scholars in Alexandria. He certainly continued the development of Euclidean mathe-

Archimedes. (Library of Congress)

matics by establishing numerous theorems in solid geometry.

Archimedes invented a water screw for irrigation and perhaps the compound pulley. He wrote the first proof of the law of the lever, that equal weights at equal distances from the fulcrum will balance. He also proved the basic principle of hydrostatics, that a solid immersed in a fluid is lighter than its true weight by the weight of the fluid displaced. The story that Archimedes discovered an important concept while bathing and ran naked through the streets crying, "Eureka!" ("I have found it!"), is believed to be no more than popular legend. Although his precise process is unknown, he did determine the volume of a gold crown (suspected to be partly silver) by measuring the amount of water that it displaced.

When the Roman army attacked Syracuse, Archimedes helped defend the city with missile launchers and cranes. One of many possibly fanciful stories about Archimedes relates that he was so focused on a geometrical diagram he had drawn in the dirt that he ignored an approaching Roman soldier, who killed the mathematician with a sword.

INFLUENCE   The achievements of Archimedes were not widely known during antiquity. Byzantine and Arab mathematicians exploited his methods in the early Middle Ages. His texts were translated into Latin in the twelfth and fifteenth centuries C.E., making Archimedes the principal influence on European geometers. Finally, Archimedes' skill with the mathematical technique known as the method of exhaustion was a precursor of the principles of integration.

FURTHER READING

Dijksterhuis, E. J. *Archimedes*. 2d ed. Princeton, N.J.: Princeton University Press, 1987.

Heath, Thomas L. *The Works of Archimedes*. Mineola, N.Y.: Dover, 2002.

Stein, Sherman. *Archimedes: What Did He Do Besides Cry "Eureka"?* Washington, D.C.: Mathematical Association of America, 1999.

Tuplin, C. J., and T. E. Rihill. *Science and Mathematics in Ancient Greek Culture*. New York: Oxford University Press, 2002.

Amy Ackerberg-Hastings

See also: Science; Syracuse; Technology.

Archytas of Tarentum

PHILOSOPHER, MATHEMATICIAN, AND POLITICIAN

Flourished: 400-350 B.C.E.; Tarentum, Magna Graecia (later Taranto, Italy)
Also known as: Archytus
Category: Philosophy; mathematics; government and politics

LIFE   Perhaps a friend of the philosopher Plato, Archytas of Tarentum (ahr-KIT-uhs of tuh-REHN-tuhm) is mentioned in Plato's *Menōn* (388-368 B.C.E.; *Meno*, 1769) as a great ruler of Taras or Tarentum, where he served for seven years. He is mainly known, however, as a scientist and mathematician, the founder of mathematical mechanics. He was a second-generation follower of Pythagoras, who sought to explain all phenomena in terms of numbers. Archytas's achievements in geometry, acoustics, and music theory include solving the problem of doubling the cube, the application of proportions to musical harmony, and a resultant theory of pitch intervals in which he posited that pitch is related to the movement of air in response to such stimuli as a stringed instrument. Although some of his conclusions are inaccurate, many are correct.

INFLUENCE   Only fragments of Archytas's philosophical works on subjects of mathematical or scientific nature survive. Book 8 of Euclid's *Stoicheia* (compiled c. 300 B.C.E.; *Elements*, 1570) probably borrows from Archytas. Other, nonmathematical fragments have been attributed to him but are more dubious because they are on Platonic themes.

FURTHER READING
Freeman, Kathleen. *Ancilla to the Pre-Socratic Philosophers*. Cambridge, Mass.: Harvard University Press, 1983.
Huffman, Carl A. *Archytas of Tarentum: Pythagorean, Philosopher, and Mathematician*. New York: Cambridge University Press, 2005.

Tejera, V. *Rewriting the History of Ancient Greek Philosophy.* Westport, Conn.: Greenwood Press, 1997.

Tammy Jo Eckhart

See also: Euclid; Plato; Pythagoras; Science.

Argead Dynasty

The Argead Dynasty ruled Macedonia for four centuries and included Philip II and his son, Alexander the Great, who shaped Macedonia and Greece into a world empire.

Date: c. 700-c. 311 B.C.E.
Category: Cities and civilizations
Locale: Macedonia

SUMMARY The Argead (ahr-GEE-uhd) Dynasty represented the ruling house of Macedonia for nearly four hundred years. Although the beginnings of the dynasty can be traced as far back as Karanos (eighth century B.C.E.), it was Perdiccas I (r. c. 670-652 B.C.E.) who led a disparate group of adventurers east from the Haliacmon (Aliákmon) River through northern Greece and became head of the Argeadae Macedones.

By the reign of Amyntas I (r. c. 540-498 B.C.E.), the kingdom of Macedonia stretched into Thrace. In an attempt to assimilate with Greece, Amyntas's son, Alexander I, began the pro-Hellenic policy that would characterize much of the rest of the period. Alexander's son, Perdiccas II, united many of the major Greek cities into a federation with Macedonia.

Perdiccas II's son Archelaus continued his father's pro-Hellenic policy and at the same time created routes through the heavily forested region. In part, this was to allow more rapid movements of his armies, improved with the development of iron and bronze armor and weapons.

SIGNIFICANCE It was during the reigns of Philip II of Macedonia (r. 359-336) and his son, Alexander the Great (r. 336-323), that the Greek empire became a world power, stretching to Egypt and east to India. Following the death of Alexander, the Argead lineage continued for another generation, but the kingdom was divided among Alexander's generals.

Kings of the Argead Dynasty, c. 700-311 B.C.E.

King	Reign
Perdiccas I	c. 670-652 B.C.E.
Argaios I	652-621
Philip I	621-588
Aeropos I	588-568
Alketas	568-540
Amyntas I	c. 540-498
Alexander I	before 492-c. 450
Perdiccas II	c. 450-c. 413
Archelaus	c. 413-399
Orestes	399-396
Aeropos II	396-393
Pausanias	393
Amyntas II	393
Amyntas III	393/392-370/369
Argaios II	390
Alexander II	370-368
Ptolemy Alorites	368-365
Perdiccas III	365-359
Philip II	359-336
Alexander the Great	336-323
Philip III Arrhidaeus	323-317
Alexander IV Aegeos	323-311

FURTHER READING

Ashley, James. *The Macedonian Empire*. Jefferson, N.C.: McFarland, 1998.

Hammond, Nicholas, and G. T. Griffith. *A History of Macedonia*. Vols. 1-3. Oxford, England: Clarendon Press, 1979.

Richard Adler

See also: Alexander the Great; Alexander the Great's Empire; Hellenistic Greece; Philip II of Macedonia.

Aristarchus of Samos

MATHEMATICIAN AND ASTRONOMER

Born: c. 310 B.C.E.; Samos
Died: c. 230 B.C.E.; Alexandria
Category: Mathematics; astronomy and cosmology

LIFE   Little is known of the life of Aristarchus of Samos (ar-uh-STAHR-kuhs of sah-MOHS) except that he spent at least some years at the museum in Alexandria. He is known for the first heliocentric (Sun-centered) theory of the universe. The scientist Archimedes noted that Aristarchus suggested that the Sun and fixed stars remained still while Earth rotated on its axis and revolved around the Sun.

The only work written by Aristarchus that survived is *On the Sizes and Distances of the Sun and Moon*. In this treatise, Aristarchus made the first truly scientific attempt to estimate the size of the solar system. He calculated that the Sun was eighteen to twenty times farther away from Earth than the Moon, which was actually short by a factor of twenty. Still, Aristarchus's measurement was ignored because he also thought the fixed stars were an enormous distance away compared with the Sun.

INFLUENCE   The mathematics required for the theory of a moving Earth was unreasonable according to the observations made by later Greek astronomers. Aristarchus was forgotten until mathematicians began to praise him during the Scientific Revolution of the seventeenth century in order to convince their contemporaries to accept the heliocentric system of Copernicus.

FURTHER READING

Gingerich, Owen. "Did Copernicus Owe a Debt to Aristarchus?" *Journal for the History of Astronomy* 16 (1985): 37-42.
Heath, Thomas L. *Aristarchus of Samos: The Ancient Copernicus*. Reprint. Mineola, N.Y: Dover, 2004.

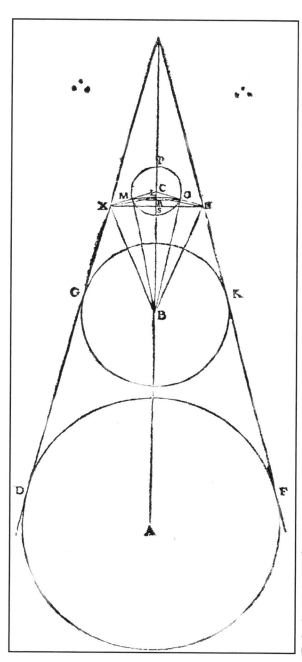

*This diagram illustrates
Aristarchus's observations
and calculations regarding
the Sun, Moon, and Earth.
He believed that Earth
rotated on its axis and
revolved around the Sun.*
(Library of Congress)

127

Hirshfield, Alan W. "The Triangles of Aristarchus." *Mathematics Teacher* 97, no. 4 (April, 2004): 228-231.

Wall, Byron Emerson. "Anatomy of a Precursor: The Historiography of Aristarchus of Samos." *Studies in History and Philosophy of Science* 6 (1975): 201-228.

Amy Ackerberg-Hastings

See also: Archimedes; Cosmology; Science.

Aristarchus of Samothrace

Scholar-librarian

Born: c. 217 B.C.E.; Samothrace
Died: c. 145 B.C.E.; Cyprus
Category: Scholarship

Life   Aristarchus of Samothrace (ar-uh-STAHR-kuhs of sa-MUH-thrays) lived in Alexandria during the reign of Ptolemy Philometor (r. 180-145 B.C.E.). He studied under Aristophanes of Byzantium and became the fifth head of the Alexandrian library. He served as a tutor to Philometor's brother, Ptolemy Euergetes II (Ptolemy VIII), and his sons, including Ptolemy VII Neos Philopator, who succeeded his father in 145 B.C.E. Ptolemy Euergetes II had Ptolemy VII murdered in 144 B.C.E. and persecuted the friends of the late king, including Aristarchus. Aristarchus escaped to Cyprus and died shortly afterward.

Aristarchus was most renowned for his Homeric scholarship. He produced two recensions of the Homeric text and commentaries on these editions. Although these works have been lost, parts of Aristarchus's scholarship have been preserved in the scholia of the Venetian codex of Homer's *Iliad* (c. 750 B.C.E.; English translation, 1611). Aristarchus also produced editions and commentaries on other poets and playwrights, including a commentary on Herodotus, the first on a prose writer. In these works, Aristarchus attempted to interpret a writer through the writer's use of language.

Influence   With Aristarchus, Homeric scholarship in Alexandria was regarded as reaching its zenith. Through his followers, his insights were preserved in the scholia. His method of interpreting a writer through the writer's works furnished a model for later scholarship.

Further Reading

Lamberton, Robert, and John J. Keaney, eds. *Homer's Ancient Readers:*

The Hermeneutics of Greek Epic's Earliest Exegetes. Princeton, N.J.: Princeton University Press, 1992.

Pfeiffer, R. *History of Classical Scholarship.* Oxford, England: Oxford University Press, 1968.

Albert T. Watanabe

See also: Alexandrian Library; Herodotus; Homer; Ptolemaic Dynasty.

Aristides of Athens

STATESMAN AND MILITARY LEADER

Born: Late sixth century B.C.E.; place unknown
Died: c. 467 B.C.E.; place unknown
Also known as: Aristides the Just
Category: Military; government and politics

LIFE   Aristides (ar-uh-STID-eez) of Athens commanded his tribal contingent when the Athenians defeated the Persians at the Battle of Marathon (490 B.C.E.), and he served as archon in 489 B.C.E. In 482 B.C.E., political rivalry led to his ostracism. However, he returned to Athens in 480 B.C.E. under the general recall of ostracized citizens at the time of Xerxes I's invasion of Greece, and he led the Athenian forces that fought as part of the Greek army that defeated the Persians at the Battle of Plataea (479 B.C.E.).

The next year, when the Spartan Pausanias led a naval expedition eastward against the Persians, Aristides was in command of the supporting Athenian fleet. After Pausanias fell from favor, Aristides, who enjoyed the confidence of the allied Greeks, was instrumental in founding (477 B.C.E.) the Delian League, a confederacy whose purpose was to continue the war against Persia under Athenian leadership.

INFLUENCE   Aristides' influence was both moral and political. His reputation for integrity provided a paradigm for later generations, and the Delian League became the instrument by which Athens established its maritime empire.

FURTHER READING

Herodotus. *The Histories.* Translated by Robin Waterfield. New York: Oxford University Press, 1998.
Plutarch. *The Rise and Fall of Athens: Nine Greek Lives by Plutarch.* Translated by Ian Scott-Kilvert. London: Penguin, 1960.

Sekunda, Nicholas. *Marathon, 490 B.C.: The First Persian Invasion of Greece*. Westport, Conn.: Praeger, 2005.

Hubert M. Martin, Jr.

See also: Athenian Empire; Athens; Marathon, Battle of; Pausanias of Sparta; Plataea, Battle of; Xerxes I.

Aristides of Miletus

WRITER

Born: c. late second century B.C.E.; place unknown
Died: c. early first century B.C.E.; place unknown
Category: Literature

LIFE Nothing is known about the life of Aristides of Miletus (ar-uh-STID-eez of mi-LEE-tuhs) except that his name is associated with the *Milesian Tales*, a collection of Greek short stories, often erotic or obscene in nature. Whether he is the actual author or only the compiler of these

Aristides of Miletus.
(F. R. Niglutsch)

tales, of which only a single fragment remains, is uncertain. The historian Plutarch reports that a copy of Aristides' book was found among the effects of a Roman officer following the Battle of Carrhae in 53 B.C.E. The *Milesian Tales* was translated into Latin by Cornelius Sisenna. Ten fragments of this Latin translation survive. Some of these tales may include the story of "The Widow of Ephesus" told in Petronius Arbiter's *Satyricon* (c. 60 C.E.; *The Satyricon*, 1694) and the story of the ass, which is the main plot of Lucius Apuleius's *Metamorphoses* (second century C.E.; *The Golden Ass*, 1566).

INFLUENCE Aristides' *Milesian Tales* may represent the beginning of the Greco-Roman short-story genre and had a significant effect on the development of the ancient novel, especially in Rome, where the term "Milesian tale" came to mean any erotic story. Aristides' work influenced not only Latin novels such as Petronius Arbiter's *Satyricon* and Lucius Apuleius's *Metamorphoses* but also later works such as Boccaccio's *Decameron: Precipe Galetto* (1349-1351 C.E.; *The Decameron*, 1620).

FURTHER READING
Trenkner, Sophie. *The Greek Novella in the Classical Period*. New York: Garland, 1987.
Walsh, P. G. *The Roman Novel*. London: Bristol Classical, 1995.

Thomas J. Sienkewicz

See also: Literature.

Aristippus

PHILOSOPHER

Born: c. 435 B.C.E.; Cyrene, Cyrenaica (now in Libya)
Died: 365 B.C.E.; Athens, Greece
Category: Philosophy

LIFE   Because Aristippus (ar-uh-STIHP-uhs) left no writings for posterity, what is known about him is derived from secondary sources, the most notable of which is Xenophon's *Apomnēmoneumata* (c. 381-355; *Memorabilia of Socrates*, 1712). It appears that Aristippus was born in North Africa in the city of Cyrene, in what is currently Libya but was then Cyrenaica. His family was reputed to have had considerable influence and to have been sufficiently rich to support the young Aristippus in his travels and studies.

Aristippus studied with Socrates, attracted to this pivotal Athenian philosopher by his obvious humanity, his fun-loving qualities, his cordiality, and, most important of all, his indisputable intellectual superiority. Aristippus spent considerable time in Athens during its Golden Age, its most significant period of intellectual influence. He also went to Syracuse, where he taught rhetoric and was associated with the court of Dionysius, an ill-tempered, often rude tyrant. Aristippus returned to his native Cyrene to begin a school of philosophy. He remained there for several years until his ultimate return to Athens, where he spent the remainder of his life.

Schooled by Socrates, the great master of the Sophist philosophy based on dialogue and structured argument, Aristippus had been exposed continually to the prevailing Socratic theory of innate ideas—to the notion that ideal forms exist, while the objects of the "real" world are mere imitations of the ideal forms (the word "idea" is derived from a Greek word meaning "shape" or "form"). Aristippus early questioned this notion, believing rather that all individuals experience and perceive things around them in unique and individual ways.

In modern philosophical terminology, Aristippus would likely be classified as a relativist. For him, no physical object (table, chair), quality (blue), or concept (goodness) in the real world possesses generalized qualities de-

Aristippus.

tached from the specific object, quality, or concept. To him, perception, which is wholly individual and idiosyncratic, determines what any object or concept communicates to any single individual. These notions led Aristippus to the conclusion that there exists no explicit, objective, and absolute world identically perceived by all people. He further posited that it is impossible to compare the experiences of different people accurately, because all individuals can know are their own perceptions and reactions.

Aristippus further contended that, from birth, all living humans seek pleasure and avoid pain. He contended that life must be lived in pursuit of pleasure. His one caveat was that pleasure must be defined by all people for themselves, that there is no universal pleasure. Some people, therefore, find the greatest pleasure in leading law-abiding, virtuous lives, whereas others find it in raucous, drunken revelry. Aristippus did not make moral judgments about where individuals sought and found their pleasures.

Aristippus also argued that the source of pleasure is always the body—which, he was quick to point out, includes the mind. For him, pleasures were most fully and satisfactorily experienced in the present. Memories of pleasures past or the contemplation of pleasures promised at some future date are weak semblances of pleasures that are immediately enjoyable.

The school of philosophy that Aristippus founded at Cyrene, based on concepts such as these, was designated the Hedonistic school, "hedonistic" being derived from the Greek word for "pleasure." Hedonism was closely akin in many ways to the Cynicism of Antisthenes, who, like Aristippus, questioned the existence of universals. Together, Antisthenes and Aristippus formulated the Nominalist theory of universals, which flew in the face of Socrates' and Plato's realism.

INFLUENCE   Perhaps Aristippus's greatest contribution to Western thought came in his questioning of Socrates' theory of ideas. In disputing these theories, he focused on individual differences and arrived at a philosophy infinitely more relativistic than the prevailing philosophies of his day. In a sense, Aristippus took the earliest tentative steps in a march of insurgent ideas that led inevitably to the Reformation of the sixteenth century.

If the Cynics, under the leadership of Antisthenes, represented the school of apathy in the ancient world, the Cyrenaics, following the lead of Aristippus, represented the school of happiness. These ideas ran counter to the prevailing philosophy emerging from Athens and were considered both exotic and quixotic by the most influential thinkers of the day. As Athens skulked into defeat and steady decline, however, many of its citizenry found Hedonism—and Epicurus's refinement of it, Epicureanism—quite to their liking.

FURTHER READING
Durant, Will. *The Story of Philosophy*. New York: Simon & Schuster, 1967.

Feldman, Fred. *Pleasure and the Good Life: Concerning the Nature, Varieties, and Plausibility of Hedonism.* Oxford, England: Clarendon Press, 2004.

Fuller, B. A. G. *A History of Ancient and Medieval Philosophy.* Revised by Sterling M. McMurrin. New York: Henry Holt, 1955.

Hamlyn, D. W. *A History of Western Philosophy.* New York: Viking, 1987.

Kenny, Anthony, ed. *The Oxford History of Western Philosophy.* New York: Oxford University Press, 1994.

Renault, Mary. *The Last of the Wine.* New York: Random House, 1975.

R. Baird Shuman

See also: Antisthenes; Cynicism; Epicureanism; Epicurus; Hedonism; Philosophy; Socrates; Sophists.

Aristophanes

PLAYWRIGHT

Born: c. 450 B.C.E.; Athens, Greece
Died: c. 385 B.C.E.; Athens, Greece
Category: Theater and drama

LIFE   Aristophanes (ar-uh-STAHF-uh-neez) is considered the greatest writer of Greek comedy, and his plays have been produced for centuries because of their wit, comic invention, poetic language, and characterization. Politically, Aristophanes was noted for his aristocratic, rather than democratic, views of government. Very little is known of the life of Aristophanes; even the dates given for his birth and death vary as much as five to ten years. His parents were Philippus and Zenodora, and their son was born into the Athenian township of Cydathenaeon of the tribe Pandionis. The father was a landowner in Aegina, which gave the young playwright certain status, and he may even have owned land at a young age. He may not have been out of his teens when his first play, *The Banqueters* (427 B.C.E.), which is no longer extant, was produced to great applause. As to his appearance, he was certainly bald by the time he produced *Eirēnē* (*Peace*, 1837) in 421 B.C.E. His vitality must have been great, since he produced and acted in several of his earlier plays.

Aristophanes inherited the traditions of the Greek Old Comedy, consisting of broad political and personal abuse, low-comedy farce of an earthy nature, inappropriate flights of poetic fancy, and theatrical conventions of costume, mask, music, and dance. The Age of Pericles allowed its comedians great license and freedom for political satire, a tradition which Aristophanes followed assiduously. He hated the age of decadence, compromise, departure from the vigorous way of life, the "new" sophistries and systems. He used his plays to influence the political, moral, and religious life of his times, and his was a vigorous campaign. Under their farcical exteriors, his plays were serious allegories aimed at the emotions rather than the intellect he so mistrusted. His art passed through three major periods and bridged the gap between the Old Comedy and the New.

Principal Works of Aristophanes

Acharnēs, 425 B.C.E. (*The Acharnians*, 1812)
Hippēs, 424 B.C.E. (*The Knights*, 1812)
Nephelai, 423 B.C.E. (*The Clouds*, 1708)
Sphēkes, 422 B.C.E. (*The Wasps*, 1812)
Eirēnē, 421 B.C.E. (*Peace*, 1837)
Ornithes, 414 B.C.E. (*The Birds*, 1824)
Lysistratē, 411 B.C.E. (*Lysistrata*, 1837)
Thesmophoriazousai, 411 B.C.E. (*Thesmophoria-zusae*, 1837)
Batrachoi, 405 B.C.E. (*The Frogs*, 1780)
Ekklesiazousai, 392 B.C.E.? (*Ecclesiazusae*, 1837)
Ploutos, 388 B.C.E. (*Plutus*, 1651)

In the first of the extant plays, *Acharnēs* (425 B.C.E.; *The Acharnians*, 1812), Aristophanes won the first prize at the Lenaea in 425 B.C.E., a remarkable feat for the young actor-director-playwright. This play is remarkable as well in that he introduces the antiwar theme for the first time in history, and he played the part of the protagonist, a simple country man who thoroughly routs the antagonist, a warmonger. *Hippēs* (424 B.C.E.; *The Knights*, 1812), following the next year, so soundly berated the tyrant and usurper Cleon that litigation was put in motion to prove the playwright of foreign birth and therefore disqualify him from competition. Continuing the one-play-a-year routine, Aristophanes presented next *Nephelai* (423 B.C.E.; *The Clouds*, 1708), satirizing the modern sophistries personified, although unfairly, by Socrates. This was one of his most widely read and discussed plays. Athens's love of litigation, which Aristophenes thought wasteful of time and energy, he attacked in *Sphēkes* (422 B.C.E.; *The Wasps*, 1812); in the second part he demonstrates how the populace could have benefited from art, literature, and music were it not for this involvement in demagoguery. *Peace* returns to his original theme, suggesting strongly that Athens should accept the Spartan peace offer and demonstrating the contrast of rural peace and strident war.

In his middle period, Aristophanes wrote his best-known and greatest plays. *Ornithes* (414 B.C.E.; *The Birds*, 1824) the play he liked best and one containing some of the greatest lyric poetry of all time, advances the utopian theory that humankind should begin to build a simpler kingdom. The plan fails when this heavenly birdland is overrun by the same old Athenian complications: litigation, demagoguery, and warfare. *Lysistratē* (411 B.C.E.; *Lysistrata*, 1837) takes its name from the feminist protagonist, who decides that women can end the sad spectacle of war by resisting men's amorous advances. The play's risqué wit and humor make this one of the best comedies of manners and the most frequently produced Greek play of the modern theater. The *Thesmophoriazousai* (411 B.C.E.; *Thesmophoria-zusae*, 1837), presented that same year, continues a theme begun earlier, that of dramatic criticism, especially of Euripides, whom Aristophanes criticized as unfairly as he did Socrates and for about the same reasons. In *Batrachoi* (405 B.C.E.; *The Frogs*, 1780) he combines many elements of criticism—of state, art, reason—into a masterpiece of theater in which Dionysus goes to the underworld to bring back the greatest poet for troubled times. The chorus of frogs chides, admonishes, and exhorts, while the arguments for and against finally agree on Aeschylus, the tragedian of the great period of Greek drama.

Aristophanes. (Library of Congress)

141

Aristophanes' last period bridges the final gap from the old Dionysian revel to the bourgeois comedy of Menander. The *Ekklesiazousai* (392 B.C.E.?; *Ecclesiazusae*, 1837) fails to support the facetious view held in *Lysistrata*, for when women intrude themselves into office they establish a novel form of communism, foreshadowing platonic sophistries and satirizing them in advance.

Ploutos (388 B.C.E.; *Plutus*, 1651), the last extant play under the old master's name, appeared probably in the year before Aristophanes' death. This work looks backward to the preoccupation of the middle period with mythological themes; blind Plutus is given sight and wisdom to see that wealth belongs to those who can sanely use it, while the way of the foolish is poverty. This play, with its simple (and not topical) allusions, struck a vibrant chord for playgoers and readers from antiquity down through the Renaissance.

INFLUENCE   Aristophanes' three sons carried on the dramatic tradition with some success, for one play—probably written by the father—won a prize in 387 B.C.E. The youngest son evidently won honors in the New Comedy. Centuries later, the plays of Aristophanes exerted considerable influence on English satire, especially on William Congreve, Ben Jonson, Henry Fielding, Somerset Maugham, and Noël Coward.

FURTHER READING
Bloom, Harold, ed. *Aristophanes*. Broomall, Pa.: Chelsea House, 2002.

Bowie, A. M. *Aristophanes: Myth, Ritual, and Comedy*. New York: Cambridge University Press, 1993.

Reckford, Kenneth J. *Aristophanes' Old-and-New Comedy*. Chapel Hill: University of North Carolina Press, 1987.

Russo, Carlo Ferdinando. *Aristophanes: An Author for the Stage*. Translated by Kevin Wren. New York: Routledge, 1994.

Silk, M. S. *Aristophanes and the Definition of Comedy*. Oxford, England: Oxford University Press, 2002.

Spatz, Lois. *Aristophanes*. Boston: Twayne, 1978.

Taaffe, Lauren K. *Aristophanes and Women*. New York: Routledge, 1993.

Jonathan L. Thorndike

See also: Aeschylus; Cleon of Athens; Euripides; Literature; Performing Arts; Socrates; Sports and Entertainment.

Aristotle

Philosopher

Born: 384 B.C.E.; Stagirus, Chalcidice, Greece
Died: 322 B.C.E.; Chalcis, Euboea, Greece
Category: Philosophy

LIFE Aristotle (ar-uhs-TAHT-uhl), one of the world's greatest philosophers, was born in Stagirus, a little town on the peninsula of Chalcidice. He was the son of Nicomachus, a physician, and Phaestis. The family was middle class, of moderate means. While Aristotle was yet a child his father became court physician to Amyntas II of Macedonia, the grandfather of Alexander the Great. From birth Aristotle, as the son of a physician, was a member of the Asclepiadae guild. His interest in science and particularly in biology was only natural, for his family had a long tradition in medicine. He was soon without parents, however, because they died when he was a boy. He became a ward of a friend and relative of the family, Proxenus.

At eighteen he became a student under Plato at the Academy in Athens, not primarily because he was interested in philosophy but because the Academy offered the best education in Greece in science and other basic studies. Aristotle distinguished himself as a student, even though there were some who were irritated by his interest in dress and by his lisping, mocking air. He remained with the Academy, always a central figure, but becoming increasingly critical of some of Plato's ideas until Plato's death in 347 B.C.E.

When Speusippus became the Academy's leader after Plato's death, Aristotle accepted the invitation of Hermias, the king of Atarneus in Mysia, to join him there and become part of a philosophical circle. While with Hermias, Aristotle spent a considerable part of his time studying marine biology along the Aeolic coast. He also found time to admire and marry Hermias's niece and adopted daughter, Pythias, with whom he had a daughter of the same name.

After spending three years in Mysia, following the assassination of Hermias by agents of the Persians, Aristotle moved to Mytilene on the island of Lesbos, where he continued his independent biological research.

Principal Works of Aristotle

The works listed here date to Aristotle's Second Athenian Period (335-323 B.C.E.), except for *Zoology*, which is dated to the Middle Period (348-336 B.C.E.):

Analytica priora (*Prior Analytics*, 1812)
De poetica (*Poetics*, 1705)
Analytica posterioria (*Posterior Analytics*, 1812)
Aporemata Homerika (*Homeric Problems*, 1812)
Aristotelous peri geneseōs kai phthoras (*Meteoroligica*, 1812)
Athenaiōn politeia (*The Athenian Constitution*, 1812)
De anima (*On the Soul*, 1812)
Ethica Nicomachea (*Nicomachean Ethics*, 1797)
Metaphysica (*Metaphysics*, 1801)
Organon (English translation, 1812)
Physica (*Physics*, 1812)
Politica (*Politics*, 1598)
Technē rhetorikēs (*Rhetoric*, 1686)
Tōn peri ta zōia historiōn (*Zoology*, 1812)
Topica (*Topics*, 1812)

He then left to undertake the tutelage of Alexander, the thirteen-year-old son of Philip II of Macedonia who would one day become known as Alexander the Great. Philip, who had known Aristotle since boyhood, was aware of Aristotle's reputation as a brilliant scientist and philosopher. Aristotle gave Alexander the usual Greek education, with emphasis upon Homer and the dramatists, and with considerable discussion of the philosophy and art of politics. The work was conducted at Pella and later at Mieza. It was virtually terminated when Alexander was appointed regent for his father in 340 B.C.E., while Philip was engaged in a campaign to complete the subjugation of all Greece. Aristotle settled in Stagirus and became friends with Antipater, later regent in Greece.

When Philip was assassinated in 336 B.C.E., Aristotle returned to Athens to continue his scientific work. At about that time Speusippus, Plato's successor at the Academy, died, and Xenocrates of Chalcedon was appointed in his place. Aristotle was not tempted to return to the Academy; instead, he decided to start a new school in the Lyceum, a grove sacred to Apollo Lyceius, located to the northeast of Athens. He rented some buildings there and acquired pupils. Because of Aristotle's custom of walking up and down under a covered court, or *peripatos*, with a group of students while lecturing or discussing some philosophical or scientific matter, his group became known as the Peripatetics. The subjects that needed special study and individual attention were taught in the mornings to small groups, while those that could adequately be taught to larger numbers were reserved for the afternoons or evenings. Emphasis was upon biology, history, and philosophy. During the twelve years he was at the Lyceum, Aristotle gave hundreds of lectures, of which some notes are extant and constitute the material which has come to be identified as his works.

Shortly after his return to Athens from Macedonia, Aristotle's wife died. He formed a lasting union out of wedlock with a woman of Stagirus,

Aristotle. (Library of Congress)

145

Herpyllis, with whom he had a son, Nicomachus, whose name has been used to distinguish the *Ethica Nichomachea* (*Nicomachean Ethics*, 1797), that version of Aristotle's ethics recorded by his son, from the *Eudemian Ethics*, the version of a pupil, Eudemus.

Alexander died in 323, and as a result of ensuing anti-Macedonian feeling, Aristotle was charged with impiety, the same capital charge that led to the death of Socrates. The charge, founded on nothing more than some poetry that Aristotle had written twenty years before to honor the memory of Hermias, was provoked by Aristotle's continued friendship with Antipater of Macedonia. Aristotle retreated to Chalcis, accompanied by several of his followers, and died there the following year. His will provided for the emancipation of some of his slaves and protected the rest from being sold.

INFLUENCE   Aristotle classified the sciences; added to the scientific data in many fields, particularly in biology; encouraged and developed ideas in ethics and politics; and developed logic as a science of reasoning. The Lyceum, largely because of the creative energy of its founder, soon became the outstanding school in Greece, outranking the Academy, and Aristotle—as the most encompassing mind of the age—achieved a preeminence which the ensuing two thousand years have not dispelled. Through Aristotle's influence, not only his own work and that of the Peripatetics but also the teachings of earlier Greek philosophers from Thales to Plato were synthesized and preserved. No other Greek philosopher, with the exception of Plato, has had a greater an influence on scientific, ethical, and logical thought in Western civilization.

FURTHER READING

Ackrill, J. L. *Essays on Plato and Aristotle*. New York: Oxford University Press, 1997.

Adler, Mortimer J. *Aristotle for Everybody: Difficult Thought Made Easy*. New York: Scribner's, 1997.

Bar On, Bat-Ami, ed. *Engendering Origins: Critical Feminist Readings in Plato and Aristotle*. Albany: State University of New York Press, 1994.

Barnes, Jonathan, ed. *The Cambridge Companion to Aristotle*. New York: Cambridge University Press, 1995.

Crivelli, Paolo. *Aristotle on Truth*. New York: Cambridge University Press, 2004.

Edel, Abraham. *Aristotle and His Philosophy*. New Brunswick, N.J.: Transaction Books, 1996.

Falcon, Andrea. *Aristotle and the Science of Nature: Unity Without Uniformity*. New York: Cambridge University Press, 2005.

Gerson, Lloyd P. *Aristotle and Other Platonists*. Ithaca, N.Y.: Cornell University Press, 2005.

Hughes, Gerard J. *Aristotle on Ethics*. New York: Routledge, 2001.

McLeisch, Kenneth. *Aristotle*. New York: Routledge, 1999.

Robinson, Timothy A. *Aristotle in Outline*. Indianapolis, Ind.: Hackett, 1995.

Strathern, Paul. *Aristotle in Ninety Minutes*. Chicago: Ivan Dee, 1996.

Young, Mark A. *Negotiating the Good Life: Aristotle and the Civil Society*. Burlington, Vt.: Ashgate, 2005.

Janet M. Luehring

See also: Alexander the Great; Antipater; Philip II of Macedonia; Philosophy; Plato; Speusippus.

Aristoxenus

PHILOSOPHER AND MUSIC THEORIST

Born: 375-360 B.C.E.; Tarentum (now Taranto, Italy)
Died: Date unknown; probably Athens, Greece
Category: Music; philosophy

LIFE   Aristoxenus (ar-ihs-TAWK-see-nuhs) received his earliest musical training at the hands of his father, Spintharus, who enjoyed some reputation as a musician. He later studied with Lamprus of Erythrae, of whom little is known. Aristoxenus moved to Athens, where he studied with the Pythagorean Xenophilus. He also studied at the Lyceum with Aristotle. Because Aristoxenus later competed, although unsuccessfully, with Theophrastus, a colleague, for headship of the Lyceum around 322, it may be assumed that Aristoxenus was a superior student and respected in scholarly circles.

Aristoxenus was a prolific writer, with one source attributing more than 450 works to him, although only a few fragments have survived. The writings cover a variety of topics, including works on music, biography, history, and philosophy. The most important of the extant fragments pertain to music. Numbering among the music fragments that survive are parts of three books titled *Harmonika stoicheia* (*The Harmonics*, 1902). In addition, there is a fragment on rhythm, consisting of approximately 250 lines.

Aristoxenian theory articulated a system that addressed the issues of pitch, intervals, genera, systems, modes, and modulation as they applied to melody. The smallest consonant interval recognized in his system was a perfect fourth, which also formed the fixed outer boundary of a four-note unit called a tetrachord. The tetrachord was a kind of building block. The combining of the tetrachords produced three important larger theoretical structures known as the Greater Perfect System, the Lesser Perfect System, and the Immutable System.

Aristoxenus's approach to the theory of music, conceived around 320 B.C.E., was unique for his time. A superior student of Aristotelian logic who was familiar with the "new math," geometry, Aristoxenus turned both

148

logic and geometry to his advantage as he defined the way subsequent theorists were to look at the discipline of music. His treatise was not simply an exercise in abstract logic. He elevated the musician's "ear" to a level equal with the intellect. By doing so, he recognized the value and importance of the commonsense judgment of the practicing musician.

Aristoxenus's writings clearly challenged both the teachings of Pythagoras, who flourished around 530 B.C.E. and whose reputation and writings were legendary by the time of Aristoxenus, and those of a group known as the Harmonists. The supporters of Pythagoras's theories about music were scientists and mathematicians who were not interested in explanations or observations about the interplay of musical elements or about the science of music itself. They believed that understanding numbers was central to understanding the universe, and, therefore, it was quite logical to express musical intervals, of key importance to the Pythagoreans, in terms of mathematical ratios.

The Harmonists, criticized by Aristoxenus for failing to establish a rigorous system, were interested in the practical and empirical aspects of music theory but fell short of articulating an acceptable system. They were preoccupied with the identification and measurement of microintervals, which emphasized the study of certain scales to the exclusion of others.

A key factor in Aristoxenus's approach was his description of sound as a continuum, or line, along which the pitch could come to rest at any point, permitting him the freedom to create intervals of varying sizes without regard to whether the interval could be expressed using rational numbers. While abstract mathematical expression of a musical interval had become most important to the Pythagoreans and the Harmonists, Aristoxenus focused instead on the development of a system that would afford him the freedom and flexibility to identify subtleties of scalar structure. He based his system on judgments made by the ear and then represented it through geometric application.

INFLUENCE   Aristoxenus was the earliest writer on music theory known to address practical musical concerns. When he took the unique position that the ear, along with the intellect, should be used in the study of music, he established a precedent that ultimately altered the course of music theory. In effect, he redefined what music theory was, taking it out of the hands of the scientists and mathematicians and creating a new discipline that focused only on the interrelationship of musical elements. His arguments, which owed much to Aristotelian influence and methodology, enabled him to produce a clearly defined and organized system of music theory.

FURTHER READING

Aristoxenus. *Aristoxenou harmonika stoicheia = The Harmonics of Aristoxenus*. Edited by Henry Stewart Macran. New York: Olms, 1990.

Barker, Andrew. "Music and Perception: A Study in Aristoxenus." *Journal of Hellenic Studies* 98 (1978): 9-16.

Crocker, Richard. "Aristoxenus and Greek Mathematics." In *Aspects of Medieval and Renaissance Music*, edited by Jan LaRue. New York: Pendragon Press, 1978.

Franklin, John Curtis. "Diatonic Music in Greece: A Reassessment of Its Antiquity." *Mnemosyne* 55, no. 6 (November, 2002): 669-702.

Gibson, Sophie. *Aristoxenus of Tarentum and the Birth of Musicology*. New York: Routledge, 2005.

Henderson, Isobel. "Ancient Greek Music." In *Ancient and Oriental Music*, edited by Egon Wellesz. Vol. 1 in *The New Oxford History of Music*. 2d ed. New York: Oxford University Press, 1990.

Lippman, Edward. *Musical Thought in Ancient Greece*. New York: Da Capo Press, 1975.

Rowell, Lewis. "Aristoxenus on Rhythm." *Journal of Music Theory* 23 (Spring, 1979): 63-79.

Winnington-Ingram, R. P. "Aristoxenus." In *New Grove Dictionary of Music and Musicians*, edited by Stanley Sadie. 2d ed. New York: Grove's Dictionaries, 2001.

Michael Hernon

See also: Aristotle; Philosophy; Pythagoras; Science; Theophrastus.

Art and Architecture

Greece is celebrated for its preclassical and classical artistic and architectural accomplishments.

Date: 2500-31 B.C.E.
Category: Art and architecture

PRECLASSICAL HELLADIC CIVILIZATIONS   These civilizations, from circa 2500 to 1000 B.C.E., arose on the Peloponnese and the islands of the Aegean Sea. Principal among these was the Minoan civilization (c. 2500-1200 B.C.E.) on the island of Crete, a center of maritime traffic and cultural exchange. King Minos's palace at Knossos (c. 1500 B.C.E.) is among the largest of the unfortified Minoan palaces; its rambling, mazelike plan may have inspired the myth of the Minotaur. Among the remarkable fresco fragments from Knossos is a portrait of a pretty green-eyed brunette nicknamed *La Parisienne* (c. 1500 B.C.E.) because of the subject's uncanny resemblance to the young women of Paris. Also represented are frescoes (such as the *Toreador fresco*, also known as *The Bull-Games*, c. 1500 B.C.E.) of bull vaulting, a ritual that involved grasping the horns of a charging bull and somersaulting over, or perhaps onto, the animal's back.

Minoan Kamares ware ceramic vessels such as the *Octopus Jar*, Gournia (c. 1600 B.C.E.), recovered near Phaestus, bear painted images of sea life, decorative whorls, and other sea-inspired patterns. Glazed statuettes of an unknown Minoan goddess or priestess, including the *Snake Goddess*, Knossos (c. 1600 B.C.E.), standing bare-breasted with open bodice and grasping a writhing snake in each hand, are also common.

In contrast, Mycenaean art (c. 1500-1200 B.C.E.) exhibits the warlike character of the Mycenaean kings inhabiting the Greek Peloponnese. Important citadel palaces at Tiryns and nearby Mycenae were protected by massive stone walls pierced by long corbeled galleries. Beehive tombs, such as the misnamed Treasury of Atreus at Mycenae (c. 1250 B.C.E.), employ corbeling to generate high ogival domes, some more than 40 feet (12 meters) in height and diameter. Relief carving above the lintel of the lion gate at Mycenae (c. 1250 B.C.E.) depicts two imposing heraldic lions, now

The Acropolis. (F. R. Niglutsch)

partially ruined, flanking a column of the "inverted" Minoan type, evidence that such columns were revered as cult objects. Ancient Mycenae bore the Homeric epithet "rich in gold," and the Mycenaean taste for metal craft is evident in artifacts recovered from shaft graves, including bronze dagger blades inlaid with gold and silver and gold repoussé work made by hammering a relief image from thin sheet metal. One example of this metalwork is the Vaphio cup (c. 1650-1450). Mycenaean repoussé funerary masks, such as the *Mask of Agamemnon* (c. 1550-1500 B.C.E.), bore a stylized likeness of the deceased.

Cycladic art (c. 2500-2000 B.C.E.) encompasses the Bronze Age cultures of the Cyclades Islands, which, because of their physical insularity, lagged somewhat behind the more developed cultural centers at Crete and the mainland. Marble plank idols ranging in size from several inches (five or six centimeters) to more than four feet (slightly over a meter) in length often accompany burials and most probably represent a goddess of rebirth. Seated male musicians holding lyrelike instruments made up a later three-dimensional variant in the *Harp Player* from Keros (c. 2500-2200 B.C.E.). Similar clay figures found on Crete and the Greek mainland suggest that these cultures enjoyed some contact, though not intensive enough to inspire a significant intermingling of traditions.

CLASSICAL GREECE   The Hellenic Age (fifth and fourth centuries B.C.E.) marks the rise of the Greek city-states following the Persian armada's defeat at the Battle of Salamis (480 B.C.E.). The art of Classical Greece, with Athens as its cultural epicenter, existed in service of philosophical ideals expressed through reasoned aesthetic principles. Its development can be traced through several evolutionary phases and substyles; in ceramics, simple repetitive geometric style designs, as in the Dipylon Vase (eighth century B.C.E.), evolve into increasingly complex representational images in black figure style, such as the François Vase (c. 570 B.C.E.), and a later red figure style represented by Euphronius's *Death of Sarpedon* (c. 515 B.C.E.).

Sculpture was the favored art form of the ancient Greeks. Sculpted marble figures of the Archaic period (800-500 B.C.E.) manifest an "Egyptian stride," especially evident in the nude male kouros figures, grave memorials formerly thought to represent the god Apollo (female counterparts are called kore). Earlier Archaic figures such as *Kouros from Tenea* (c. 570 B.C.E.) appear stylized and tentative. Faces present a generic type stamped with a distinctive "archaic smile" whose very ubiquity suggests a meaning other than happiness—perhaps the facial rigor of the deceased as a funerary marker. In just over one hundred years, however, the Greek kouroi sculptors mastered the subtleties of anatomical representation, including the elegant counterpoise of hip and shoulder when body weight is shifted onto one leg, called ponderation, as can be seen in *Kritios Boy*, Athens (c. 480 B.C.E.).

In Greek philosophy, as in Greek art, perfection of form was thought to go hand in hand with perfection of concept: For a thing to be perfect, it had to look perfect as well. Therefore, later Classical sculptors (c. fifth century B.C.E.) developed canons of proportion thought to yield an ideal figure, as in Polyclitus's *Doryphorus* (c. 440 B.C.E.). Most Greek marble carvings were painted, especially facial details and drapery, to enhance their verisimilitude; the pristine appearance of classical sculpture is entirely an accident of time.

Classical Greek architecture used mortarless post-and-lintel construction techniques. Temple forms are varied, but most incorporate a rectangular *naos* (or cella) fronted or surrounded by columns supporting a spanning entablature and gabled roof. The pediment, or triangular area beneath the roof gables, was frequently adorned with sculpture. Three Classical orders are readily identified by their distinctive column capitals: the Doric Order with its plain cushionlike capitals; the Ionic Order with its elegant scroll-shaped volutes; and the Corinthian Order, originating from Asia Minor, with its bundled acanthus leaves.

The most famous examples of classical architecture are the temples on the Athenian Acropolis (literally, "hill city"), built in gratitude to the protector goddess Athena Parthenos. The Parthenon, a Doric temple with Ionic features (built by architects Ictinus and Callicrates in 447-432 B.C.E.), originally housed a 40-foot (12-meter) gold and ivory statue of Athena (now lost) by the sculptor Phidias, as well as the treasury of the Delian League. The Parthenon's original relief carvings and pediment statues (by the workshop of Phidias) are now in the British Museum. The Erechtheum, a rambling Ionic structure built by Mnesicles (fl. fifth century B.C.E.) to commemorate a contest between Athena and Poseidon, contains within its compass several cult items: a sacred olive grove, a stone marked by Poseidon's trident, a saltwater spring, and the tomb of the semilegendary hero Erechtheus; therefore, the Erechtheum is asymmetric and built on two different levels. The south Porch of Maidens is famous for its caryatids, female figures used as supporting columns. The Propylaea built by Mnesicles, gateway to the Acropolis, contained a picture gallery-museum in its north wing.

The later period following the death of Alexander the Great of Macedo-

The Erechtheum, built by Mnesicles, is known for its Porch of Maidens with caryatids, female figures used as columns. (PhotoDisc)

nia (r. 336-323) was regarded as a decadent epoch by Roman scholars such as Pliny the Elder, who called it Hellenistic (meaning "Greek-like"); it has since come to be appreciated in its own right, however, for its distinctive emphasis on realism, movement, and emotion. Among the many Hellenistic masterpieces are the *Nike of Samothrace* (c. 190? B.C.E.) and *Laocoön* by Agesander, Polydorus, and Athenodorus of Rhodes (c. 100 B.C.E.), a work much admired by Michelangelo. Many surviving classical sculptures are actually Roman marble copies of lost Greek originals.

FURTHER READING

Belozerskaya, Marina, and Kenneth Lapatin. *Ancient Greece: Art, Architecture, and History*. Los Angeles: J. Paul Getty Museum, 2004.

Boardman, John. *The Archaeology of Nostalgia: How the Greeks Re-Created Their Mythical Past*. London: Thames & Hudson, 2002.

_____. *Greek Art*. 1964. Reprint. London: Thames and Hudson, 1985.

Bonnefoy, Yves. *Mythologies*. Translated by Wendy Doniger. Chicago: University of Chicago Press, 1991.

Martin, Roland. *Greek Architecture*. London: Phaidon, 2003.

Osborne, Harold, ed. *The Oxford Companion to Art*. Oxford, England: Oxford University Press, 1970.

Larry Smolucha

See also: Achilles Painter; Amasis Painter; Apollodorus of Athens (artist); Artemis at Ephesus, Temple of; Mycenae, Palace of; Parthenon; Phidias; Zeus at Pergamum, Great Altar of.

Temple of Artemis at Ephesus

This temple for the goddess Artemis is one of the Seven Wonders of the World.

Date: c. 700 B.C.E.-262 C.E.
Category: Art and architecture; religion and mythology
Locale: Ancient city of Ephesus, near modern Selçuk, Turkey

SUMMARY   The foundation of the temple of Artemis at Ephesus (AHRT-ih-muhs at e-FUH-suhs) dates back to the seventh century B.C.E., but it is best known for the great marble structure that was built between 560 and 550 B.C.E. sponsored by King Croesus of Lydia and designed by the architect Chersiphron. The temple was dedicated to Artemis, goddess of the hunt, whose presence at the temple was believed by the citizens of Ephesus to provide them with wealth and protection. Legend has it that a man named Herostratus, in an attempt to immortalize his name, burned the temple to the ground on the night Alexander the Great was born in 356 B.C.E.

A new temple, larger and more impressive than the first, was built on the same spot. The high terraced base of the temple was rectangular, measuring 380 by 180 feet (115 by 55 meters), with 127 Ionic columns 62 feet (19 meters) high. The architects were Paeonius and Demetrius. The temple suffered at the hands of the Goths in 262 C.E. and was abandoned with the coming of Christianity to the Roman Empire. It no longer stands.

SIGNIFICANCE   The temple of Artemis at Ephesus was the second largest temple in the ancient Greek world, and tourists, pilgrims, and devotees paid homage by coming from far and wide.

FURTHER READING
Clayton, Peter A., and Martin J. Price. *The Seven Wonders of the Ancient World.* New York: Routledge, 1988.

This engraving shows the temple of Artemis at Ephesus as it might have looked in ancient times.

Pedley, John. *Sanctuaries and the Sacred in the Ancient Greek World.* New York: Cambridge University Press, 2005.

Scherrer, Peter, ed. *Ephesus: The New Guide.* Authorized by Österreichisches Archáologishes Institut and Efes Müzeski Selçuk. Translated by Lionel Bier and George M. Luxan. Rev. ed. Turkey: Ege Yayinlau, 2000.

Seval, Mehlika. *Let's Visit Ephesus.* Istanbul: Minyatur, 1998.

Whitley, James. *The Archaeology of Ancient Greece.* New York: Cambridge University Press, 2001.

John A. Nichols

See also: Art and Architecture; Croesus; Mythology; Paeonius; Polyclitus.

Artemisia I

QUEEN OF HALICARNASSUS (R. C. 500 B.C.E.)

Born: Late sixth century B.C.E.; probably Halicarnassus, Caria, Asia Minor
(now Bodrum, Turkey)
Died: Probably mid-fifth century B.C.E.; place unknown
Category: Government and politics; women

LIFE Artemisia I (ahrt-uh-MIHZ-ee-uh) came to the throne of Halicarnassus upon the death of her husband. Her city-state was under the suzerainty
of the Persian Empire. When Xerxes I invaded Greece in 480 B.C.E., Artemisia
contributed five ships that she commanded because of her "spirit of adventure
and manly courage," according to the historian Herodotus.

Artemisia distinguished herself in the campaign's first major action, off
the coast of Euboea. No details are given of Artemisia's skill during this
first encounter, but no one contradicted her when she alluded to it later in
conference with Xerxes. In that conference, Artemisia disagreed with all of
Xerxes' other advisers, telling him not to attack the Greek fleet. Xerxes admired her courageous stand but conceded to the majority and ordered his
fleet to advance to Salamis, off the coast from Athens.

The narrow waters off Salamis negated the superior numbers of the Persian fleet, and the smaller and more maneuverable Greek ships soon gained
the upper hand. Chased by an Athenian ship, Artemisia rammed an allied
ship. This convinced her pursuers that she was Greek or had changed sides,
so they turned away. Xerxes, watching the battle, assumed the ship that she
rammed was Greek. Seeing her "success" in the midst of his fleet's defeat,
he is said to have remarked, "My men have turned into women, my women
into men."

INFLUENCE Artemisia had limited impact, but had her advice been followed before Salamis, all Greek and European history may have been
changed.

FURTHER READING

Herodotus. *The Histories*. Translated by Robin Waterfield. New York: Oxford University Press, 1998.

Lightman, Marjorie, and Benjamin Lightman. *Biographical Dictionary of Ancient Greek and Roman Women: Notable Women from Sappho to Helena*. New York: Facts On File, 2000.

Paul K. Davis

See also: Salamis, Battle of; Xerxes I.

Artemisia II

RULER OF CARIA (R. 377-C. 350 B.C.E.)

Born: Date unknown; place unknown
Died: c. 350 B.C.E.; Halicarnassus, Turkey
Category: Government and politics; women

LIFE   Named after her more famous predecessor who fought against the Greeks for the Persians at the Battle of Salamis in 480 B.C.E., Artemisia II (ahrt-uh-MIHZ-ee-uh) was the wife and also the sister of Mausolus. For twenty-four years (377-353 B.C.E.), Mausolus ruled a small section of the Persian Empire along the Aegean Sea in southwestern Turkey. From the capital in Halicarnassus, together they extended their territory over other cities and conquered the island of Rhodes. Although Persian, the couple admired the Greek culture and did their best to promote it in the cities under their rule. On the death of Mausolus in 353 B.C.E., Artemisia succeeded him. A revolt by the Rhodians occurred, and a fleet of ships was sent to capture the city of Halicarnassus. Learning of the attack, Artemisia commanded her navy to anchor in a secret location, and when the time was right, they attacked and defeated the rebellion.

INFLUENCE   Artemisia ordered the construction of an Ionic-style tomb for her husband's ashes. The greatest Greek artists were commissioned to create the tomb, which when complete was considered one of the Seven Wonders of the Ancient World. Artemisia never lived to see the finished tomb, dying only three years after her husband. She also was entombed in the structure. The magnificence of the completed tomb resulted in the coinage of the word "mausoleum" after Mausolus, Artemisia's husband.

FURTHER READING
Boardman, John, et al. *Greece and the Hellenistic World.* Oxford, England: Oxford University Press, 1988.
Hornblower, S. *Mausolus.* Oxford, England: Oxford University Press, 1982.

Lightman, Marjorie, and Benjamin Lightman. *Biographical Dictionary of Ancient Greek and Roman Women: Notable Women from Sappho to Helena*. New York: Facts On File, 2000.

John A. Nichols

See also: Halicarnassus Mausoleum; Mausolus.

Aspasia of Miletus

RHETORICIAN

Born: c. 475 B.C.E.; Miletus, Asia Minor (now in Turkey)
Died: After 428 B.C.E.; probably Athens, Greece
Category: Scholarship; oratory and rhetoric; women

LIFE Aspasia of Miletus (as-PAY-shee-uh of mi-LEE-tuhs) appears to have been well educated in rhetoric before arriving at Athens (c. 445 B.C.E.), where her exceptional intellect and beauty caught the attention of Pericles, a foremost Athenian statesman. After divorcing his wife, Pericles lived openly with Aspasia, and their home became a meeting place for the

Aspasia of Miletus.
(Library of Congress)

most famous thinkers and writers of the Classical era. Ancient sources refer to Aspasia's ability to discuss rhetoric, philosophy, and politics. Socrates and Plato were said to comment that Aspasia was one of the most intelligent persons of their day. A strong woman in a patriarchal society, Aspasia drew the barbs of critics who accused her of unduly influencing Pericles and inciting Athenian hostilities against other city-states. Contemporary comedies depicted Aspasia and Pericles in unflattering terms and were probably inspired more by political motives than actual fact. After the death of Pericles (429 B.C.E.), Aspasia continued to exert considerable influence over the intellectual life of Athens.

INFLUENCE   In a culture in which women were secluded and denied an education, Aspasia was able to make her intellectual abilities known. Her achievements, mentioned by respected Greek and Roman writers, give insight into an otherwise silent Athenian female population.

FURTHER READING

Henry, Madeleine M. *Prisoner of History: Aspasia of Miletus and Her Biographical Tradition*. Oxford, England: Oxford University Press, 1995.

Lightman, Marjorie, and Benjamin Lightman. *Biographical Dictionary of Ancient Greek and Roman Women: Notable Women from Sappho to Helena*. New York: Facts On File, 2000.

Powell, Anton. *The Greek World*. London: Routledge, 1995.

Sonia Sorrell

See also: Pericles; Women's Life.

Athenian Democracy

Athens developed the unique principles of government that resulted in the emergence of the first democracy in Western civilization.

Date: Sixth century B.C.E.
Category: Government and politics

SUMMARY   The development of Athenian democracy began in the late seventh century B.C.E. as a result of social and economic tensions in the city-state between the ruling nobility and the common population. In an effort to address the turmoil, the Athenian aristocrat Solon, around 594 B.C.E., divided society into four census groups based on wealth and established a city council of four hundred citizens. Eligibility for council service was extended to include not only the aristocracy but also a broader segment of the city-state's overall population. All male citizens, regardless of wealth, were permitted to vote in the Ecclesia, or Assembly of the People. Under Solon's reforms, wealth, rather than birth, determined who would hold political office. Solon's reforms eased strife in Attica temporarily, but social and political divisions continued to fuel instability which eventually gave way to a tyranny under Pisistratus. His rulership resulted in a decline of aristocratic authority in the city with a commensurate growth in the governmental power of the demos, or citizen population, which provided Pisistratus political support.

Following overthrow of the tyranny in the late sixth century B.C.E., Athenian nobles attempted to restore their rule in the city but were stopped around 508 B.C.E. by constitutional changes introduced by the statesman Cleisthenes. Under his reforms, the entire citizen population of Attica was enrolled in demes, or village units; a regional cross section of demes was then grouped into territorial tribes. The tribal arrangement distributed all citizens, rural or urban, regardless of clan, family, or wealth, into ten new political divisions, thereby diminishing the role of local and factional interests in the politics of the city-state. These changes served to form a more homogenous system of government.

Athenian government was now delegated to two bodies: a boule, or council of five hundred citizens that replaced the older Solonian Council of Four Hundred, and the Ecclesia. The boule handled the daily affairs of government and prepared legislation to be acted on by the citizen assembly, and the Ecclesia dealt with the larger matters of government, such as foreign policy. These two organs governed in conjunction with ten magistrates called *strategoi* who were each elected annually by tribe, rather than appointed by lot as were all other officials of the city. Through these reforms, Athenian government was now in the hands of the demos, with only the poorest citizens unable to hold government office. Later reforms introduced by the statesmen Ephialtes and Pericles in the fifth century B.C.E. removed the remaining vestiges of oligarchic authority and gave way to full direct democracy.

Ostracism

According to Aristotle, Cleisthenes of Athens introduced the practice of ostracism (*ostrakophoria*) during a reform of the Athenian constitution around 508 B.C.E. It was first used in 487 B.C.E., to ostracize Hipparchus, son of Charmus, and fell out of use after the ostracism of Hyperbolus c. 417 B.C.E. Prominent men who were ostracized include Aristides of Athens, Themistocles, Cimon, and Thucydides, son of Melesias.

In midwinter, Athenians gathered to decide whether to hold a vote on ostracism. At this vote, citizens would write the name of another citizen who they judged to be threatening the stability of the state. When enough votes were gathered, the person was ostracized. He had to leave within ten days and remain away for ten years, although he retained his property and his citizenship.

SIGNIFICANCE   The principles of government which evolved in ancient Athens contributed to the broadening of democratic ideas in the Hellenistic world and to the unique political tradition that emerged in later Western civilization.

FURTHER READING

Hansen, M. H. *The Athenian Democracy in the Age of Demosthenes: Structure, Principles, and Ideology.* Cambridge, Mass.: Blackwell, 1991.

Rhodes, P. J., ed. *Athenian Democracy.* New York: Oxford University Press, 2004.

Stockton, David. *The Classical Athenian Democracy.* New York: Oxford University Press, 1990.

Donathan Taylor

See also: Athens; Cleisthenes of Athens; Ephialtes of Athens; Four Hundred, The; Government and Law; Pericles; Pisistratus; Solon.

Athenian Empire

Athens transformed a defensive alliance against Persia into a political empire, preventing the peaceful unification of Greece and leading to the Peloponnesian War.

Date: 478-431 B.C.E.
Also known as: Delian League
Category: Cities and civilizations; government and politics; expansion and land acquisition
Locale: Athens, Ionia, and other Greek city-states

SUMMARY   After the Persian invasion of Greece had been repulsed in the spring of 479 B.C.E., delegates from the liberated Greek cities of Ionia and Athens assembled and agreed to combine forces in a league whose stated aims were to protect the Aegean area from fresh Persian offensives and to ravage Xerxes I's territory. Pausanias of Sparta (c. late sixth century-c. 470 B.C.E.) had been the commander in chief of the allied Greeks. His behavior was so arrogant and brutal, however, that the allies rejected all Spartan leadership. Aristides of Athens (c. 525-c. 467 B.C.E.) became the allied leader, accompanied by his younger colleague Cimon (c. 510-c. 451 B.C.E.).

The headquarters of this confederacy was located on the sacred island of Delos, and it came to be called the Delian League. In the beginning, an assembly of representatives determined policy, with each state, large or small, exercising one vote. Each member contributed either ships or money; the respective assessments of ships and money were the work of Aristides, whose determinations were so fair that he was called "The Just." The money was kept on Delos under the supervision of a board of Athenians called Hellenic Treasurers. Fleet and army were both commanded by Athenians because Athens was the largest and most powerful of the allied states, and Athenians had won great prestige in both war and peace.

At first, all went well. The league fleet maintained the security of the Aegean and even successfully attacked the Persian-held island of Cyprus.

167

Such victories led some members of the confederacy to regard the Persian menace as broken, and about 470 B.C.E., Naxos, tired of onerous naval service, seceded. The Athenians, supported by a majority of the allies, felt that the withdrawal of Naxos might portend the dissolution of the league to Persia's advantage. Naxos was therefore besieged and reduced to obedience. This act set an important precedent. Moreover, the league's assessment of the situation was confirmed the next year, when the reconstituted Persian navy sailed toward the Aegean but was defeated in the Battle of Eurymedon (c. 467 B.C.E.) by the league fleet ably commanded by Athens' Cimon.

Because providing ships year after year was a hardship for some members, Athens, on the suggestion of Cimon, introduced the policy of allowing any state to convert its obligation to one of paying money. The exact date of this change is unknown; it probably occurred in the mid-460's B.C.E., at the height of Cimon's power and prestige. Gradually most confederates made payments until, by 445, only seven states of a regular membership of some 150 still contributed triremes. At the time the change must

ATHENIAN EMPIRE, 5TH CENTURY B.C.E.

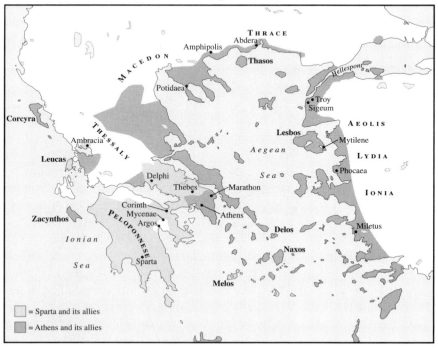

168

have seemed statesmanlike, but it actually cloaked a great danger to the league. As time went on, only the Athenians and the few other states with fleets were capable of serious naval action; the ships of the money-paying cities decayed, and their crews lacked practice. The Athenians, meanwhile, not only increased the size of their navy but also introduced improved models of triremes and new naval tactics, so that their navy was a virtually invincible force by the 440's.

In another unintended way, Cimon furthered Athenian imperialism. League member Thasos seceded in 465 B.C.E. It was defeated at sea and then besieged by the Athenians, and it finally appealed to Sparta for help. Athens and Sparta remained formally allied, but Sparta, fearing Athens' growing power, agreed to aid Thasos. Before they could act, a severe earthquake struck Sparta, causing much destruction and many deaths. Seizing this opportunity, Sparta's subject-peoples revolted and eventually were besieged at Ithome. Meanwhile, the Thasians, lacking Spartan aid, surrendered.

Sparta, recognizing Athenian prowess in siege operations, appealed to Athens for help. Cimon, relatively conservative and pro-Spartan, argued in favor; his more democratic, anti-Spartan opponent Ephialtes of Athens (d. 461 B.C.E.), against. Cimon prevailed and was chosen to lead the assisting army. Yet the Spartans, probably fearing both the presence of an Athenian army in their territory and the effects of Athenian liberalism on current and would-be rebels, changed their minds. Delivering a "slap in the face," they asked the Athenians to leave but retained their other allies. As a result, Cimon's pro-Spartan policy was repudiated, and he was ostracized in 461 B.C.E. His conservative institutional ally, the council of the Areopagus, was stripped of most of its powers by Ephialtes. Athens became more democratic, more anti-Spartan, and almost immediately, more imperial.

In 460 B.C.E., the Delian confederates attacked the Persians in Egypt, but the offensive ended with the annihilation of a league fleet in 454 B.C.E. For a time, it seemed that Persian naval forces might again invade the Aegean. To meet the immediate danger posed to the league's treasure on the unfortified island of Delos, it was agreed to move the fund to the heavily guarded Acropolis at Athens. When peace was made with Persia in 448 B.C.E., however, the money was not moved back. The leaders of Athens assumed sole control of this enormous sum of five thousand talents and insisted that the annual sums thereafter be paid to Athens. During the following decades, this money was used to maintain the Athenian navy, to erect the remarkable series of buildings on the Acropolis, and to finance future wars. Meet-

Cimon courting the favor of the Athenians. (F. R. Niglutsch)

ings of the league's assembly stopped; the league had become the Athenian Empire.

Some members of the league strongly objected to this new regime and rebelled against it, but their naval weakness made them easy to suppress. Rebellious states were compelled to accept democratic, pro-Athenian governments; other states had their legal and commercial relations with Athens subjected to regulation. A few were forced to accept Athenian garrisons or to cede territory for Athenian settlers. Pericles (c. 495-429 B.C.E.) was mainly responsible for this program. He envisioned an idealized Athens, both as a supreme military power and as a model of political organization and advanced culture. "Our state," he said, "is the education of Hellas."

Pericles' more extreme acts of imperialism were condemned by conservatives such as the statesman and historian Thucydides (c. 459-c. 402 B.C.E.), but by the 440's some thousands of Athenians received wages for various services from the annual payments of the allies. As a result the majority backed Pericles, and Thucydides was ostracized. "It may have been wrong to acquire the empire," said Pericles, "but it would certainly be dangerous to let it go." Therefore, while defense had dictated the punishment of Naxos, imperial power compelled the Athenians to keep their grip on their former allies. Athens, in its own eyes "the educator of Hellas," was the tyrant-city to other Greeks. When the Peloponnesian War broke out in 431 B.C.E., most Greeks supported Sparta in the hope of seeing Athenian power destroyed.

SIGNIFICANCE   Athenian imperialism was regrettable because Athens was, in most respects, the most advanced state in Greece. It was democratic. It tolerated free speech to a remarkable degree. Athens provided work for its poor and treated its slaves with relative humanity. Artists, poets, and scholars came to Athens from all parts of the Hellenic world so that the city became the cultural and philosophical center of Greece, a first "world city." Yet the Athenians' passion for empire turned much of the world against them and perhaps prevented the Delian League from becoming a vehicle for the gradual and voluntary unification of the numerous small, quarrelsome Greek states.

The possibility of this transformation highlights the relationship between internal politics and foreign policy. The early Delian League was nonimperial largely because Athens was balanced internally—in leadership, between Ephialtes and Cimon; institutionally, between the council of Areopagus and a popular assembly. The events about 462 B.C.E. permanently upset these balances, opening the way for imperial policies. In time, Pericles became as dominant internally as Athens did externally. Each had ceased to be a first among equals, the condition necessary for a peaceful transformation.

FURTHER READING

Carnes, Mark C., and Josiah Ober. *The Threshold of Democracy: Athens in 403 B.C.* 3d ed. New York: Pearson/Longman, 2005.

Fornara, Charles W., and Loren J. Samons II. *Athens from Cleisthenes to Pericles.* Berkeley: University of California Press, 1991.

Hornblower, Simon. *The Greek World, 479-323 B.C.* 3d ed. New York: Routledge, 2002.

Kagan, Donald. *Pericles of Athens and the Birth of Democracy.* New York: Free Press, 1991.

Meier, Christian. *Athens: A Portrait of the City in Its Golden Age.* New York: Metropolitan Books/H. Holt, 1998.

Podlecki, Anthony J. *Perikles and His Circle.* New York: Routledge, 1998.

Thorley, John. *Athenian Democracy*. 2d ed. New York: Routledge, 2004.

Wartenberg, Ute. *After Marathon: War, Society, and Money in Fifth-Century Greece*. London: British Museum Press, 1995.

Samuel K. Eddy; updated by John F. Wilson

See also: Athens; Cimon; Ephialtes of Athens; Pausanias of Sparta; Pericles.

Athenian Invasion of Sicily

The Athenian invasion of Sicily failed when the invasion force was totally destroyed, setting Athens on its course to inevitable defeat in the Peloponnesian War.

Date: June, 415-September, 413 B.C.E.
Category: Wars and battles
Locale: Syracuse and its environs, island of Sicily

SUMMARY Following the successful conclusion of the series of wars with Persia during the sixth century B.C.E., the Greek city-states gradually settled into a system of conflicting alliances headed by Athens on one hand and Sparta on the other, or they tried to maintain neutrality between these two great powers. In 477 B.C.E., Athens became head of the Delian League, supposedly a purely defensive association of some 150 Greek city-states. Within fifty years, the Delian League had grown to encompass more than 250 city-states and was, for all practical purposes, the Athenian Empire, with all league riches flowing into Athens and with Athens setting league foreign policy.

Sparta, Athens' major Greek rival, watched its northern neighbor grow steadily more powerful, especially at sea, where the Spartans were weakest. According to the early historian Thucydides, it was this fear of Athenian expansion that led to the outbreak of the Peloponnesian War in 431 B.C.E. It would last, with several interruptions caused by uneasy truces that pretended to be peace, until the final and apparently utter defeat of Athens in 404 B.C.E. One of the factors that led directly to the downfall of Athens was the disaster that overtook its expedition against the city of Syracuse, on the island of Sicily, in 415-413 B.C.E.

The first phase of the war, known as the Archidamian War for the name of the Spartan king who began it, ended inconclusively in 421 B.C.E. The years from 421 through 415 B.C.E. were known as the Peace of Nicias, for Nicias (c. 470-413 B.C.E.), the Athenian leader who negotiated a treaty with the Spartans. In Athens, the young and brilliant but unscrupulous Alcibiades (c. 450- 404 B.C.E.), a ward of the great Athenian leader Pericles, urged a renewal of the conflict and an invasion of Sicily. He claimed this invasion would cut off Sparta's vital supply of Sicilian wheat. It is also thought that Alcibiades may have dreamed of further conquests of southern Italy or Carthage.

Although the invasion plan was resisted by Nicias of Athens and other conservative leaders, it was enormously popular, and, in June, 415 B.C.E., the Athenians launched what was then an enormous fleet of at least 134 warships carrying between 5,000 and 6,500 heavy infantry (hoplites) and light

The Athenians are defeated in the Battle of Syracuse. (F. R. Niglutsch)

armed troops. In joint command of the expedition were Alcibiades, Nicias, and Lamachus, the last more a professional soldier than a politician.

Just before the armada sailed (some sources say the very night before), a number of religious statues throughout Athens were mutilated. Because these Herms, as they were known, were sacred to Hermes, the god of travel, the act could be seen either as a bad omen or as a deliberate sacrilege; in either event, considerable suspicion fell on Alcibiades, largely because of his scandalous past, which included participation in mocking celebrations of some of the Greeks' most solemn religious mysteries. Alcibiades was recalled after the fleet had sailed. Fearing for his life, he fled to Sparta and urged a strong defense of Syracuse and a prompt attack on Athens.

In the absence of Alcibiades, the Athenian expedition sailed on and landed in Sicily. Lamachus urged an immediate attack on Syracuse, which might well have carried the city, but Nicias preferred caution. When Lamachus was killed in an early skirmish, Nicias procrastinated and the campaigning season of 415 B.C.E. ended with Syracuse scarcely damaged. The Athenians were forced to withdraw into winter quarters, while the Syracusans appealed for and received help from their mother city of Corinth and its ally Sparta. The Spartans sent one contingent under Gylippus (c. 450-400 B.C.E.) and the Corinthians another under Gongylus.

In 414 B.C.E., Athenian reinforcements arrived in Sicily, and Nicias pressed the siege of Syracuse, a strong, walled city built on a peninsula that separates a large bay, the Grand Harbor, from the sea. The Athenians seized part of the Grand Harbor, fortified it, and blockaded the city by the sea, hoping by building a wall across the landward end of the peninsula to isolate Syracuse completely and force its surrender through lack of food. Lacking a siege train of battering rams, catapults, and similar weapons, the Athenians had no choice but to attempt the long and arduous process of starving out their opponents—or to have the city betrayed by a faction within its walls. Starvation or betrayal were, in fact, the typical fashion in which sieges were conducted during classical times because a walled city such as Syracuse was, for all practical purposes, invulnerable to assault. After months of inaction, and at the moment when the Athenian strategy seemed about to force the city's surrender, Gongylus slipped inside the city to report Gylippus's approach with relief forces. Gylippus's strategy was to extend a counterwall from Syracuse at right angles to Nicias's wall and head off its completion. During the summer, fierce combat ranged around the ends of the two walls. By a narrow margin, Gylippus carried his fortifications past those of Nicias and thus frustrated the Athenian offensive. In the autumn, operations stalled, and Nicias asked for reinforcements.

During the winter of 414-413 B.C.E., although under Spartan attack on the Greek mainland, the Athenians dispatched seventy-three additional triremes and five thousand hoplites under the command of Demosthenes (d. 413 B.C.E.). Their arrival barely restored the balance in favor of the Athenians. Fresh naval forces had reached Syracuse from the Peloponnesus and parts of Sicily. The Syracusans had made a bid for victory, and in June and July, 413 B.C.E., they had won a series of naval actions in the Grand Harbor. It was at this point that Demosthenes had arrived, reestablished Athenian naval supremacy, and dashed Syracusan hopes.

Demosthenes and Nicias next decided to capture Gylippus's counterwall to retrieve gains made in the campaign of the year before. The Athenian army went forward by night and came extremely close to success, but in the darkness, it lost cohesion and was repulsed. Demosthenes promptly advised Nicias to begin immediate withdrawal by sea, but once more Nicias delayed, believing an eclipse of the Moon an omen against evacuation. The Syracusans then resumed their naval offensive and, in September, defeated the Athenian fleet in a great battle in the Grand Harbor, compelling Nicias to resort to the forlorn hope of escaping by land. Complete disaster followed. The Syracusan cavalry and light troops harried their enemy and wore them down under a hail of missiles until Nicias surrendered. The Syracusans executed both Nicias and Demosthenes and imprisoned their men in stone quarries for months. Those who did not die under these conditions were sold into slavery.

SIGNIFICANCE   This military defeat of Athens marked the beginning of the end for the city's struggle in the Peloponnesian War, primarily because it struck at Athens' political solidarity. At first enthusiastically united behind Alcibiades' scheme, the city was devastated first by his defection to the Spartans and then by the complete disaster that overtook the bulk of its relatively limited armed forces. Athens experienced a crisis of confidence from which it never fully recovered.

Although the Sicilian disaster encouraged some revolts within the Athenian Empire and lured Persia into an alliance with Sparta, its main effect—and Alcibiades' enduring legacy—was to sow distrust and dissension within Athens. It was this internal disarray, which brought distrust to its citizens and timidity to its military commanders, that led to its eventual collapse and final surrender in 404 B.C.E.

FURTHER READING

Ellis, Walter M. *Alcibiades*. New York: Routledge, 1989.

Hornblower, Simon. *The Greek World, 479-323 B.C.* 3d ed. New York: Routledge, 2002.

Kagan, Donald. *The Peace of Nicias and the Sicilian Expedition*. Ithaca, N.Y.: Cornell University Press, 1981.

Kallet, Lisa. *Money and the Corrosion of Power in Thucydides: The Sicilian Expedition and Its Aftermath*. Berkeley: University of California Press, 2001.

Roisman, Joseph. *The General Demosthenes and His Use of Military Surprise*. Stuttgart: F. Stiner, 1993.

Strauss, Barry S., and Josiah Ober. *The Anatomy of Error: Ancient Military Disasters and Their Lessons for Modern Strategists*. New York: St. Martin's Press, 1990.

Thucydides. *The Peloponnesian War*. Translated by Richard Crawley. Edited by Robert B. Strassler, with an introduction by Victor Davis Hanson. New York: Simon and Schuster, 1998.

Worthington, Ian, ed. *Demosthenes: Statesman and Orator*. New York: Routledge, 2000.

Samuel K. Eddy; updated by Michael Witkoski

See also: Alcibiades of Athens; Archidamian War; Athens; Demosthenes; Nicias of Athens; Peloponnesian Wars; Syracuse.

Athens

Site of the earliest democracy of Western civilization, Athens was the cultural center of Greek civilization from the Classical through the Roman periods.

Date: 3000 B.C.E.-700 C.E.
Category: Cities and civilizations
Locale: Southern Greece, in Attica

BACKGROUND   The city of Athens developed around the Acropolis, a rocky hill rising from the central plain of Attica about five miles (eight kilometers) from the Saronic Gulf. Traces of habitation first appear in the late Neolithic period (c. 3000 B.C.E.), and Athens became an important center in the late Bronze Age (1600-1100 B.C.E.). A Mycenaean palace stood on the Acropolis, which was girded by massive fortifications. These remains lend some support to the tradition that in this period the hero Theseus united all of Attica under Athenian leadership.

Although Athens escaped the destruction endured elsewhere in Greece in the twelfth century B.C.E., the city still entered the Dark Ages of Greece (c. 1000-800 B.C.E.), a period of poverty and depopulation. Athens recovered earlier than other parts of Greece, but it failed to join the colonizing movement of the eighth and seventh centuries B.C.E., when Greek cities sent out colonies to deal with growing populations. One theory holds that Athens suffered a sharp decline in population because of a severe drought around 700 B.C.E.

During the Dark Ages the Athenians replaced their king with officials called archons. By 700 B.C.E., nine archons were elected each year, and they governed Athens with the council of the Areopagus. Around 630 B.C.E., Athenian nobleman Cylon tried unsuccessfully to seize power and make himself tyrant. The failed coup created intense infighting and perhaps led to the legislation of Draco (c. 621 B.C.E.). Later generations remembered Draco's laws as "written in blood" because of their severity.

By 600 B.C.E., Athens faced a severe economic crisis as farmers were

The Parthenon and other buildings atop the Acropolis of Athens.
(R. S. Peale and J. A. Hill)

falling into debt, and nonaristocrats resented the excesses of aristocratic government. The reforms of Solon (c. 594 B.C.E.) addressed this crisis by canceling debts, promoting trade, and reforming Athenian government. Citizens could appeal the decisions of aristocratic judges, and nonaristocrats gained some access to political office. These reforms were only partly successful, and in about 560 B.C.E., Pisistratus became tyrant. Under his reign and that of his sons, Athens enjoyed increasing prosperity. Pisistratus reorganized religious festivals, built the first large stone temples on the Acropolis, and started a temple to Olympian Zeus. New public buildings and a fountain house were erected in the marketplace, and Athenian pottery dominated foreign markets.

DEMOCRATIC REFORMS   The overthrow of the tyranny in 510 B.C.E. was followed by the democratic reforms of Cleisthenes in 508 B.C.E., who sought to break aristocratic control of government. Cleisthenes created ten regionally based tribes and established a council of five hundred citizens, fifty from each tribe, to prepare business for the assembly. He also insti-

179

tuted the practice of ostracism, by which the Athenians could exile potentially dangerous citizens for ten years.

After these reforms, Athens reached its military, political, and cultural zenith. The Athenians defeated the Persians at Marathon in 490 B.C.E., and a decade later, the Athenian navy helped overcome the Persians at Salamis (480 B.C.E.). Athens, however, was sacked. When the Athenians returned in 479 B.C.E., they fortified the city but left their temples in ruins as symbols of Persian impiety. After peace was formally concluded with Persia in 448 B.C.E., Pericles proposed rebuilding the city's temples. This building project began in 447 B.C.E., and over the next forty years, brilliant marble buildings, including the Parthenon, Propylaea, and Erechtheum, rose on the Acropolis and throughout Athens. Meanwhile, Greek artists and intellectuals flocked to the city. Itinerant teachers called Sophists taught anyone who could afford their fees. The historian Herodotus visited Athens while composing his history of the Greco-Persian Wars. The tragedians Aeschylus, Sophocles, and Euripides and the comic poet Aristophanes produced plays that laid the foundation for Western drama.

THE ADVANCE OF DEMOCRACY   The fifth century B.C.E. also saw the blossoming of democracy. In 462 B.C.E., Athenian Ephialtes deprived the Areopagus of its remaining political powers. Pericles later instituted pay for jury service and public office, thereby enabling poor citizens to participate fully in public affairs. Ironically, the advance of democracy at Athens was accompanied by Athenian imperialism abroad. In 478 B.C.E., the Athenians founded the Delian League, an alliance of Greek cities to fight the Persians. This league, however, pursued Athenian interests, and the Athenians continued to collect funds from their allies even after war with Persia was over. These funds helped finance Pericles' building program.

Athenian democracy was overthrown after the Peloponnesian War (431-404 B.C.E.). Although democratic government was soon restored, the Athenians never regained their former power. Still, the fourth century was not entirely one of decline. Despite the execution of Socrates in 399 B.C.E., philosophy flourished. Plato established a school in the Academy, a gymnasium just outside the city. His student Aristotle set up another school known as the Lyceum. Oratory was perfected by Isocrates, Aeschines, and Demosthenes. Spurred by the speeches of Demosthenes, the Athenians made one final stand against Philip II of Macedonia. Although Philip defeated the Athenians at Chaeronea (338 B.C.E.), Athens was spared destruction.

Athens remained a cultural center during the Hellenistic and Roman periods. Hellenistic kings adorned the city with new buildings, and several philosophical schools developed, most notably the Stoic and Epicurean. The Athenians initially enjoyed good relations with Rome, but when they joined Mithradates VI Eupator in a war against Rome, Lucius Cornelius Sulla sacked the city (86 B.C.E.). Still, Athens continued to attract patrons, and the city prospered under the Roman Empire. In the second century C.E., the emperor Hadrian initiated a building program and finished the temple of Olympian Zeus, and Athens again became a center of learning.

Athens was sacked in 267 C.E. by the Herulians, a Germanic tribe. The city was rebuilt on a smaller scale, but rhetoric and philosophy continued to be taught. After the emperor Justinian I closed the philosophical schools in 529 B.C.E., Athens lost this last link with its glorious past and quickly sank into obscurity.

FURTHER READING

Camp, John M. *The Athenian Agora: Excavations in the Heart of Classical Athens*. London: Thames and Hudson, 1986.

Frantz, Alison. *Late Antiquity, A.D. 267-700*. Vol. 24 in *The Athenian Agora*. Princeton, N.J.: American School of Classical Studies at Athens, 1988.

Habicht, Christian. *Athens from Alexander to Antony*. Translated by Deborah Lucas Schneider. Cambridge, Mass.: Harvard University Press, 1999.

Hurwit, Jeffrey M. *The Athenian Acropolis: History, Mythology, and Archaeology from the Neolithic Era to the Present*. Cambridge, England: Cambridge University Press, 1999.

Meier, Christian. *Athens: A Portrait of the City in Its Golden Age*. Translated by Robert and Rita Kimber. New York: Metropolitan Books, 1998.

Thorley, John. *Athenian Democracy*. 2d ed. New York: Routledge, 2004.

Waterfield, Robin. *Athens: A History, from Ancient Ideal to Modern City*. New York: Basic Books, 2004.

James P. Sickinger

See also: Aeschines; Aeschylus; Alcibiades of Athens; Apollodorus of Athens (artist); Apollodorus of Athens (scholar and historian); Aristides of

Athens; Aristophanes; Aristotle; Athenian Democracy; Athenian Empire; Athenian Invasion of Sicily; Chaeronea, Battle of; Cimon; Cleisthenes of Athens; Cleon of Athens; Crates of Athens; Critias of Athens; Draco; Draco's Code; Ephialtes of Athens; Euripides; Hippias of Athens; Marathon, Battle of; Military History of Athens; Mithradates VI Eupator; Nicias of Athens; Parthenon; Peloponnesian Wars; Pericles; Phidias; Pisistratus; Plato; Salamis, Battle of; Socrates; Solon; Solon's Code; Sophocles; Thirty Tyrants.

Attalid Dynasty

Under the Attalids, Pergamum became a powerful city-state and a center of Hellenistic civilization.

Date: c. 282-133 B.C.E.
Category: Cities and civilizations
Locale: Ancient Pergamum, west central Anatolia, Turkey

SUMMARY   Philetaerus (c. 343-263 B.C.E.) was the founder of the Attalid (AHT-uh-lihd) Dynasty. With Roman support, Philetaerus freed himself (c. 282 B.C.E.) from the influence of rival powers in the area. With the treasure he had accumulated, he began the policy of the beautification of Pergamum continued by his successors. Efficient use of Pergamene resources as well as heavy taxation kept the treasury filled. The Attalids became known for their fabulous wealth. Eumenes I (r. 263-241 B.C.E.), nephew and successor of Philetaerus, continued the consolidation of power but could not rid Pergamum of the burdensome tribute exacted by the savage neighboring Gauls (Celts).

Kings of the Attalid Dynasty, c. 282-133 B.C.E.

King	Reign
Philetaerus	c. 282-263 B.C.E.
Eumenes I	263-241
Attalus I	241-197
Eumenes II	197-160/159
Attalus II	160/159-138
Attalus III	138-133

Relief from the oppressors was achieved in 236 B.C.E. by his cousin and successor, Attalus I (269-197 B.C.E.; r. 241-197 B.C.E.), "the Savior," first to be designated king. An excellent general and astute diplomat, Attalus conquered much of Asia Minor. Pergamum became the strongest military and economic power in the area. Because an important harbor, the nearby coastal city of Ephesus, was under its control, Pergamum also ranked as a maritime power. Eumenes II (r. 197-160/159 B.C.E.), eldest son of Attalus I, brought Pergamum to the zenith of its power and influence. He wanted his city to be successor to the Golden Age of Athens, and Pergamum became one of the principal conduits through which Greek culture and tradition passed into the Roman civilization. Pergamum became a major manufacturer and exporter of parchment, the scraped skins of calves and sheep to which the city gave its name, fine fabrics, pitch, and art objects. Artists flocked to the city and achieved a distinctive Pergamene style. The Pergamum library was second in size and excellence only to that of Alexandria, Egypt.

The great artistic achievement of Eumenes II was the construction of the Great Altar of Zeus (180-175 B.C.E.), one of the few top-level Hellenistic architectural and sculptural works. The altar's eye-level frieze is filled with greater than life-size writhing and sinuous figures depicting the mythological battle between the gods and the giants but actually commemorating the battle with and victory over the Gauls. Attalus II (r. 160/159-138 B.C.E.), second son of Attalus I, loyally supported and continued the policies of his brother, but by increasing dependence on Rome, he ultimately made Pergamum a pawn of Roman policy. Attalus III (r. 138-133 B.C.E.), "the Benefactor," successor of Attalus II, son of Eumenes II and last of the Attalids, was noted chiefly for his "Testament" ceding Pergamum to Rome.

SIGNIFICANCE   A remarkable group of rulers (except for its last member), the Attalids changed Pergamum from a minor hill fortress into an influential and powerful city-state as well as a major center of Hellenistic civilization.

FURTHER READING

Erskine, Andrew, ed. *A Companion to the Hellenistic World*. Malden, Mass.: Blackwell, 2003.

Fleming, William. "Pergamon." In *Arts and Ideas*. New York: Holt, Rinehart and Winston, 1997.

Hansen, Esther Violet. *The Attalids of Pergamon.* 2d ed. Ithaca, N.Y.: Cornell University Press, 1971.

Nis Petersen

See also: Eumenes II; Hellenistic Greece; Zeus at Pergamum, Great Altar of.

Bacchylides

POET

Born: c. 520 B.C.E.; Iulis, Island of Ceos (now Kéa, Greece)
Died: c. 450 B.C.E.; Place unknown
Also known as: Bakchylides
Category: Poetry; literature

LIFE Bacchylides (buh-KIHL-uh-deez) was the nephew of Simonides of Ceos. Like his contemporary Pindar, he composed odes to be sung to musical accompaniment of lyres and pipes (reed instruments) and to be danced by choruses. Of his nine books of poems collected in the Hellenistic period, a papyrus discovered in 1896 has preserved substantial portions of fourteen epinician (victory) odes and six dithyrambs. Two recipients of his victory odes, Hieron I of Syracuse and Pytheas of Aegina, were also celebrated by Pindar. His odes, like Pindar's, contain aphoristic reflections, mythological vignettes, advice, prayers, and praise of achievement, but his style is considerably simpler and less difficult to translate than Pindar's.

His dithyrambs feature mythological narratives such as Menelaus's mission to Troy to recover Helen, Deianira's destruction of her husband Heracles, and Theseus's voyage to confront the Minotaur, while one presents a dramatic dialogue between the chorus and Aegeus, king of Athens.

INFLUENCE Because only a few short fragments of his poetry were known before the papyrus was published, Bacchylides' influence was negligible. Furthermore, he was overshadowed by Pindar, to whom antiquity judged him inferior.

FURTHER READING

Bacchylides. *Bacchylides: A Selection*. Edited by H. Maehler. New York: Cambridge University Press, 2004.
Burnett, A. P. *The Art of Bacchylides*. Cambridge, Mass.: Harvard University Press, 1985.

Campbell, D. A. *Greek Lyric*. Cambridge, Mass.: Harvard University Press, 1992.

Fear, David. "Mapping Phleoious: Politics and Myth-Making in 'Bacchylides 9.'" *Classical Quarterly* 53, no. 2 (2003): 347-367.

Hutchinson, G. O. *Greek Lyric Poetry: A Commentary on Selected Larger Pieces*. New York: Oxford University Press, 2001.

Maehler, H. *Die Lieder des Bakchylides*. Vol. 1. Leiden, Netherlands: E. J. Brill, 1982.

William H. Race

See also: Hieron I of Syracuse; Literature; Lyric Poetry; Pindar.

Bion

POET

Born: Probably second century B.C.E.; Phlossa, near Smyrna (now in Turkey)
Died: Probably second century B.C.E.; Sicily?
Also known as: Bion of Smyrna
Category: Poetry; literature

LIFE The Greek bucolic poet Bion (BI-uhn) was born in the village of Phlossa, near Smyrna, and later moved to Sicily. Almost nothing else is known of his life, and even the approximate times of his birth and death are based upon metrical analysis of his few surviving poems. He is often referred to as Bion of Smyrna to distinguish him from the philosopher Bion of Borysthenes. A verse epitaph to Bion was traditionally attributed to Moschus of Syracuse, a pastoral poet who was writing at about 150 B.C.E., but this poem is now considered to be later in origin.

Bion's "Lament for Adonis," his only surviving work to have had any appreciable influence on later poets, was written to celebrate the first day of the festival of Adonis, an important figure in Greek mythology. A handsome young man loved by the goddess Aphrodite, Adonis died in a hunting accident. According to one version of the myth, the gods, in order to comfort the broken-hearted Aphrodite, agreed to permit Adonis to leave Hades for six months of each year. Thus Adonis came to represent the cyclical nature of the cosmic order, and his death was associated with the annual change of seasons. The annual Athenian festival in his honor was held in late summer. Aside from Bion's "Lament for Adonis," some other works dealing with this myth are the fifteenth *Idyl* of Theocritus, the third book of *The Library*, by Apollodorus (second century B.C.E.), and the tenth book of Ovid's *Metamorphoses* (c. 8 C.E.; English translation, 1567).

INFLUENCE Poets who are designated as pastoral (from Latin *pastor*, or shepherd) or bucolic (from Greek *boukolos*, shepherd)—such as Bion, Moschus, and the earlier and more famous third century B.C.E. poet

Theocritus—adopted an artificial set of poetic conventions based on the lives of shepherds. These conventions established a poetic tradition that runs through Vergil, whose *Eclogues* (43-37 B.C.E.; also known as *Bucolics*; English translation, 1575) and *Georgics* (c. 37-29 B.C.E.; English translation, 1589) were extremely influential, into the Renaissance and on into later times. Some notable examples of such poetry are *Arcadia* (1504), by Jacopo Sannazaro; *The Shepheardes Calender* (1579), by Edmund Spenser; "Lycidas" (1638), by John Milton; "Endymion" (1818), by John Keats; and "Adonais" (1821), by Percy Bysshe Shelley.

The last-named of these poems appears to have been directly influenced by Bion's most famous surviving poem, the "Lament for Adonis," and by the "Lament for Bion," once attributed to Moschus. In fact, Shelley prefaces "Adonais" with a four-line Greek quotation from the latter poem and later (stanza 36) paraphrases part of this quotation in his own text. In this poem can be seen how the pastoral poet employs the mechanism of the shepherds' artificial world to address a personal crisis, since Shelley is actually writing about the recent death of the poet John Keats.

Another notable work influenced by Bion is the Victorian pastoral elegy "Thyrsis" (1866), by Matthew Arnold, a lament for the passing of Arnold's friend the poet Arthur Hugh Clough. Arnold acknowledges his debt by devoting lines 81 through 90 to Bion.

Bion's "Lament for Adonis" has been translated by several different persons, including J. M. Edmonds, Arthur S. Way, and Elizabeth Barrett Browning. The anonymous "Lament for Bion" has been translated by Way and by Andrew Lang, among others.

FURTHER READING

Edmonds, J. M., ed. and trans. *The Greek Bucolic Poets*. New York: Macmillan, 1912.

Fantuzzi, Marco. *Tradition and Innovation in Hellenistic Poetry*. New York: Cambridge University Press, 2004.

Gow, A. S. F., trans. *The Greek Bucolic Poets*. 1953. Reprint. Hamden, Conn.: Archon Books, 1972.

Lambert, Ellen Zetzel. *Placing Sorrow: A Study of the Pastoral Elegy Convention from Theocritus to Milton*. Chapel Hill: University of North Carolina Press, 1976.

Reed, J. D., ed. *Bion of Smyrna: The Fragments and the Adonis*. New York: Cambridge University Press, 1997.

Rosenberg, D. M. *Oaten Reeds and Trumpets: Pastoral and Epic in Virgil, Spenser, and Milton*. Lewisburg, Pa.: Bucknell University Press, 1981.

Robert W. Haynes

See also: Bucolic Poetry; Literature; Moschus of Syracuse.

Brasidas of Sparta

MILITARY LEADER

Born: Date unknown; place unknown
Died: 422 B.C.E.; Amphipolis, Macedonia
Also known as: Brasidas, son of Tellis
Category: Military

LIFE Brasidas (BRAS-uh-duhs), the finest Spartan general of the Archidamian War (431-421 B.C.E.), first gained notice in 431 B.C.E., when he saved the city of Methone from Athenian assault. In subsequent years, he advised Spartan naval commanders, always advocating aggressive action, and gallantly led an unsuccessful landing attempt on Athenian-held Pylos.

In 424 B.C.E., he rescued the city of Megara from Athenian attack, then marched into Thrace, where he won over various communities, in particular the important Athenian colony of Amphipolis. In 423 B.C.E., he secured two more cities, Mende and Scione, but could not prevent the Athenians from besieging Scione or retaking Mende and other sites. However, when the Athenian leader Cleon went against Amphipolis in 422 B.C.E., Brasidas surprised his army and routed it with heavy losses, killing Cleon but losing his own life as well. Their deaths allowed the war-weary Athenians and Spartans to end hostilities, at least for the moment.

INFLUENCE Brasidas won Sparta's only genuine successes of the Archidamian War. The loss of Amphipolis grieved the Athenians for generations and resulted in the exile from Athens of the historian Thucydides, keeping him out of the war and allowing him to write much of his *Historia tou Peloponnesiacou polemou* (431-404 B.C.E.; *History of the Peloponnesian War*, 1550).

FURTHER READING
De Souza, Philip. *The Peloponnesian War, 431-404 B.C.* New York: Routledge, 2003.

Hanson, Victor Davis. *A War Like No Other: How the Athenians and Spartans Fought the Peloponnesian War*. New York: Random House, 2005.

Kagan, Donald. *The Peloponnesian War*. New York: Viking, 2003.

Powell, Anton. *Athens and Sparta*. New York: Routledge, 1996.

Thucydides. "History of the Peloponnesian War." In *The Landmark Thucydides: A Comprehensive Guide to the Peloponnesian War*, edited by Robert B. Strassler. New York: Free Press, 1996.

Scott M. Rusch

See also: Archidamian War; Cleon of Athens; Peloponnesian Wars; Thucydides.

Bucolic Poetry

The Sicilian-Alexandrian poet Theocritus began the bucolic genre, which was a popular mode in the Hellenistic era and inaugurated the pastoral tradition.

Date: Third century B.C.E.
Category: Literature; poetry

SUMMARY   Though attempts have been made to trace Greek bucolic (byew-KO-lihk) poetry to earlier nature rituals and hymns, as well as to nature descriptions by early poets such as Homer and Hesiod, scholars are agreed that bucolic poetry as such begins only with Theocritus (c. 308-c. 260 B.C.E.). Theocritus was born in Syracuse, the major city of Greek Sicily, and the Sicilian landscape provided the setting for his bucolic poetry. Like later pastoral poets, though, Theocritus made his career in the great metropolis of his day, in his case the Hellenized Egyptian city of Alexandria, capital of the Ptolemaic kingdom where he published his *Idylls*. Not all of Theocritus's poetry was bucolic—strictly speaking, "bucolic" means only poetry celebrating specifically rural scenes—but Theocritus set the tone for bucolic poetry in several ways.

His depiction of the countryside casts it as an ideal of a simple, pleasant life where shepherds are free to live and love. Yet there is also a realistic strain in the work of Theocritus. His country people live humbly, eat everyday food, and feel common emotions of disappointment, envy, and death. The role of the poet is itself a subject for bucolic poetry, as poets compete to see who can write the finest verse and the shepherd becomes a representation of the poet as self-conscious maker. Despite their humble state, Theocritus's shepherds are daring in their love lives, feeling passion for the goddess Aphrodite and the nymph Galatea.

The tradition of Theocritus was continued in the next centuries by Moschus of Syracuse (c. 175-c. 125 B.C.E.) and Bion (second century B.C.E.). Commentators have noted that this body of poetry, with its evocation of rustic earthiness, emerged when the Mediterranean world was becoming more urbanized and when the sophistication and cosmopolitanism of the Hellenistic era were at their height. The interest in the bucolic seemed to be either nostalgic or a quest for what was absent within society.

The bucolic poet Theocritus. (Hulton Archive/Getty Images)

SIGNIFICANCE   Moschus wrote epic and epigram as well as bucolic, but Bion explicitly imitated Theocritus and promulgated the idea of the bucolic as a standing genre at which each new poet could try his or her hand. Moschus and Bion are often overshadowed by Theocritus, but they assured the continuity of the genre. The Greek bucolic tradition was a crucial influence on Vergil's *Eclogues* (43-37 B.C.E., also known as *Bucolics*; English translation, 1575) and, through him, on the pastoral tradition in European poetry in general. Later pastoral poetry became more moralistic and philosophical, moving away from the naturalism and lyricism of Theocritus. Nevertheless Theocritus, as much as any Greek poet, can be said to have founded an enduring tradition in later literature.

FURTHER READING

Anagnostou-Laoutides, Evangelia. *Eros and Ritual in Ancient Literature: Singing of Atalanta, Daphnis, and Orpheus.* Piscataway, N.J.: Gorgias Press, 2005.

Fantuzzi, Marco, and Richard Hunter. *Tradition and Innovation in Hellenistic Poetry.* New York: Cambridge University Press, 2004.

Halperin, David. *Before Pastoral: Theocritus and the Ancient Tradition of Bucolic Poetry.* New Haven, Conn.: Yale University Press, 1983.

Rosenmeyer, Thomas G. *The Green Cabinet.* Berkeley: University of California Press, 1969.

Nicholas Birns

See also: Bion; Elegiac Poetry; Iambic Poetry; Literature; Lyric Poetry; Moschus of Syracuse; Theocritus of Syracuse.

Calendars and Chronology

Greek cities each had their own distinctive calendars, which represent various attempts to marry the incommensurate cycles of the Moon and the Sun.

Date: c. 1370-31 B.C.E.
Category: Mathematics; astronomy and cosmology

THE BRONZE AGE   The earliest evidence for Greek calendars comes from the Linear B tablets recovered from Knossos on Crete (c. 1370 B.C.E.) and Pylos in southern Greece (c. 1200 B.C.E.). They represent ritual calendars, in which the offerings to be made to the gods were listed month by month. The word for "month" is *me-no*, which suggests a relationship with the Moon and therefore a lunar calendar, but how this system might have been correlated with the seasonal, solar year is unknown. From Knossos are preserved the names of eight months, and from Pylos three, but the two sites share none in common. All apparently derive from gods or localities, and four names resemble later historical months—*di-wi-jo* (Dios), *ra-pa-to* (Lapato), *di-pi-si-jo* (Dipsios), and *ka-ra-e-ri-jo* (Klareon)—but this is the only evidence for any continuity.

HOMER AND HESIOD   Within Homer's *Iliad* (c. 750 B.C.E.; English translation, 1611) and *Odyssey* (c. 725 B.C.E.; English translation, 1614) are reflections of the use of the Sun as a measure of the seasonal year, although lunar months are also referred to, for instance as a means of counting the length of a pregnancy. While no calendar as such appears, the risings and settings of stars are used as signals for periods in the seasonal year.

This mechanism is more developed in Hesiod's *Erga kai Emerai* (c. 700 B.C.E.; *Works and Days*, 1618), which is partly an account of the agricultural year. The poet provides ten observations of five stars or constellations, which help distinguish four seasons. Accompanying this star-lore are other signs from the natural world, such as the arrival of migrating birds.

The Moon too is occasionally used to signal the proper time for farming activities. Star-based almanacs remained in use throughout the Greek and Roman periods, providing historians such as Thucydides (c. 459-c. 402 B.C.E.) with fixed points to which they could attach events more securely than if they relied solely on the discordant, local state calendars.

CLASSICAL GREEK CALENDARS   The city-states of Greece all kept lunar calendars, but the start of the year differed from city to city. Each city began its year with the first new Moon after a key point of the solar year, but this could be the summer or winter solstice or the spring or autumn equinox. This combination of lunar and solar phenomena made the beginning of the year mobile within a certain period of time, exactly like Christian Easter. A mixture of observation and schematic calculation seems to have been used in deciding when a month started and when it ended, with the start being marked by the evening sighting of the new Moon's crescent.

The Athenian year began after the summer solstice, midway through a Julian year. The names of the months—Hekatombaion, Metageitnion, Boedromion, Pyanepsion, Maimakterion, Poseideon, Gamelion, Anthesterion, Elaphebolion, Mounichion, Thargelion, and Skirophorion—reflect religious festivals that took place in the month. A year consisted usually of twelve lunar months, with an occasional thirteenth added (or intercalated) in an attempt to bring the lunar year of 354 days, with its alternating months of 30 and 29 days, into alignment with the solar year of 365.25 days.

Various systems of intercalation were devised to attain this realignment, notably the eight-year cycle and the nineteen-year (or Metonic) cycle, the latter named after the Athenian Meton, who invented it in the 430's B.C.E. In the eight-year cycle, three of the lunar years were given an extra month, while in the Metonic cycle seven years gained one. The four-yearly games at Delphi and Olympia were governed by eight-year cycles, while Athens at times regulated its calendar with the Metonic cycle, with intercalary months added every second, fifth, eighth, tenth, thirteenth, sixteenth, and eighteenth year.

It is impossible to synchronize the Greek cities' calendars except in ideal terms. Interstate decrees, financial statements, and even slave manumissions are particularly helpful in establishing broad synchronisms, as they often include correspondences between the calendars of two cities.

HELLENISTIC CALENDARS As a result of the conquests of Alexander the Great, the Macedonian calendar not only was widespread throughout the Greek world but also was assimilated into Egypt and the former Persian Empire. Its months were Dios, Apellaios, Audnaios, Peritios, Dystros, Xanthikos, Artemisios, Daisios, Panemos, Loios, Gorpiaios, and Hyperberetaios. The new year began after the autumn equinox. The Persian Empire used the old Babylonian lunisolar calendar, regulated by its own independent nineteen-year cycle. The Macedonian calendar slotted into this much older, but very similar, system without any loss. In Egypt, however, a calendar of 365 days was used, with twelve months each of thirty days being followed by five extra (epagomenal) days. The Macedonian calendar was absorbed into this system but lost its lunar character entirely, as the Macedonian months were made to fit the regular Egyptian ones.

CHRONOLOGY In Athens, one political year was distinguished from another on official documents by the names of the secretary of the first month's standing-committee (prytany) of the council. Lists of the principal annual magistrates (archons) were also drawn up, allowing events in individual years to be attached to the archonship. Relative chronology could be constructed from this system. For example, the Parian Marble (264/263 B.C.E.) lists various events, dating them from the year of its carving in "the archonship of Astyanax(?) at Paros and Diognetos at Athens."

Different eras existed. There were "liberation" eras; for example, the era of Tyre started in 126/125 B.C.E., when the city broke free of Seleucid rule, and lasted into the seventh century C.E. A king's regnal years could also distinguish one year from the next; for example, the capture of Babylon in 312 B.C.E. marked the first year of the reign of Seleucus I Nicator. Augustus's victory at Actium in 31 B.C.E. became the start of another era for some cities. The best-known era is that of the Olympiads, the four-year periods of the Olympic Games, starting traditionally in 776 B.C.E. This was formulated by Timaeus (c. 350-260 B.C.E.) and Eratosthenes (c. 285-c. 205 B.C.E.). As the Olympic year began in midsummer, however, it straddled the second half of one Julian year and the first half of the next; for example, the third year of the sixth Olympiad (Ol. 6, 3) is equivalent to 754/753 B.C.E.

FURTHER READING

Bickerman, E. J. *Chronology of the Ancient World.* Rev. ed. London: Thames and Hudson, 1980.

Hannah, Robert. *Greek and Roman Calendars: Constructions of Time in the Classical World.* London: Duckworth, 2005.

Samuel, Alan E. *Greek and Roman Chronology: Calendars and Years in Classical Antiquity.* Munich, Germany: Beck, 1972.

Robert Hannah

See also: Athens; Crete; Eratosthenes of Cyrene; Hesiod; Historiography; Linear B; Olympic Games; Seleucus I Nicator; Thucydides.

Callicrates

ARCHITECT

Flourished: Fifth century B.C.E.; Athens, Greece
Also known as: Kallikrates
Category: Art and architecture

LIFE Callicrates (kuh-LIHK-ruh-teez) and Ictinus (also known as Iktinos) were the architects of the Parthenon (temple of Athena Polias) on the Acropolis in Athens, built between 447 and 432 B.C.E. The Parthenon was the first building erected on the Acropolis in Pericles' grand rebuilding plan. Work on the Parthenon was described in a lost book by Ictinus and Carpion. Callicrates is also credited with the plan of the temple of Athena Nike ("Victory") or Athena Asteros ("Without Wings"), authorized by the Athenian senate in 449 B.C.E. and constructed between 427 and 424 B.C.E. This Ionic temple was the fourth and last building constructed in Pericles' rebuilding plan.

The Athenian temple on the Illissus River also appears to have been designed by Callicrates, on the plan of the temple of Athena Nike. A Doric temple built on the island of Delos has also been attributed to Callicrates on the basis of its style and affinities with the Parthenon. This temple was dedicated by the Athenians in 425 B.C.E.

INFLUENCE The classical style of architecture created by Callicrates influenced temple design of the Greeks and Romans and architecture of the Renaissance and beyond.

FURTHER READING

Beard, Mary. *The Parthenon*. London: Profile, 2002.
Biers, William R. *The Archaeology of Greece: An Introduction*. 2d ed. Ithaca, N.Y.: Cornell University Press, 1996.
Dinsmoor, William Bell. *The Architecture of Ancient Greece*. New York: W. W. Norton, 1975.

Neils, Jenifer, ed. *The Parthenon: From Antiquity to the Present.* New York: Cambridge University Press, 2005.

Sally A. Struthers

See also: Art and Architecture; Athens; Ictinus; Parthenon.

Callimachus

POET

Born: c. 305 B.C.E.; Cyrene, Cyrenaica (now in Libya)
Died: c. 240 B.C.E.; Alexandria, Egypt
Category: Poetry; literature

LIFE   Very little is known about the life of Callimachus (kuh-LIHM-uh-kuhs). He was born about 305 B.C.E. in the Greek colony of Cyrene, in modern Libya. He came from a prominent family, and his works suggest that he was frankly homosexual. His literary output seems to have been extensive, for ancient literary sources refer to many works by him in both prose and poetry; however, only a few poetic works—some of them fragmentary—exist today. Many of his other works seem to have been scholarly efforts: a catalog of books in the great library at Alexandria, various encyclopedias, and a life of Democritus. He is remembered for championing the shorter literary genres, such as the epyllion, an abbreviated epic treating a single episode in detail. He excelled at composing epigrams on many subjects, and he wrote numerous elegies on topics derived from Greek myths. Probably as a result of his influence, the best extant poems from Alexandria exploit these modes.

Callimachus's literary career developed not in Cyrene but in Alexandria during the period of that city's dominance of the Mediterranean world's intellectual life. Exactly when Callimachus arrived in Alexandria is impossible to say, but he apparently went there in his youth and studied under an Aristotelian philosopher named Praxiphanes. Alexandria enjoyed an extraordinary cultural blossoming in the thirty years or so following the rise to power in 323 B.C.E. of the Egyptian general Ptolemy, who annexed Cyrene to his kingdom and became an enthusiastic patron of art and learning. The bustling city had a Jewish quarter, the Greeks had their section, and the Egyptians maintained their original holdings.

The famous museum (the Shrine of the Muses) at Alexandria, begun in 294, expanded into a dominating university resplendent with botanical and zoological gardens and an observatory. The university's many accomplishments in mathematics, astronomy, engineering, and medicine included both Euclid's *Elements* (c. 300 B.C.E.) and Apollonius of Perga's theory of conic sections.

When Callimachus, the young provincial from Cyrene, came upon this scene, he apparently settled there immediately. Some scanty evidence suggests that he may have begun his career as a schoolteacher, but before long he was one of the scholars diligently taking advantage of the Royal Library that flourished under the patronage of Ptolemy II. It was at this congenial institution that Callimachus wrote his poems, carried on his scholarship, and earned his reputation as an outspoken critic.

Two important themes emerge in Callimachus's work. He is often quoted as saying, broadly, that a big book is a bad book. What he meant by this—if he indeed actually said it—may have been nothing more than an understandable complaint by a librarian about the cumbersome nature of large scrolls. However, the remark probably reflects his well-known contempt for the epic; in one epigram he spits out, "I hate epic poetry." It is not surprising that Callimachus preferred Hesiod to Homer.

One tradition in scholarship identifies Callimachus as an antagonist (as far as literary theory goes) of his contemporary Apollonius Rhodius, a supporter of the Homeric style in poetry. Better evidence of his views emerges from his attack in *Aitiōn* (*Aetia*, 1958), or "the sources of the myths," on the Telchines. The Telchines were mythological people supposedly from Crete and Rhodes and associated with the origins of metal-smithing. Callimachus used their reputation for sorcery to identify them with three of his literary enemies: the Alexandrian poets Asclepiades and Posidippus and the phi-

Principal Works of Callimachus

Aitiōn (*Aetia*, 1958)

Epigrammata (*Epigrams*, 1793)

Ekalē (*Hecale*, 1958)

Hymni (*Hymns*, 1755)

Iamboi (*Iambi*, 1958)

Lock of Berenice, 1755

Pinakes

losopher Praxiphanes of Mitylene. They are the ignorant ones who, he says, "grumble at my poetry, because I did not accomplish one continuous poem of many thousands of lines." Poems, he concludes, "are far shorter for being sweet." Another persistent theme, in *Aetia* and elsewhere, is Callimachus's rebelliousness—his fierce determination to go his own way and "tread a path which carriages do not trample." Such a course will be narrow, but it will be fresh and it will be one's own.

INFLUENCE   Among other poets flourishing in the last two centuries B.C.E., the little-known Cyrenian poet Philostephanus, who wrote of landscapes, and Euphorion, who continued Callimachus's devotion to the short poem, may be called followers of Callimachus. The prominent Latin poets Moschus and Parthenius both composed epyllia, and Vergil's early pastorals may also owe something to Callimachus. The Augustan poets Ovid and Propertius were major disciples: Propertius was even known as "the Roman Callimachus," while Ovid's *Metamorphoses* (c. 8 C.E.; English translation, 1567) are epyllia that are often judged Callimachean in spirit.

Despite their disagreements over Homer's merits, the Alexandrian poets of Callimachus's era were generally traditionalists, and the museum and its library enabled them to master much of the ancient world's learning. They were keen craftsmen, intent on technique, who nevertheless usually followed the old forms. In all these aspects of his time, Callimachus was a consummate Alexandrian.

FURTHER READING

Acosta-Hughes, Benjamin. *Polyeideia: The Iambi of Callimachus and the Archaic Iambic Tradition*. Berkeley: University of California Press, 2002.

Calame, Claude. "Legendary Narratives and Poetic Procedure in Callimachus's 'Hymn to Apollo.'" In *Hellenistica Gronigana: Proceedings of the Gröningen Workshops on Hellenistic Poetry*, edited by Annette Harder. Gröningen, Germany: Egbert Forster, 1993.

Cameron, Alan. *Callimachus and His Critics*. Princeton, N.J.: Princeton University Press, 1995.

Ferguson, John. *Callimachus*. Boston: Twayne, 1980.

Gutzwiller, Kathryn. *Poetic Garlands: Hellenistic Epigrams in Context*. Berkeley: University of California Press, 1998.

Hollis, A. S. Introduction to *Callimachus' "Hecale."* Oxford, England: Clarendon Press, 1990.

Thomas, Richard F. "Callimachus Back in Rome." In *Hellenistica Gronigana: Proceedings of the Gröningen Workshops on Hellenistic Poetry*, edited by Annette Harder. Gröningen, Germany: Egbert Forster, 1993.

Tress, Heather van. *Poetic Memory: Allusion in the Poetry of Callimachus and the "Metamorphoses" of Ovid*. Boston: Brill, 2004.

Williams, Frederick. "Callimachus and the Supranormal." In *Hellenistica Gronigana: Proceedings of the Gröningen Workshops on Hellenistic Poetry*, edited by Annette Harder. Gröningen, Germany: Egbert Forster, 1993.

Frank Day

See also: Alexandrian Library; Apollonius Rhodius; Elegiac Poetry; Hellenistic Greece; Literature; Ptolemaic Egypt.

Carthaginian-Syracusan War

This war for control of Sicily resulted in a military stalemate.

Date: 481-480 B.C.E.
Category: Wars and battles
Locale: Western Mediterranean region

SUMMARY   It was in Carthage's national interest to protect Sicily, Sardinia, and its Greek Sicilian allies in order to secure and expand its commercial trading empire and, perhaps more important, to control the route to Spain and its rich mineral resources. However, the development of a very virulent form of Greek nationalism in Greek Asia and in Sicily became an extreme threat to the strategic realization of those interests. In 514 B.C.E., the Spartan prince Dorieus, a Greek nationalist, set out to colonize Carthage's Tripolitania province aided by Cynrenaica's Greeks. However, Dorieus and his allies were ejected from Tripolitania, only to return a few years later to colonize a Carthaginian region in western Sicily. Carthage and its Greek Sicilian allies reacted very quickly, and Dorieus and his military cohort were killed in a minor battle. Later, Dorieus would be viewed as a martyr by all Greek nationalists in Sicily led by the emerging Siceliot tyrants.

In this context, the Carthaginian-Syracusan War had its historical origins in the rise of the Greek Siceliot tyrants, whose central objective was to push Carthage out of Sicily and Sardinia. Beginning in 498 B.C.E., Hippocrates of Gela (d. 491 B.C.E.), one of the first Siceliot tyrants, spent eight years looting and subjugating Greek colonies in northeastern Sicily and threatening Carthage. The uneasy political existence between the Greek Siceliot tyrants and Carthage centered on their joint occupation of Sicily and Carthage's intent to protect its security and economic interests.

In 491 B.C.E., Hippocrates died and was succeeded by one of his captains, Gelon (d. 478 B.C.E.). A supporter of the patriotic war ideology, Gelon quickly declared war against Carthage and its main allies in the western Sicily region. His central goal was to terminate Carthage's influ-

The Battle of Himera. (F. R. Niglutsch)

ence in the Gulf of Gabes and, if possible, eject Carthage from Sicily (and Sardinia) altogether. Gelon and his allies were largely unsuccessful because of inadequate military resources and Carthaginian resistance. However, in 485 B.C.E., the displaced aristocracy of the city-state Syracuse asked Gelon to restore it to royal power. Instead, Gelon quickly occupied Syracuse, eliminated all internal threats, and ruthlessly transformed it into the most powerful state in Greek Sicily.

Meanwhile, Carthage grew concerned with Gelon and his allies and worried that their military machinations in western Sicily were becoming increasingly dangerous. In 480 B.C.E., the sudden displacement of an important Greek Sicilian ally, Terillos of Himera, from his city-state convinced Carthage to invade western Sicily with large army and naval forces. Led by Hamilcar (d. 480 B.C.E.) the Magonid, Carthage anticipated very strong military resistance from Gelon and his Greek Sicilian allies to the restoration to power of Terillos in Himera. Before the battle, Hamilcar of Carthage had an army of about 30,000 foot soldiers and a strong cavalry force, and Gelon of Syracuse had an army of no more than 24,000 foot soldiers and 2,000 horses.

The Battle of Himera (480 B.C.E.) was decided by good intelligence

207

rather than by a regular military battle. The historical record indicates that Gelon intercepted a Carthaginian communication indicating precisely where Hamilcar the Magonid would be on the day of the battle and had his cavalry forces kill Hamilcar. Gelon also set ablaze Carthage's naval squadron. The Carthaginian army and its allies were disoriented by the death of their commander and dissolved as a serious fighting unit when attacked by Gelon's forces.

SIGNIFICANCE   Carthage sued for peace in the aftermath of the Battle of Himera. Because Gelon was not in a political position to exploit the defeat, he settled for a large silver payment as tribute. Carthage, deeply shaken by the defeat, turned inward and began the subjugation of African territories.

FURTHER READING
Caven, Brian. *The Punic Wars*. New York: St. Martin's Press, 1980.
Goldsworthy, Adrian Keith. *The Punic Wars*. London: Cassell, 2000.
Warmington, B. H. *Carthage*. New York: Frederick A. Praeger, 1969.

Michael J. Siler

See also: Gelon of Syracuse; Syracuse.

Cassander

KING OF MACEDONIA (R. 305-297 B.C.E.)

Born: c. 358 B.C.E.; place unknown
Died: 297 B.C.E.; place unknown, probably Macedonia
Category: Government and politics

LIFE   Cassander (kuh-SAN-duhr), who represented his father, Antipater, Alexander the Great's regent, joined Alexander in fighting at Babylon in 324 B.C.E. After Alexander's death in 323 B.C.E., the succession fell to Philip Arridaeus (Alexander's mentally impaired half brother, known as Philip III) as regent and Alexander IV (Alexander's infant son). When Antipater died in 319 B.C.E., Polyperchon became regent while Cassander remained in a subordinate role. Cassander formed an alliance with Antigonus I Monophthalmos against Polyperchon; they invaded Macedonia but were unsuccessful. In 318 B.C.E., Olympias, Alexander the Great's mother, in an attempt to gain power for herself and her grandson Alexander IV, murdered Philip III and forced his wife, Eurydice, to commit suicide. Olympias claimed to rule for her grandson, but Cassander besieged her in Pydna in 316 B.C.E., forced her to surrender, and put her on trial for the murders she had ordered. She was condemned to death and killed by the relatives of her victims. Cassander, now regent, married Alexander the Great's half sister Thessalonice.

In 316 B.C.E., Cassander refounded Thebes, which Alexander had destroyed earlier. Around 310 B.C.E., he had Alexander IV and his mother murdered but did not assume the throne himself. Around 305 B.C.E., Cassander assumed the title of king. With Antigonus's death in 301 B.C.E., Cassander's title became secure. In 297 B.C.E., he died, leaving the throne to his son Philip IV, who ruled for only four months before dying. Cassander's younger sons Antipater and Alexander V quarreled and lost the kingdom to Demetrius Poliorcetes, the son of Antigonus I Monophthalmos.

INFLUENCE   Cassander ended Argead rule in Macedonia and made possible the rise of new and independent Hellenistic kingdoms.

FURTHER READING

Green, Peter. *Alexander to Actium: The Historical Evolution of the Hellenistic Age*. Reprint. Berkeley: University of California Press, 1993.

Hammond, N. G. L., and F. W. Walbank. *A History of Macedonia*. Vol. 3. Oxford, England: Clarendon Press, 1988.

Will, Édouard. *Cambridge Ancient History*. Vol. 7. Cambridge, England: Cambridge University Press, 1984.

Martin C. J. Miller

See also: Alexander the Great; Alexander the Great's Empire; Antigonid Dynasty; Antipater; Hellenistic Greece; Olympias.

Battle of Chaeronea

Macedonia's victory over Greece effectively ended the era of the Greek city-state.

Date: August 2, 338 B.C.E.
Category: Wars and battles
Locale: Chaeronea, in Boeotia northwest of Thebes

SUMMARY Philip II of Macedonia (r. 359-336 B.C.E.) modernized the Macedonian army. He taught his factious nobility to serve him loyally, using heavy cavalry, and created a highly professional phalanx of infantry. In the 340's B.C.E., Philip began to penetrate southward through Thessaly while the Greek states were distracted by their perpetual feuds.

War broke out between Macedonia and a united Greece in 340 B.C.E. The decisive battle was probably fought in Chaeronea (kehr-uh-NEE-uh) on August 2, 338 B.C.E. Thebans and Boeotians held the Greek right flank, the Athenians the left, and various allies from central Greece and the Peloponnese the center. The Greek phalanx hoped to crush the enemy by its usual straightforward attack. Philip, a master of innovation, combined use of cavalry and infantry. His right, pretending retreat, lured the Athenians into a charge. The Greek center and left moved obliquely to keep in close ranks. Into this hole the eighteen-year-old crown prince Alexander (later, the Great) led the Macedonian cavalry in wedge formation against the Thebans. Crack units of Macedonian infantry followed. After heroic resistance the Thebans were beaten; the other Greeks, panic-stricken, broke and ran.

SIGNIFICANCE As a result of this battle, the independent city-states of Greece came under Macedonian control. In 337 B.C.E., Philip organized the Hellenic League with its seat at Corinth. He served as president of the league, and member cities were forbidden to wage war with each other and were forced to follow Philip's foreign policy.

FURTHER READING

Hammond, N. G. L. *Philip of Macedon*. Baltimore: Johns Hopkins University Press, 1994.

Hornblower, Simon. *The Greek World, 479-323 B.C.* 3d ed. New York: Routledge, 2002.

Lendon, J. E. *Soldiers and Ghosts: A History of Battle in Classical Antiquity*. New Haven, Conn.: Yale University Press, 2005.

Montagu, John Drogo. *Battles of the Greek and Roman Worlds: A Chronological Compedium of 667 Battles to 31 B.C., from the Historians of the Ancient World*. Mechanicsburg, Pa.: Stackpole Books, 2000.

Thomas J. Sienkewicz

See also: Alexander the Great; Philip II of Macedonia.

Cimon

MILITARY LEADER

Born: c. 510 B.C.E.; place unknown
Died: c. 451 B.C.E.; Near Citium (now Larnaca), Cyprus
Also known as: Kimon
Category: Military

LIFE   Cimon (SI-muhn) was the son of Miltiades the Younger, the hero of the Battle of Marathon (490 B.C.E.), and a Thracian princess. Although Miltiades died in disgrace because of unpaid debts, Cimon restored the

Cimon.
(Library of Congress)

213

family honor by settling them. His heroic action at the Battle of Salamis (480 B.C.E.) brought him renown, and afterward, he was consistently elected *strategos* (general). He was a leader of the conservative party in Athens and stressed the necessity of an alliance with Sparta against the Persians. His handsome stature, successful policies of consolidating the Delian League, and victorious campaigns against Persia maintained his popularity until 461 B.C.E. Then after Sparta humiliated Athens by rejecting the city's help in putting down a revolt of the helots (Spartan serfs), the democratic opposition led by Pericles and Ephialtes of Athens sent him into exile. Pericles later recalled him, and he died on campaign against Persia.

INFLUENCE   Cimon was the leading general of Athens and the Delian League from the time of Athenian statesman Themistocles to that of Pericles. Although a leader of the conservative party, he strengthened the position of democratic Athens as the leading city in Greece and successfully fought against the Persians.

FURTHER READING
Meier, Christian. *Athens: A Portrait of the City in Its Golden Age*. London: John Murray, 1998.

Montagu, John Drogo. *Battles of the Greek and Roman Worlds: A Chronological Compedium of 667 Battles to 31 B.C., from the Historians of the Ancient World*. Mechanicsburg, Pa.: Stackpole Books, 2000.

Plutarch. *Plutarch's Lives: The Dryden Translation, Edited with Notes by Arthur Hugh Clough*. New York: Modern Library, 2001.

Frederick B. Chary

See also: Athens; Ephialtes of Athens; Greco-Persian Wars; Marathon, Battle of; Miltiades the Younger; Pericles; Salamis, Battle of.

Classical Greece

Greek culture reached its apex, producing philosophers, tragedians, orators, and buildings such as the Parthenon. Its city-states rose and fell as military powers, and Greek dominion reached the eastern and western basins of the Mediterranean.

Date: 500 B.C.E.-323 B.C.E.
Category: Cities and civilizations
Locale: Greek peninsula, southern Italy, Sicily, eastern Mediterranean

HISTORY The Panhellenic religious and cultural developments of the seventh and sixth centuries B.C.E. provided impetus, but two events played a signal role in the making of Classical Greece, giving it a definition and figure that differentiates it from its Archaic antecedent. The first was the deposition of the tyrants. Tyrants (from *tyrannos*, a word possibly of Lydian extraction) had dominated the poleis, or city-states, during the late seventh and sixth centuries B.C.E. Tyrants usually came to power at the instigation of the lower economic classes and were in many cases a forerunner to democratic government. Although tyrants were usually no worse than their aristocratic predecessors (and in some cases they were considerably better), tyranny seldom lasted more than two generations. The tyrants were for the most part gone by the end of the sixth century B.C.E., although tyranny did last longer in Sicily, where it was even revivified in the fourth century B.C.E.

By the end of the sixth century B.C.E., the best-known Greek states had developed the system of government they would maintain throughout the Classical period: Athens had democracy, put in place by Cleisthenes; Sparta was ruled by a dual kingship and military aristocracy; Corinth had an elected council and a board of magistrates; and Thebes and the other cities of Boeotia were governed by the somewhat enigmatic Boeotarchs. Sparta in this period took the lead in Greek affairs, helping to depose many of the tyrants, developing the Spartan Alliance, and entering into international relations with Lydia.

The second major event was the conflict with Persia. When Persia defeated the Lydian kingdom of Croesus and gained control of the lucrative Greek cities of Ionia and western Asia Minor, a collision with the mainland Greeks became inevitable. The conflict was accelerated by the expansionist policies of the Persian king Darius the Great, who crossed over into Europe and annexed portions of Thrace and eventually extended Persian rule to the Danube. When the Ionian states rebelled against Persia in 499 B.C.E., the Athenians and Eretrians exacerbated a volatile situation by assisting their fellow Ionians and sending troops to aid the rebels. One detachment sacked the Persian regional capital, Sardis, in 494 B.C.E.

Darius suppressed the revolt and determined to punish the Athenians and Eretrians for their role in aiding the rebels. He also intended an eventual annexation of mainland Greece. In 490 B.C.E., a Persian expedition sacked Eretria and deported the population to Asia but was subsequently defeated at Marathon by the combined forces of Athens and Plataea.

Under Darius's successor, Xerxes I, Persia mounted a true invasion. The Persians won a victory at Thermopylae and killed the Spartan king Leonidas in 480 B.C.E., but the Greeks won a subsequent naval victory at Salamis later that same year and then scored a decisive victory on land at Plataea in 479 B.C.E. A subsequent engagement at Mycale crippled the Persian fleet. At the same time, Gelon, the tyrant of Syracuse, crushed a synchronously timed invasion of Sicily by Carthage, defeating the Carthaginians at Himera and breaking Carthaginian power in the west for two generations.

The defeat of the Persians left Athens and Sparta as the dominant powers in mainland Greece. Sparta did little to exploit its advantage, content to preserve the status quo. By contrast, the Athenians, whose city had been sacked twice by the Persians during the invasion, resolved to continue the war in order to liberate the Greek cities of Asia Minor. Athens and the Greek maritime powers created an alliance known as the Delian League because the treasury of the league was kept at Delos, the island sacred to Apollo. Under the leadership of the Athenian Cimon, the league vigorously prosecuted the war, winning a great double victory at the Eurymedon River circa 466 B.C.E.

At home, Athens radicalized its democracy under Ephialtes and Pericles. It continued to pursue an aggressive foreign policy against Sparta and Persia, consolidated its leadership of the Delian League, and transformed it into the Athenian Empire. Athens removed the treasury of the league from Delos to Athens and used the revenues to finance its own building projects, imposed terms and garrisons on the other cities in the league, required all members to use Athenian coinage and standards, and ordered the other cities to bring offerings to the Great Panathenaic festival every four years.

These policies caused rebellions throughout the league and eventually caused Sparta to bring an army into Attica. Pericles, the architect of Athenian policy, was able to negotiate a withdrawal of the Spartan army and a Thirty Years' Peace (445 B.C.E.). The peace left Athens free to consolidate its empire but laid the groundwork for the Peloponnesian War by essentially dividing Greece into two armed camps.

Hostilities with Sparta and its allies exploded in 431 B.C.E. for a variety of reasons. The first ten years of the war, known as the Archidamian War (431-421 B.C.E.), were inconclusive, although Athens suffered greatly from the plague in 429-428 B.C.E. The Peace of Nicias guaranteed a fifty-year truce, but Athens opted to break the peace by invading Syracuse, the wealthiest Greek city in the west. The invasion ended disastrously for Athens and renewed the general war with Sparta. Athens suffered a final humiliating defeat at Aegospotami in 405 B.C.E. and surrendered the next year, enduring the loss of its democracy and the imposition of a Spartan garrison on the Acropolis.

Sparta was unable to hold Athens for long, and the democracy was restored in 401 B.C.E. Sparta embarked on an interventionist foreign policy under Agesilaus II, who was forced ultimately to sell out the Greek cities in Ionia in order to gain Persian aid in controlling affairs in mainland Greece. Athens, Thebes, Argos, and Corinth, in a rolling system of alliances, opposed Sparta. Spartan power was finally broken at Leuctra in 371 B.C.E., and Thebes and the Boeotian League enjoyed a brief hegemony under Epaminondas, but he was killed at the indecisive Battle of Mantinea (362 B.C.E.), and Thebes never recovered its position.

The last few decades of the Classical era witnessed the growth of Macedonia under Philip II. He first consolidated his own power in Macedonia, then exploited the chaotic conditions in Greece after Mantinea to gain a foothold in Greece. He intervened in the Third Sacred War (357 B.C.E.-346 B.C.E.), was invited by Isocrates to lead a Greek invasion of Persia, and eventually overwhelmed Greek opposition to Macedonian domination at Chaeronea in 338 B.C.E. His son and successor Alexander the Great took two years to consolidate his own position, defeating Celtic tribes in the north and west of Macedonia and then quelling any possible Greek opposition by annihilating Thebes. Alexander then led his army into Persia, where he overwhelmed Persian opposition at Granicus, Issus, and Gaugamela. He took over Darius III's throne and reached as far as southern Russia, Afghanistan, and India before returning to Babylon and dying in 323 B.C.E.

In western Greece, Syracuse remained the dominant state. After the invasion by Athens, internal difficulties led to a restoration of the system of tyranny that had been jettisoned sixty years earlier when Syracuse overthrew the unfortunate Thasyboulos. The new tyrant, Dionysius the Elder, warred almost incessantly against Carthage and gained control of much of Sicily and Magna Graecia before a serious defeat at Cronium (375 B.C.E.). His son Dionysius the Younger, briefly a student of Plato, attempted to consolidate Syracusan power in Sicily but saw his position usurped by his uncle, Dion, who held Syracuse until his murder in 354 B.C.E.. Dionysius the Younger eventually recovered Syracuse but was defeated by the Corinthian Timoleon, who sent Dionysius the Younger into exile at Corinth. Timoleon made peace with Carthage and was able to consolidate his power at Syracuse until his retirement from public life, caused by encroaching blindness. He died about 334 B.C.E.

PERFORMING ARTS   In Athens, the fifth century B.C.E. was the era of the theater. At the festival of the City Dionysia, Athenian citizens watched the tragedies of Aeschylus, Sophocles, and Euripides. The tragedians competed with one another, both for the right to have plays funded and to perform them. The *Oresteia* (458 B.C.E.; English translation, 1777) of Aeschylus is the only surviving trilogy from ancient Greece, and Sophocles' *Oidipous Tyrannos* (c. 429 B.C.E.; *Oedipus Tyrannus*, 1715) remains the most famous of all Greek plays. Aristophanes was the leading comic poet of Athens. His comedies mocked the leading citizens of Athens and denounced the excesses of the prowar parties. His most famous work, the *Lysistratē* (411 B.C.E.; *Lysistrata*, 1837), has remained a staple of pacifism to the present day.

LANGUAGE AND LITERATURE   The fifth century was the age of Pindar, whose *Epinikia* (498-446 B.C.E.; *Odes*, 1656) celebrated the glories of athletic victory. Bacchylides of Ceos, a proximate contemporary, wrote epinician (victory) odes and dithyrambs, while Simonides, also of Ceos, wrote hymns and epitaphs to celebrate and to mourn the fallen of the Greco-Persian Wars. The same century also saw the development of historical writing. Herodotus wrote *Historiai Herodotou* (c. 424 B.C.E.; *The History*, 1709), focusing on the war against Persia and recording a great deal of ethnographic, religious, and sociological information on Greece as well as Egypt, Persia, and other states of the Near East. Thucydides wrote the definitive history of the Peloponnesian War, and where his account breaks off in about 410 B.C.E., it is picked up by Xenophon, whose *Ellīnika* (411-362

B.C.E.; *History of the Affairs of Greece*, also known as *Helenica*, 1685) extends the account to the second Battle of Mantinea in 362 B.C.E. Xenophon also gave the world one of the great "true" adventure stories, the *Kurou anabasis* (between 394 and 371 B.C.E.; *Anabasis*, also known as *Expedition of Cyrus* and *March Up Country*, 1623), an account of the expedition of 10,000 Greek mercenaries, called the March of the Ten Thousand, against the Persian king Artaxerxes II, and their subsequent escape.

Xenophon and the March of the Ten Thousand reach the sea's edge. (F. R. Niglutsch)

The late fifth and fourth centuries B.C.E. also saw the development of oratory as an art form. The canonical Attic orators practiced at this time. Lysias, a metic (resident noncitizen) of Athens was the master of the simple, smooth style of Attic Greek. Demosthenes, who spoke out repeatedly against Philip II of Macedonia, earned a place in history for himself with his Philippic orations, which were later copied by Cicero in his writings against Marc Antony.

PHILOSOPHY The three most famous figures of Greek philosophy belong to this period. Socrates was an Athenian stonecutter who abandoned his trade to inquire into the nature of humankind, thus moving philosophy from natural science to ethics. He wrote nothing, and his greatest contribution was as a teacher to Plato. He was executed by the state for impiety and corruption of the youth. His great disciple, Plato, authored a number of works in dialogic form in which Socrates challenges the conventional wisdom of his interlocutor and works through logical analysis to educate. Plato's greatest works are the *Politeia* (c. 388-368 B.C.E.; *Republic*, 1701), *Symposion* (c. 388-368 B.C.E.; *Symposium*, 1701), *Phaedros* (c. 388-368 B.C.E.; *Phaedrus*, 1792), and *Phaedōn* (c. 388-368 B.C.E.; *Phaedo*, 1675).

Aristotle, born in Stagirus in Chalcidice, came to Athens at the age of seventeen to study with Plato and remained at the Academy until Plato's death in 347 B.C.E. He later tutored Alexander the Great (then a boy) and finally returned to Athens in 335 B.C.E., establishing his own school at a grove sacred to Apollo Lyceius and the Muses. His extensive works include the *Physica* (c. 335-323 B.C.E.; *Physics*, 1812), *Metaphysica* (c. 335-323 B.C.E.; *Metaphysics*, 1801), *Technt rhetorikīs* (c. 335-323 B.C.E.; *Rhetoric*, 1686), and *Ethica Nicomachea* (c. 335-323 B.C.E.; *Nicomachean Ethics*, 1797).

RELIGION AND RITUAL The Panhellenic aspects of Greek religion focused on the major festivals and shrines. From the eighth century B.C.E., Delphi had been predominant for the worship of Apollo, and its influence grew in the Classical period as it became the place to which the Greek cities resorted for information, approbation, and direction from the god. It played a particularly important part in the Greco-Persian Wars, although it did lose some of its authority. It was pro-Spartan during the Peloponnesian War and later was pro-Macedonian, suggesting either a great conservatism or a keen if sometimes errant estimate of comparative military force by Apollo and his minions.

The city of Athens opened its Panathenaic and Dionysia festivals to foreigners, but perhaps its most famous ritual was the Eleusinian Mysteries, held at the village of Eleusis and sacred to Demeter. Other significant sites included Delos, sacred to Apollo, the Heraion at Argos, the temple of Artemis Orthia at Sparta, and the shrine of Zeus at Dodona.

The great spiritual longing that would characterize the Hellenistic Age seems not yet apparent in the Classical period, although, in addition to the rites of Demeter at Eleusis, there is substantial evidence for Orphic and Dionysiac practice at this time.

WOMEN'S LIFE   The condition of women varied considerably from one Greek state to another, and it is a mistake to view any one instance as paradigmatic. In Athens, women were generally isolated from men, to the extent that the better houses included separate women's quarters. Nonetheless, women did play a central role in family ritual and held important roles in burial practices. The principal female festival at Athens was the Thesmophoria. Spartan women were, by contrast, able to own property and were noted for the extensive freedom of behavior and movement they enjoyed. Educated women from Ionia and the Greek cities of Asia Minor were actively sought as courtesans, and it is from this group that Aspasia of Miletus, the mistress of Pericles, was drawn. Women were also noted for acts of great heroism. The poet Telesilla of Argos (whose work survives in nine fragments only) led a group of women who repelled Spartan invaders under Cleomenes after the Argive army was defeated at Sepeia.

ECONOMICS   By the Classical period, most of the Greek world had adopted coined money. The availability of coinage made easier the acquisition and preservation of capital and encouraged both commerce and private wealth. Trade was conducted on an international basis, with Greek cities acquiring goods from across the Mediterranean basin, the Black Sea, inland Europe, and Asia. Greek wares reached the Atlantic coast and India. Athens, Corinth, Rhodes, and the cities of the Asiatic coasts (depending on political conditions) were all leading market cities.

GOVERNMENT AND LAW   The major cities of Greece had, for the most part, established forms of government before the Classical period. Each city was essentially self-governing, although owing to victory or defeat in war or the dominance of one power or another in the shifting alliances that characterized the period, the larger powers sometimes gained control of the internal government and foreign policy of their allies. Nor were the governments entirely static. Athens revised its democratic practices on more than one occasion, even going so far as to vote the democracy out of existence in 411 B.C.E. under the stress of the Greco-Persian Wars. The Thebans and the other states of the Boeotian confederacy were under the rule of the Boeotarchs. Sparta was governed by two kings who operated at the direction of the board of ephors (magistrates), a *gerousia* (council of elders), and an assembly of citizen-soldiers. Corinth enjoyed for the most part a rule of stable oligarchy, although it did flirt briefly with democracy. Argos established a type of democracy sometime after 480 B.C.E.

The famous law code of Gortyn, in Crete, which dates from the fifth century, gives an idea of both the substantive and procedural laws that might have been common throughout the Greek states. Most knowledge about the laws in Athens, however, comes from the large number of speeches preserved from the law courts of the late fifth and fourth centuries B.C.E.

WAR AND WEAPONS   Greece defeated Persia in no small part because of its naval supremacy. Athens built a substantial fleet of triremes (warships) to keep its maritime empire in charge. On land, hoplite warfare reigned supreme during the Classical period. The later fifth and the fourth centuries B.C.E. saw the first widespread use of mercenary soldiers in Greece. The preferred weapon of the hoplite was the spear, backed by the use of a short, straight sword. Hoplite armies were effective against cavalry on even terrain, but when scattered or on broken ground, they were much more vulnerable. The Thebans under Epaminondas proved the ultimate effectiveness of cavalry backed by heavy infantry, particularly at Leuctra in 371 B.C.E. Philip II and Alexander the Great perfected such tactics.

EDUCATION AND TRAINING   Sparta demanded that every boy enter the army at age seven and remain there until his retirement from active service. In addition to military skills, young men learned to read and write and received some instruction in music. Women were educated in gymnastics, dancing, and music. Elementary education at Athens might consist of a boy hearing a *grammatistes*, who taught reading, writing, literature, and the elements of arithmetic; a *kitharistes* who taught music; and a *paidotribes*, who taught physical education. Evidence from vase painting suggests that upper-class young women might receive education in all three areas as well. Higher education in professional fields was available, as was advanced study at the philosophical schools. Plato's Academy, Aristotle's Lyceum, and Isocrates' school of rhetoric were the most famous. Professional itinerant educators known as Sophists taught rhetoric, logic, and other skills. Schools are mentioned in other cities as well (for example, Troezen and Mycalessus), but little is known of how they functioned.

ARCHITECTURE AND CITY PLANNING   The fifth century B.C.E. witnessed the great period of Athenian building. A wall was built around the city in 479 B.C.E., replacing an Archaic wall, and the famous Long Walls were built to connect the city to the Piraeus in the 450's. The Piraeus, a harbor complex built to accommodate the new Athenian navy as well as to foster trade, was laid out on a rectangular plan by the architect Hippodamus of Miletus, who was also responsible for planning the Panhellenic colony at Thurii (443 B.C.E.).

On the Acropolis, most of the original buildings had been destroyed by Persian invaders. In the 450's B.C.E., the major building projects were begun, and Phidias's colossal statue of Athena Promachus was erected. Phidias superintended the overall work on the Acropolis. The Parthenon was completed by 432 B.C.E.: Ictinus and Callicrates were the architects. Mnesicles was responsible for the Propylaea, finished in the same year, and the latter part of the fifth century B.C.E. saw the completion of the Erechtheum. An earlier building program under Cimon had seen a substantial rebuilding of the Agora, including the famous Stoa Poecile. The shape of the fifth century B.C.E. Theater of Dionysus is a matter of considerable dispute. In imitation of Athens, however, substantial theaters were built at Epidaurus and Megalopolis. Megalopolis, founded by Epaminondas as the center of the Arcadian League, was perhaps the most ambitious foundation of the fourth century B.C.E. until Alexander founded Alexandria in Egypt to provide him communication by sea with Europe.

CALENDARS AND CHRONOLOGY   The Greek world had no universal calendar. The Athenian calendar, the best known, was a twelve-month lunar calendar of approximately 354 days with an occasional thirteenth month added to restore pace with the solar year. The names of some individual months are known from other cities. Years were generally reckoned on the four-year cycle of the Olympic Games, while an individual year might be known from a particular officeholder (in Athens, for example, the Archon Eponymous).

MEDICINE AND SCIENCE   Medicine developed greatly during the Classical period. Hippocrates of Cos was said by Plato to be the first who attempted to treat the body as a whole, although the body of works that have come down in the Hippocratic corpus show no overt signs of such concern. It is likely that the peripatetic Hippocrates left disciples throughout the Greek world who followed in outline, at least, his theories. However, the popularity of the cult of Asclepius at Epidaurus, the use of incubation in Asclepian rites, and the persistent use of charms and amulets suggest that nonrational elements continued to exercise a strong influence on Greek medical practice. The great scientific and astronomical discoveries of the Hellenistic Age lay in the future, but some progress was made in mathematics and natural science by both Plato and Aristotle. The expedition of Alexander the Great into Persia and Central Asia greatly increased knowledge in geography, botany, and biology.

TRANSPORTATION AND NAVIGATION   The Greeks of the Classical period continued to improve on their shipbuilding. The trireme was the principal warship in Classical times, replacing the *pentekontor* in the late sixth century B.C.E. It was fairly narrow, with a removable mast that was taken down and sometimes put ashore before battle. The regular merchant vessels were much squarer, relying primarily on sail power, although they could use long sweeping oars for maneuverability. The original merchant ships had one mast, although later a forward mast was added. The sailing season generally fell between March and October. Ships did not tack well, and there were no instruments such as the sextant or compass to assist in finding position at sea.

SPORTS AND ENTERTAINMENT   The Olympic Games, celebrated every fourth year, remained the most important of the athletic festivals of this period. In addition, Panhellenic games were celebrated at Corinth (Isthmian Games), Nemea (Nemean Games), and Delphi (Pythian Games). Two of the most famous athletes of the Classical period were Theagenes of Thasos, who won nine Nemean and ten Isthmian Games, and Dorieus of

Rhodes, whose victories in boxing and the *pankration* (a type of "no-holds-barred" wrestling) extended over a career of at least twenty-six years.

VISUAL ARTS Athenian red-figured pottery came into use around 530 B.C.E. and dominated throughout the Classical period. Vase painting became less stiff although still idealized. A freer style of painting characterized fourth century B.C.E. vases. In sculpture, Phidias completed the monumental Athena Promachos for the Acropolis in the 450's. The sculptures of the pediment are either his work or were done under his direction. There was some larger painting done on walls at this period, particularly by Micon and Polygnotus, who decorated the Stoa Poecile and the Theseum. Zeuxis of Heraclea was perhaps the best known of all the painters of the Classical period, known for his use of shading and highlighting. A famous story alleges that his painting fooled birds.

CURRENT VIEWS Much scholarship has focused on integrating the cultural and religious elements of the Classical period with the more familiar politics and literature. There has been a rejection of the Apollonian/Dionysian split favored by philosopher Friedrich Nietzsche in favor of an attempt to find the unity that underlies the rationalism of Plato and Aristotle, the mysticism of Eleusis, the superstition of Delphi, and the ordinary savagery of Greek warfare and politics. In addition, comparative evidence is being mined for insights into the lives of women and the political underclasses in Greek society, and much more work is being done on those elements that connect Classical Greece to its own Archaic past. There has also developed a greater appreciation of the role that cultural exchange with Asia, other parts of Europe, and Egypt played in the development of Classical Greece.

FURTHER READING

Brunschwig, Jacques, and G. E. R. Lloyd, eds. *Greek Thought: A Guide to Classical Knowledge.* Cambridge, Mass.: Belknap Press of Harvard University Press, 2000.

Bryant, Joseph M. *Moral Codes and Social Structure in Ancient Greece: A Sociology of Greek Ethics from Homer to the Epicureans and Stoics.* Albany: State University of New York Press, 1996.

Gagarin, Michael. *Early Greek Law.* Berkeley: University of California Press, 1986.

Hammond, Nicholas G. L. *A History of Greece to 322 B.C.* 3d ed. Oxford, England: Oxford University Press, 1986.

Harris, Edward Monroe, and Lene Rubinstein, eds. *The Law and the Courts in Ancient Greece*. London: Duckworth, 2004.

Meadows, Andrew, and Kirsty Shipton. *Money and Its Uses in the Ancient Greek World*. Oxford, England: Oxford University Press, 2001.

Rhodes, P. J., ed. *Athenian Democracy*. New York: Oxford University Press, 2004.

Roberts, J. W. *The City of Sokrates: An Introduction to Classical Athens*. London: Routledge and Kegan Paul, 1998.

Stockton, D. *The Classical Athenian Democracy*. New York: Oxford University Press, 1990.

Wiles, David. *Tragedy in Athens: Performance Space and Theatrical Meaning*. Cambridge, England: Cambridge University Press, 1997.

Joseph P. Wilson

See also: Aegospotami, Battle of; Alexander the Great; Archaic Greece; Archidamian War; Aristophanes; Aristotle; Art and Architecture; Aspasia of Miletus; Athenian Empire; Athenian invasion of Sicily; Athens; Bacchylides; Calendars and Chronology; Callicrates; Carthaginian-Syracusan War; Chaeronea, Battle of; Cimon; Coins; Delphi; Demosthenes; Dionysius the Elder; Dionysius the Younger; Education and Training; Eleusinian Mysteries; Epaminondas; Gelon of Syracuse; Gortyn's Code; Government and Law; Greco-Persian Wars; Hellenistic Greece; Herodotus; Hippocrates; Ictinus; Leonidas; Leuctra, Battle of; Lysias; Mantinea, Battles of; Medicine and Health; Military History of Athens; Mycenaean Greece; Olympic Games; Oratory; Parthenon; Peloponnesian Wars; Performing Arts; Pericles; Phidias; Philip II of Macedonia; Philosophy; Pindar; Plato; Polygnotus; Religion and Ritual; Sacred Wars; Salamis, Battle of; Science; Socrates; Sports and Entertainment; Syracuse; Theater of Dionysus; Thermopylae, Battle of; Thucydides; Timoleon of Corinth; Trade, Commerce, and Colonization; Transportation and Navigation; Trireme; Warfare Before Alexander; Women's Life; Xenophon; Xerxes I; Zeuxis of Heraclea.

Cleisthenes of Athens

ARCHON OF ATHENS (525/524 B.C.E.)

Born: c. 570 B.C.E.; place unknown
Died: After 507 B.C.E.; place unknown
Also known as: Kleisthenes of Athens
Category: Government and politics

LIFE   Born into Athens' most powerful family, the Alcmaeonids, Cleisthenes (KLIS-thuh-neez) of Athens held the archonship in 525/524 B.C.E., but soon afterward his family was driven into exile by the tyrant Hippias of Athens. Spending lavishly at Delphi to influence the oracle to pressure the Spartans, Cleisthenes convinced Cleomenes I of Sparta to overthrow the tyranny in 510 B.C.E., but in the ensuing factional struggles, he was outdone by his rival Isagoras, who was elected archon in 508/507 B.C.E. In reaction, Cleisthenes appealed to the people, leading Isagoras to call in Cleomenes, but popular support for Cleisthenes sent Isagoras and the Spartan king packing.

Refashioning Solon's constitution in order to create a less fractious government and enhance his own political position, Cleisthenes then established the basic machinery of the fifth century B.C.E. democracy, creating the ten tribes and the Council of Five Hundred. He also created the institution of ostracism and established contacts with Persia in order to protect the new government from the Spartan threat, which ended with the failed Peloponnesian invasion of 507 B.C.E. Having thus set Athens on the path from an aristocratic tribal state to a true democracy, Cleisthenes disappeared, presumably dying of old age.

INFLUENCE   Whatever Cleisthenes' personal motives, the government he created enabled the development of the fifth century B.C.E. democracy and all that would mean to the West.

FURTHER READING

Aristotle. *The Politics, and the Constitution of Athens.* Rev. ed. Edited by Stephen Everson. New York: Cambridge University Press, 1996.

Burn, A. R. *Persia and the Greeks: The Defense of the West, 546-478 B.C.* Stanford, Calif.: Stanford University Press, 1984.

Forsdyke, Sara. *Exile, Ostracism, and Democracy: The Politics of Expulsion in Ancient Greece.* Princeton, N.J.: Princeton University Press, 2005.

Herodotus. *The Histories.* Translated by Robin Waterfield. New York: Oxford University Press, 1998.

Hignett, C. *A History of the Athenian Constitution.* Oxford, England: Oxford University Press, 1952.

Rhodes, P. J., ed. *Athenian Democracy.* New York: Oxford University Press, 2004.

Thorley, John. *Athenian Democracy.* 2d ed. New York: Routledge, 2004.

Richard M. Berthold

See also: Athenian Democracy; Athens; Cleomenes I; Delphi; Hippias of Athens; Solon's Code.

Cleisthenes of Sicyon

Statesman and Military Leader

Born: Seventh century B.C.E.; Greece
Died: c. 570 B.C.E.; Greece
Also known as: Kleisthenes of Sikyon
Category: Military; government and politics

Life Cleisthenes (KLIS-thuh-neez) was tyrant of Sicyon (SIHS-ee-ahn) from about 600 to 570 B.C.E. At war with Argos, Cleisthenes of Sicyon banned the Homeric epics because of their praise of the Argives, stripped honors from Adrastus, an Argive hero buried in Sicyon, and gave the Sicyonian tribes new names differing from the Dorian names used at Argos.

Cleisthenes took part in the First Sacred War (c. 595 B.C.E.) and won the chariot race at the Pythian Games (582 B.C.E.), after which he dedicated two buildings at Delphi. The metopes from one of these buildings are among the finest examples of Archaic Greek sculpture. After winning the chariot race at Olympia (c. 576 B.C.E.), he invited the best of the Greeks to compete for the hand of his daughter Agariste. After entertaining and testing the suitors for a full year, Cleisthenes chose Megacles of Athens as his son-in-law.

Influence Cleisthenes' career shows how a tyrant could use religious and cultural propaganda and illustrates a tyrant's concern for magnificence and display. He was the grandfather of Cleisthenes of Athens and an ancestor of Pericles and Alcibiades of Athens.

Further Reading

Griffin, Aubrey. *Sikyon*. Oxford, England: Clarendon Press, 1982.
Ogden, Daniel. "Cleisthenes of Sicyon, Leuster." *Classical Quarterly* 43 (1993): 353-363.

Sealey, Raphael. *A History of the Greek City States*. Berkeley: University of California Press, 1976.

George E. Pesely

See also: Agariste; Alcibiades of Athens; Cleisthenes of Athens; Pericles; Sacred Wars.

Cleomenes I

KING OF SPARTA (R. C. 519-490 B.C.E.)

Born: Date unknown; Sparta, Greece
Died: c. 490 B.C.E.; Sparta, Greece
Category: Government and politics; military

LIFE Cleomenes I (klee-AHM-uh-neez) succeeded his father, King Anaxandrides, to the throne around 519 B.C.E. Initially, his half brother Dorieus challenged his ascendancy, but Cleomenes was planted firmly in power when Dorieus left Sparta to establish a colony elsewhere.

Cleomenes I wanted to fight against Athens's tyranny and to expand Sparta's boundaries and influence outward, even into Greece. After a naval failure, he led a land expedition against Athens that succeeded in trapping the Athenian dictator, Hippias, and members of his government on the Acropolis. Spartans captured Hippias's children as they were being smuggled out of Athens and ransomed them to force Hippias to accede to the Spartans' demands and leave the city.

Overseen by Cleomenes I, Cleisthenes and Isagoras ruled Athens. Years later, when a struggle between them threatened civil war, Cleomenes ordered Cleisthenes out of Athens. He exiled seven hundred supporting Athenian families and threatened to replace Cleisthenes' Council of Five Hundred with a three-hundred-member council supportive of Isagoras. Isagoras was Cleomenes' protégé, and Athenians did not appreciate his efforts to install him on their throne. Struggles continued until Isagoras's entire party was executed. Isagoras was able to escape.

Cleisthenes and his seven hundred supporting families returned to Athens and began negotiations with Darius of Persia for a possible alliance. On hearing of Athens's deceit, Cleomenes gathered an army to attack the city. Cleomenes' co-monarch, Demaratus, joined the military forces to demonstrate unanimous Spartan support for the campaign. Cleomenes' main goal for the attack on Athens was to return Isagoras to the throne, not to punish it for its recent negotiations with Persia, as many thought. When Demaratus discovered the true nature of the campaign, the two monarchs argued. Co-

231

rinthian forces who had joined the Spartans refused to participate and went home. The campaign failed.

Early in the fifth century, Sparta's ancient enemy, Argos, refused to pay tribute. Cleomenes led his armies northward to Argosian territory to reestablish Sparta's authority. Before crossing the Erasinos River, Spartans offered sacrifices to the gods for support. Believing the sacrifices did not satisfy the gods, Cleomenes boarded his men on ships and instead attacked the Argosians at Sepeia. His victory was complete by about 494 B.C.E., but, in a controversial move, Cleomenes pursued a number of Argosians to a grove where they had taken refuge. Calling them out under the pretense of arranging for their ransom, Cleomenes executed fifty of Argos's leading citizens. Again citing religious reasons, he decided not to attack Argos and went home.

Three years later, a Persian invasion of Athens appeared imminent. Cleomenes received word that a number of local islands were paying homage to King Darius the Great of Persia, in particular the strategically located Aegina. Athens appealed to Cleomenes for support. Cleomenes led military forces to Aegina in 491 B.C.E. to arrest leading members of the offending parties. He was met by Krio, known as "the Ram." Krio refused to acknowledge Cleomenes' power to arrest, stating that he did not have Spartan governmental support for his campaign. If Sparta supported his cause, Krio asserted, both Spartan kings would have come to Aegina. Because of arguments between the monarchs in the struggle against Athens, Spartan law forbade any two rulers from participating together in the same campaign.

Cleomenes believed his co-king, Demaratus, was behind Krio's words and decided to try to remove him from office. He revived old rumors that Demaratus was illegitimate and therefore had no claim to the Spartan throne. When the oracle at Delphi was consulted as to his paternity, she affirmed his illegitimate status, and Spartans replaced Demaratus with his enemy Leotychides. Rumors began that Cleomenes had bribed the prophetess.

For a few months, Cleomenes and Leotychides worked well together. They further strengthened the Peloponnese against the Persian threat and managed to arrest Aeginetan leaders who opposed them. However, reports of Cleomenes' bribery of the Delphic oracle grew. Cleomenes became so unpopular that he was forced to flee to Thessaly and later Arcadia. While in Arcadia, Cleomenes put together a military force to retake his own city. He was recalled to Sparta where, on his return, his family had him arrested.

Cleomenes reportedly stabbed himself to death; however, it is also possible that his Ephorian enemies killed him.

SIGNIFICANCE   Though some historians claim that Cleomenes I suffered from intermittent mental illness, his actions in office and on the military front show him to have been a capable strategist. Rumors of madness may have been spread by his enemies to justify forcing him out of Sparta. Though he may not have spread Spartan rule as far as he desired, Cleomenes increased Sparta's power more than any ruler before him.

FURTHER READING

Boardman, John, Jasper Griffin, and Oswyn Murray, eds. *The Oxford History of Greece and the Hellenistic World*. New York: Oxford University Press, 2001.
Forrest, W. G. *A History of Sparta, 950-192 B.C.* 2d ed. London: Duckworth, 1980.
Grimal, Pierre. *Hellenism and the Rise of Rome*. New York: Delacorte Press, 1968.
Huxley, G. L. *Early Sparta*. New York: Barnes & Noble, 1970.
Walbank, F. W. *The Hellenistic World*. Rev. ed. Cambridge, Mass.: Harvard University Press, 1993.

Leslie A. Stricker

See also: Cleisthenes of Athens; Delphic Oracle; Hippias of Athens; Leonidas.

Cleomenes II

Born: Date unknown; Sparta, Greece
Died: c. 309 B.C.E.; Sparta, Greece
Category: Government and politics; military

LIFE   A year before Cleomenes II (klee-AHM-uh-neez) ascended the throne in 370 B.C.E., the great city-state of Sparta was brutally defeated at the Battle of Leuctra in Boeotia. What was once the most feared of cities had been reduced to a seemingly benign town. Under Cleomenes II, Sparta did not try to expand so much as to defend the territory it still had.

In 362 B.C.E., Thebes threatened the peninsula. After some initial successes in relieving Sparta of some of its possessions, the Theban threat encouraged Spartans to form a new coalition with their neighbors to fight their common enemy. Sparta was defeated during the ensuing battle, but Theban armies lost their leader and, with him, the will to continue.

SIGNIFICANCE   Afterward, negotiations over the reunification of the peninsula continued. After years of arguing and contending for power, Sparta rejoined the Achaean League in 332 B.C.E. Cleomenes II reigned during a time of great trouble, and perhaps his greatest accomplishment was to have held the defeated city together and thus prepare it for a resurgence of power.

FURTHER READING

Boardman, John, Jasper Griffin, and Oswyn Murray, eds. *The Oxford History of Greece and the Hellenistic World*. New York: Oxford University Press, 2001.

Forrest, W. G. *A History of Sparta, 950-192 B.C.* 2d ed. London: Duckworth, 1980.

Grimal, Pierre. *Hellenism and the Rise of Rome*. New York: Delacorte Press, 1968.

Huxley, G. L. *Early Sparta*. New York: Barnes & Noble, 1970.

Walbank, F. W. *The Hellenistic World*. Rev. ed. Cambridge, Mass.: Harvard University Press, 1993.

Leslie A. Stricker

See also: Achaean League; Leuctra, Battle of.

Cleomenes III

KING OF SPARTA (R. 235-219 B.C.E.)

Born: Date unknown; Sparta, Greece
Died: 219 B.C.E.; Alexandria, Egypt
Category: Government and politics; military

LIFE   Cleomenes III (klee-AHM-uh-neez) was the son of Leonidas II, who ruled Sparta from 254 to 235. Leonidas and his co-monarch, Agis IV, had ascended the Spartan throne during a time of financial crisis. Agis IV attempted to institute a program of social reform in Sparta. He believed that returning to a Lycurgan form of government would help Sparta regain its former glory. He proposed land redistribution so that every freeman would share equally in the city. To reform the financial situation, Agis called for the cancellation of all debts, a measure supported by many Spartans who owed creditors and by landowners who had mortgaged their properties.

While Agis was away at war, his support diminished in Sparta. Leonidas believed part of Agis's reform strategy included removing him from office. With Leonidas's consent, Agis was tried and executed. Though Leonidas was banished and forced into exile, he later returned and regained the throne. In an effort to bring unity to the city, Leonidas induced Agis's widow, Agiatis, to marry his son, Cleomenes III. Though the marriage was arranged, Cleomenes III fell in love with his wife and was swayed by her former husband's political ideas.

When Cleomenes III ascended the throne in 235, he rededicated himself to instituting Agis IV's social reforms and restoring a Lycurgan constitution. The people of Sparta were calling for change. Most of Sparta's land was held by only one hundred families. Fewer and fewer people in the city, only about seven hundred men, could declare themselves full citizens. As years passed, increasing numbers of poor called for more equitable land distributions and cancellation of debts.

By conducting a few successful military skirmishes, Cleomenes III strengthened Sparta's position in the Achaean League and earned support from the military. His reform ideas and relatively austere lifestyle gained him support from the people; however, his reforms were strongly opposed by rich landowners. The *gerousia*, the governing body of Sparta, refused to pass his measures. In 237, Cleomenes III staged a governmental coup and rearranged Sparta's government. He abolished the *gerousia* on the grounds that Lycurgus never sanctioned its creation. In addition, Cleomenes killed or exiled many of those who opposed him. He liberated thousands of serfs by allowing them to purchase their freedom for a fee, thus increasing the treasury as well. He succeeded in canceling debts and redistributing four thousand lots of land. At the same time, Cleomenes attracted and registered thousands of new citizens.

After the liberation of the serfs, three thousand men joined Cleomenes' phalanx of soldiers. He reintroduced traditional discipline into the military, preparing them to extend Sparta's influence throughout the Peloponnese. Agis IV had strengthened Sparta's position in the Achaean League by joining Aratus of Sicyon in a joint Peloponnesian defense against the Aeto-

Cleomenes III.
(Library of Congress)

lians. However, when Cleomenes III wanted to be named commander in chief of the Achaean forces, Aratus refused to acquiesce to his demands. Cleomenes quarreled with the Achaean League and then set out to break it up. The same Aratus who had assisted Agis IV against the Aetolians called on Antigonus III Doson of Macedonia to help the league in the impending attack from Sparta.

In the meantime, Cleomenes gained support for his cause from various Peloponnesian cities. He succeeded in taking Corinth, Hermione, Troezen, Pellene, Argos, Epidaurus, Philius, and Aratus. Commoners in these cities hoped that Cleomenes III would bring his social reforms with him and re-distribute land as he had in Sparta; they surrendered without a fight.

In 222 B.C.E., Cleomenes met Doson at Sellasia in the hills of north Sparta. Doson defeated the Spartan forces and forced Cleomenes to flee to Alexandria, where he hoped to find refuge with Egyptian ruler Ptolemy III. Cleomenes, however, failed to win support among the Egyptian people. He was reportedly killed in 219 during the palace purges that surrounded the accession of Ptolemy IV.

SIGNIFICANCE   Many commoners saw Cleomenes III as liberating them from their oppressive rulers. After the death of Cleomenes, the oligarchic regime was reinstated in Sparta. Doson and his armies later occupied Sparta and revoked Cleomenes' social reform projects.

FURTHER READING

Boardman, John, Jasper Griffin, and Oswyn Murray, eds. *The Oxford History of Greece and the Hellenistic World.* New York: Oxford University Press, 2001.

Forrest, W. G. *A History of Sparta, 950-192 B.C.* 2d ed. London: Duckworth, 1980.

Grimal, Pierre. *Hellenism and the Rise of Rome.* New York: Delacorte Press, 1968.

Huxley, G. L. *Early Sparta.* New York: Barnes & Noble, 1970.

Walbank, F. W. *The Hellenistic World.* Rev. ed. Cambridge, Mass.: Harvard University Press, 1993.

Leslie A. Stricker

See also: Achaean League; Spartan Constitution.

Cleon of Athens

Political leader

Born: Date unknown; place unknown
Died: 422 B.C.E.; Amphipolis, Macedonia
Category: Government and politics

Life   Cleon (KLEE-ahn) of Athens, the first demagogue, was a tanner who made enough money to enter political life by 430 B.C.E. He was perhaps a member of the boule, or council, in 428 B.C.E., and in 427 B.C.E. in the Mytilene debate, he proposed the execution of all male Mytileneans after that town's revolt in 428 B.C.E. He was successful, but the next day, the assembly reversed its decision. In 425 B.C.E., Cleon's criticism of Nicias of Athens's ability to capture besieged Spartans on Sphacteria led to his extraordinary command, and with Demosthenes' help, he captured the Spartans. When Sparta sued for peace, Cleon blocked the proposals.

Cleon's influence was now paramount in Athens. He was elected *strategos* (general) for 424 B.C.E., increased the tribute paid by the Athenian allies and pay for the jurors, and was perhaps responsible for Thucydides' exile for failing to save Amphipolis from Sparta. In 422 B.C.E., as *strategos*, he marched to Amphipolis, where he was defeated and killed in battle by a Spartan force. The presentation of Cleon in contemporary sources by Thucydides and Aristophanes is biased, but there is no question that he was an able orator who wanted to increase Athens's power.

Influence   Cleon was the first demagogue in the Athenian democracy and set a trend for the non-noble "new politicians" who followed him, thereby changing the dynamics of Athenian political life.

Further Reading

Andrews, James A. "Cleon's Hidden Appeals (Thucydides 3.37-40)." *Classical Quarterly* 50, no. 1 (2000): 45.
Kagan, Donald. *The Archidamian War.* Ithaca, N.Y.: Cornell University Press, 1974.

Woodhead, A. G. "Thucydides' Portrait of Cleon." *Mnemosyne* 13 (1960): 289-317.

Ian Worthington

See also: Archidamian War; Aristophanes; Nicias of Athens; Thucydides.

Cleopatra VII

Queen of Upper and Lower Egypt (r. 48-30 b.c.e.)

Born: 69 b.c.e.; Alexandria, Egypt
Died: August 3, 30 b.c.e.; Alexandria, Egypt
Also known as: Cleopatra Philopator
Category: Government and politics; women

LIFE   Cleopatra VII was the third child born to Ptolemy XII Neos Diony-sus (Auletes). She was educated in Greek and Egyptian traditions and bred for politics. As a child, she showed not only a remarkable intelligence but also a talent for learning languages. She was the only member of the Ptole-maic line able to speak the common language (Egyptian) of their subjects, a skill that would serve her in uniting Upper and Lower Egypt during her reign as pharaoh (51-30 b.c.e.).

Upon the death of Ptolemy XII in 51 b.c.e., Cleopatra became queen at the age of eighteen. According to Egyptian tradition, she married her brother Ptolemy XIII, then aged ten, to serve as co-ruler with him. This was a marriage in name only, and as the elder of the sovereigns, she was free to rule as she chose.

In 48 b.c.e., Ptolemy XIII's guardians forced Cleopatra from the throne. At about this time, Roman ruler Julius Caesar arrived in Alexandria in pur-suit of Pompey the Great. He and Cleopatra met and fell in love. Caesar helped Cleopatra regain her throne, and she became co-ruler with her youn-ger brother, Ptolemy XIV.

In 47 b.c.e., Cleopatra gave birth to Caesar's son. The child, Ptolemy XV Caesar, was called Caesarion by the Egyptians. At Caesar's invitation in 46 b.c.e., Cleopatra went to stay in Rome and took Caesarion and Ptol-emy XIV with her. They remained in Rome until Caesar was assassinated in 44 b.c.e.

In 41 b.c.e., Marc Antony invited Cleopatra to Tarsus (Turkey). She and Antony fell in love, had twins, and married in 37 b.c.e. The two had ambi-tious goals for an Egyptian-Roman alliance. Antony, one of three rulers of Rome, hoped to become sole ruler. Cleopatra hoped to put their children,

Cleopatra VII is unrolled from a carpet in front of Julius Caesar. (F. R. Niglutsch)

but especially her son Caesarion, in line as future Roman rulers.

Her ambitious plans for Egypt came to ruins in 30 B.C.E. Antony mistakenly thought Cleopatra was dead and killed himself. She committed suicide soon after learning of his suicide. Upon her death, the Ptolemaic line of Egyptian pharaohs ended. Caesarion was executed by the Romans, who feared he would claim to be heir to Caesar and thus Roman ruler.

INFLUENCE Cleopatra's diplomatic acumen and facility for foreign languages allowed her to unite, for a brief time, the Upper and Lower Nile valleys, earning her the title "mistress of two lands." She successfully ruled with her two brothers and with her son, Ptolemy Caesar. Her ability to speak Egyptian, and her concern for the welfare of her subjects, earned their respect and admiration. As the last ruler of the Macedonian Dynasty in Egypt, Cleopatra kept Egypt out of Roman hands through political and romantic alliances with Julius Caesar and Marc Antony.

FURTHER READING

Burstein, Stanley M. *The Reign of Cleopatra*. Westport, Conn.: Greenwood Press, 2004.

Flamarian, Edith. *Cleopatra: The Life and Death of a Pharaoh*. New York: Harry N. Abrams, 1997.

Foss, Michael. *The Search for Cleopatra*. New York: Arcade, 1997.

Walker, Susan, and Sally-Ann Ashton, eds. *Cleopatra Reassessed*. London: British Museum, 2003.

Lisa A. Wroble

See also: Actium, Battle of; Ptolemaic Dynasty; Ptolemaic Egypt.

Coins

The Greek city-states used coins as a means of exchange as they expanded their area of settlement and became economically sophisticated in their trade relations.

Date: From c. 640 B.C.E.
Category: Economics; trade and commerce
Locale: Greece

SUMMARY   The earliest Greek trade occurred during the Neolithic era and was opportunistic in nature. In response to a particular need or an unusual situation, Greeks ventured on the sea and engaged in rudimentary barter to secure what they needed or to gain an economic advantage. The leaders of the earliest Greek communities were eager to import luxury goods such as jewelry, decorative pottery, and ornamented weapons that they ultimately used as grave goods. The Greeks usually obtained their luxury goods from Levantine or Minoan traders who called on the Greeks of the mainland at infrequent intervals.

When the Greeks needed additional food supplies or raw materials such as wood or metals, they sought to trade their locally grown produce or locally manufactured goods for that which they needed from various traders who happened into the area. In terms of competition, however, the earliest Greek traders were at a decided disadvantage because Greece offered little in the way of natural resources to use as beginning trading capital. To compensate for this deficiency, the Greeks participated in a combination of commerce and piracy, trading with or attacking passing ships as the occasion allowed.

Greek merchant adventurers traded with the people who inhabited the Aegean islands and the various peoples who lived along the coasts of the Black, Ionian, and Mediterranean Seas. With increased experience at sea and a growing familiarity with overseas territories and peoples, the Greeks began the process of overseas colonization. Over an extended period of time, from the Late Bronze Age through the Iron Age, mainland Greeks colonized the islands of the Aegean and the coastal areas of Asia Minor. The greatest period of colonization, however, occurred from about 734 to 580 B.C.E., when the Greeks succeeded in founding more than three hundred Greek communities along the Mediterranean coasts of present-day Africa, Spain, France, southern Italy, and the northern shore of the Black Sea. With the notable exception of the Greek communities of the Black Sea region, all these Greek colonies developed into independent city-states.

For the most part, the newer areas of colonization had climates similar to that of mainland Greece. This factor not only enabled the Greeks overseas to practice their usual forms of agriculture without change but also helped them to adapt to their new surroundings quickly. In addition, the colonial areas commonly offered the Greeks more economic opportunities than they had ever had before. The Greeks in colonial areas wanted to have the foods and products they were used to having in their former homelands. There developed a significant and steady trade between the mother cities of mainland Greece and the daughter cities overseas in foodstuffs (olives, olive oil, wine, grain, and fish), raw materials (timber, marble, and metal ores), and manufactured goods (such as pottery).

Through their trade and colonization efforts, the Greeks came into contact with a number of people (particularly in Asia Minor and the Levant)

The face of Philip II of Macedonia on a coin. (Library of Congress)

245

who were more economically advanced than they were and who had developed more sophisticated political organizations than they had. Some of these people had writing and numerical systems through which they could record tax collections and maintain inventory lists of produce and weapons. The traders from these more advanced economies were able to conduct more complex economic transactions than just barter. To participate in these more complicated and many times more lucrative economic transactions, the Greeks had to adjust to these new realities. In addition to adapting the Phoenician alphabet to the Greek language, the Greeks adopted and improved on a new economic development—coinage.

Both archaeology and Greek tradition attribute the beginnings of coinage to the Lydians of the interior of Asia Minor. The Greeks, having colonized the coastal areas of Asia Minor, would have come into economic contact with the Lydians at a very early date and would have been one of the first people introduced to the concept of coinage. Coinage is simply a method of designating value on a specific amount of precious metal. When a state struck or marked a coin with its mint mark, it certified the purity and weight of the precious metal in the coin and guaranteed its value. Coinage enabled an individual or state to store value or wealth in the form of a coin of precious metal that could be used again at some time in the future. The earliest coins, however, represented relatively high values and were probably issued to facilitate large payments between and among the various independent states of Asia Minor.

The Lydians appear to have struck their first coins sometime around 640 B.C.E., and the Greeks soon followed suit. The earliest Lydian coins were of electrum, an alloy of gold and silver, and the Greeks usually struck their coins in silver. Although both the Lydians and the Greeks had access to gold, they rarely coined it because it represented such a high value in relationship to silver. It was the Greeks who developed, refined, and expanded the use of coinage. The island of Aegina off the Greek mainland was the first Greek city-state to issue a large number of silver coins, and they struck them with the image of a sea turtle. Soon, the Greeks recognized the Aeginetan "turtles" as a practical coin standard and used them as a medium of exchange throughout their trading area. Aegina came to dominate the seaborne trade within Greece and the Greek trade with Egypt and the other countries of the eastern Mediterranean. With the expansion of trade, other Greek city-states struck coins and used mint marks unique to their cities as their guarantee of value.

Although there was no international regulation of coinage, the Greeks

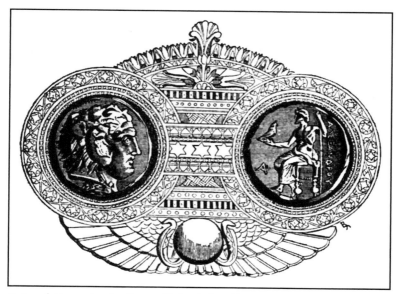

Coins of Alexander the Great. (F. R. Niglutsch)

realized early that there would be economic chaos if every Greek city-state issued coins according to its own arbitrary standard of weights and measures. Although Aegina was the earliest Greek city-state of the mainland to strike coins, its standard did not end up the sole standard for Greece. Greek city-states roughly adhered to, with local variations, one of two standards of coin weights and measures—the Aeginetan standard and the Euboic standard. Of the two weight systems, the Aeginetan system possessed the heavier weights, since it contained more silver in its coins. During the history of ancient Greece, the Euboic system gradually replaced the Aeginetan standard as the most common coin standard.

SIGNIFICANCE Whether coins were used as tribute payment or for payment for goods and services, the advent of coinage marked a great advance for the Greek city-states. When a state had to pay an obligation, the obligation did not have to be paid in bullion that would have to be weighed and assayed each time it was used in a transaction. This made trading simpler and allowed for far more complicated deals than could be accomplished by barter. Gradually by the fifth century B.C.E., Greek city-states began to mint

247

smaller denomination coinage to facilitate the economic transactions of the average person. This brought the convenience and standardization provided by the use of coins in trade to the level of the ordinary person, thereby increasing the level of economic transaction that an individual could make.

FURTHER READING

Carradice, Ian. *Greek Coins*. Austin: University of Texas Press, 1995.

Hasebroek, Johannes. *Trade and Politics in Ancient Greece*. Translated by L. M. Fraser and D. C. Macgregor. Chicago: Ares, 1978.

Lowry, S. Todd. *The Archaeology of Economic Ideas: The Classical Greek Tradition*. Durham, N.C.: Duke University Press, 1987.

Malkin, Irad. *Religion and Colonization in Ancient Greece*. Leiden, Netherlands: Brill, 1987.

Mattingly, Harold B. *From Coins to History: Selected Numismatic Studies*. Ann Arbor: University of Michigan Press, 2004.

Meadows, Andy, and Kirsty Shipton, eds. *Money and Its Uses in the Ancient Greek World*. New York: Oxford University Press, 2001.

Schaps, David M. *The Invention of Coinage and the Monetization of Ancient Greece*. Ann Arbor: University of Michigan Press, 2004.

Peter L. Viscusi

See also: Trade, Commerce, and Colonization.

Colossus of Rhodes

This enormous statue of the god Helios was constructed on the Greek island of Rhodes.

Date: Constructed 292-280 B.C.E., according to Pliny the Elder
Category: Art and architecture
Locale: City of Rhodes, Island of Rhodes

SUMMARY The Colossus (koh-LAW-suhs) was erected by the city of Rhodes to commemorate its successful resistance to Demetrius Polior-

This engraving depicts the Colossus of Rhodes astride the entrance to the harbor.
(Martin Heemskerck)

cetes' year-long siege of 305-304 B.C.E. The Rhodians financed this statue of their patron deity, the Sun god Helios, from the sale of Poliorcetes' abandoned siege equipment. The appearance of the statue, probably a standing nude male wearing a crown of Sun rays, is known only from ancient sources, mainly Strabo, Pliny the Elder, and Philon of Byzantium. Reportedly, the Rhodian sculptor Chares of Lindos, a pupil of Lysippus, was commissioned to oversee the project. The statue was composed of cast bronze sections over an iron framework and stood some 110 feet (33 meters) tall on a white marble base (compare the Statue of Liberty at 152 feet, or 46 meters). It was steadied by stones placed inside and took twelve years to complete.

The Colossus has been popularly depicted from the medieval period onward with its legs spanning the entrance to the Rhodian harbor later known as Mandraki. This reconstruction, however, is not possible, because the distance is more than 1,300 feet (396 meters). The Colossus stood only fifty-six years before it fell, broken at the knees, in an earthquake around 226 B.C.E. The statue lay in ruins until Arabs, invading Rhodes in 654 C.E., sold the remains as scrap metal to a Syrian. Tradition has it that nine hundred camels were needed to transport the fragments.

SIGNIFICANCE   The Colossus of Rhodes was the largest recorded statue from antiquity and one of the Seven Wonders of the Ancient World.

FURTHER READING

Berg, Christopher. *Amazeing Art: Wonders of the Ancient World*. New York: Quill, 2001.

Clayton, Peter A., and Martin J. Price, eds. Reprint. *The Seven Wonders of the Ancient World*. New York: Routledge, 1998.

Perrottet, Tony. "Journey to the Seven Wonders." *Smithsonian* 35, no. 3 (June, 2004): 114.

Romer, John, and Elizabeth Romer. *The Seven Wonders of the World: A History of the Modern Imagination*. New York: Henry Holt, 1995.

Lee Ann Turner

See also: Art and Architecture; Demetrius Poliorcetes; Lysippus; Strabo.

Corinna of Tanagra

POET

Flourished: Third or fifth century B.C.E.; Boeotia, Greece
Category: Poetry; literature; women

LIFE Corrina of Tanagra (kuh-RIHN-uh of TAN-uh-gruh) was either an archaizing Hellenistic poet of the third century B.C.E. or (following several ancient sources) a poet who flourished in the fifth century B.C.E. and was a rival of the Theban poet Pindar, whom she supposedly defeated five times in literary contests. Corinna is known for her choral narrative lyrics in simple diction and meter. Among her themes, addressed to the daughters of Tanagra, is "the courage of heroes and heroines in old myths."

INFLUENCE Though only fragments of her work survive, Corinna is esteemed among female poets second only to Sappho.

FURTHER READING

Barnstone, Willis. *Sappho and the Greek Lyric Poets.* New York: Schocken Books, 1988.

Mulroy, David. *Early Greek Lyric Poetry.* Ann Arbor: University of Michigan Press, 1992.

David J. Ladouceur

See also: Literature; Lyric Poetry; Pindar; Sappho.

Sack of Corinth

The sack of Corinth marked the end of Greek political autonomy and displayed the harsh tactics of mature Roman imperialism.

Date: 146 B.C.E.
Category: Wars and battles
Locale: Greece

SUMMARY Corinth's fall in the summer of 146 B.C.E. came as the final event of what the Romans called the *bellum Achaicum*, or Achaean War, the fifth Roman military intervention into the eastern Mediterranean region since 200 B.C.E. Unlike earlier invasions, which had targeted the powerful kings of Macedonia and Syria, this conflict was a war against a Greek state: the Achaean League, one of several confederacies of city-states that had come to prominence during the late Classical and Hellenistic periods. Since joining the league in 243 B.C.E., Corinth had emerged as an influential member and frequently served as a site for Achaean League congresses and meetings with foreign ambassadors. As a result, Corinth was a logical target for punitive action following the Roman victory over the league. The fame of its wealth and artistic treasures made it an even more appealing victim, and its international prominence as overseer of the Panhellenic Osthmian Games heightened the lesson of its destruction.

The motives behind Rome's halting assertion of control over Greece are extremely complex, but two things must be understood: The Romans did not set out to conquer Greece, and initially the Greeks did not find the Roman presence unwelcome. For example, the Romans undertook the Second Macedonian War (200-196 B.C.E.) against Philip V (238-179 B.C.E.) at the behest of several Greek states that had suffered Philip's depredations, and they fought the war with the support of most Greek states, including the Achaean League. Following Philip's defeat, the victorious commander Titus Quinctius Flamininus (c. 229-174 B.C.E.) held a grand Panhellenic ceremony at Corinth at which he declared the Greek states to be free and then evacuated all Roman forces from the region. The Achaeans also supported Rome in its war against Seleucid king Antiochus the Great (r. 223-187

B.C.E.), but friction soon arose as the aggressively independent Achaean general Philopoemen (c. 252-182 B.C.E.) ignored Roman appeals for restraint and forcibly incorporated the city-state of Sparta into the league. His death in 182 B.C.E. allowed a pro-Roman Achaean leader Callicrates (d. 149 B.C.E.) to adopt a more cooperative relationship with Rome, but this stance invited charges of collaboration. Stung by these attacks, Callicrates urged the Roman senate to support their Greek friends and show displeasure with their enemies—something the Romans would do with a vengeance during their next military intervention.

The Third Macedonian War (171-167 B.C.E.) revealed a hardening of Roman attitudes, not only toward defeated opponents but also toward Greek states that had displayed lukewarm support for the Roman war effort. Thus, Illyrians and Macedonians saw their monarchies abolished and their countries divided. In Epirus, the Romans sacked seventy Greek towns that had sided with Macedonia and enslaved 150,000 people. In Boeotia, the fate of Haliartos exactly presaged the doom that would later befall Corinth: slaughter, enslavement, and destruction. With the aid of a Roman garrison, the pro-Roman faction of the Aetolian League executed 550 citizens suspected of antipathy to Rome. Some one thousand leading Achaean citi-

The citadel of Corinth. (F. R. Niglutsch)

zens named by Callicrates were deported to Italy, where they remained for seventeen years. The absence of these opposition leaders at first strengthened the hand of the pro-Roman faction in Achaea, but the continued holding of the hostages engendered growing resentment.

The release of the surviving Achaean captives in 150 B.C.E., along with the death of Callicrates in the following year, stiffened the Achaean League's sense of independence at a crucial time, for Sparta had chosen this moment to reassert its autonomy and appealed to Rome. Diaeus (d. 146 B.C.E.), a rival of Callicrates, defended the Achaean position before the Roman senate, which promised to send a ten-man commission to settle the dispute. Perhaps because of the senate's preoccupation with Rome's Third Punic War (149-146 B.C.E.) against Carthage, the commission was not sent for more than a year, during which the dispute intensified. At this moment, the appearance of a pretender to the Macedonian throne brought forth the army that would soon threaten Achaea. In 148 B.C.E., Quintus Caecilius Metellus (d. 115 B.C.E.) defeated the pretender and stayed on with his army to complete the pacification of Macedonia. Again the Achaeans had supported the Roman campaign, but they did not respond positively to Metellus's initial request that they show restraint in their conflict with Sparta. A second embassy from Metellus finally convinced the league to call a truce and await the promised Roman commission.

Headed by Lucius Aurelius Orestes, the commission arrived at Corinth in the summer of 147 B.C.E. and delivered a stunning decision: It not only endorsed Sparta's secession from the league but also decreed that Corinth, Argos, Heracleia, and Orchomenos were to be detached as well. News of this ultimatum provoked a furious response throughout the city. The Roman commissioners tried in vain to save Spartans who had taken refuge with them and at one point were themselves pelted with filth. An outraged Orestes returned to Rome, where he claimed that the lives of the Roman commissioners had been in danger and demanded retaliation. Another Roman embassy accomplished little, and formal contacts between the league and the senate ceased at this point. The Achaean general Critolaus (d. 146 B.C.E.) spent the winter of 147-146 B.C.E. preparing for war, and the senate authorized Lucius Mummius to raise an army and proceed against Achaea.

When Critolaus led the Achaean League army north in 146 B.C.E. to lay siege to the rebellious town of Heracleia, he was probably unaware of Mummius's preparations. On one hand, perhaps recalling Philopoemen's successful acts of defiance, he may not have expected the Romans to back up their threats with force. Alternatively, he may have anticipated an eventual attack by Metellus but thought he had time to take up a position at Thermopylae, where he might reasonably attempt to confront Roman forces coming down from Macedonia. In any case, he was unprepared for Metellus's ferocious onslaught, which routed the Achaean army. Critolaus himself disappeared in the confusion, a victim of the battle or a suicide. Metellus then took control of the Isthmus of Corinth and tried to upstage Mummius by offering a negotiated settlement, but the Achaean leadership refused and resolved to resist with a hastily assembled force made up primarily of freed slaves. At this juncture Mummius arrived, dismissed Metellus back to Macedonia, and with a fresh army overcame Diaeus and the Achaeans in battle at the Isthmus. Diaeus fled to his home city of Megalopolis, where he killed his wife and himself to avoid capture.

The destruction of Corinth followed shortly in two phases. Two days after the battle at the Isthmus, Mummius subjected the city to a brutal sack. Most of the men were killed, the women and children enslaved, and the city systematically looted. Scores of artistic treasures were shipped back to Italy, where they adorned temples and public buildings. Some weeks after this initial sack, a ten-man commission arrived from Rome to impose a final settlement. The commissioners dismembered the Achaean League and placed Greece under the oversight of the military governor in Macedonia, which was now organized as a Roman province. As for Corinth, part of its territory was declared Roman public land and reserved for exploitation by Romans; the rest was ceded to the neighboring city-state of Sicyon, which also received control of the Isthmian Games. Finally, citing as justification the insolent treatment of Orestes' commission, the commissioners ordered that the city be razed and burned.

SIGNIFICANCE   For a century, the site remained a wasteland inhabited by a few squatters and tomb robbers, who raided the cemeteries for valuables. Thus, Corinth ceased to exist, until Julius Caesar refounded the city in 44 B.C.E. as a colony for his veterans and others. Ironically, in this reincarnation, the city would later flourish as the capital of the entire Greek region, now called the Roman province of Achaea.

FURTHER READING
Derow, P. S. "Rome, the Fall of Macedon, and the Sack of Corinth." In *Rome and the Mediterranean to 133 B.C.* Vol. 8 in *The Cambridge An-*

cient History, edited by A. E. Astin et al. 2d ed. New York: Cambridge University Press, 1990.

Erskine, Andrew, ed. *A Companion to the Hellenistic World*. Malden, Mass.: Blackwell, 2003.

Gruen, Eric S. *The Hellenistic World and the Coming of Rome*. 2 vols. Berkeley: University of California Press, 1984.

Harris, William V. *War and Imperialism in Republican Rome, 327-70 B.C.* Oxford, England: Oxford University Press, 1985.

Kallet-Marx, Robert Morstein. *Hegemony to Empire: The Development of the Roman Imperium in the East from 148-62 B.C.* Berkeley: University of California Press, 1995.

James T. Chambers

See also: Achaean League; Achaean War; Antiochus the Great; Philip V; Philopoemen.

Corinthian War

Unable to achieve victory on their own, the Spartans invited the Persians to intervene.

Date: 395-386 B.C.E.
Category: Wars and battles
Locale: Greece

SUMMARY   Both the Persians and Sparta's erstwhile allies became alarmed by the success of the Spartan expedition in Asia Minor led by Agesilaus II of Sparta.
In 395 B.C.E., the Persians bribed politicians in Argos, Corinth, Thebes, and possibly Athens to instigate a war against Sparta, and an anti-Sparta coalition was formed. After the Spartan defeat at the Battle of Haliartus in Boeotia in 395 B.C.E., Agesilaus II was recalled from Asia Minor. In 394 B.C.E., the Spartans won two land battles, but these victories were negated by the defeat at sea to the renegade Athenian general Conon, in command of the Persian fleet, which put an end to Spartan domination of the sea. Desultory fighting around Corinth ensued. In 392 B.C.E., the Spartans, worried about increasing Athenian naval activity, attempted unsuccessfully to make separate peace agreements with Persia and within Greece. Eventually the threat of renewed Athenian imperialism caused the Persians to intervene in support of Sparta and impose the King's Peace (also known as the Peace of Antalcidas) of 386 B.C.E.

SIGNIFICANCE   The King's Peace thwarted the imperial ambitions of Athens, Argos, and Thebes and confirmed Sparta's hegemony over Greece.

FURTHER READING
Hamilton, Charles D. *Sparta's Bitter Victories*. Ithaca, N.Y.: Cornell University Press, 1979.

Strauss, Barry S. *Athens After the Peloponnesian War*. Ithaca, N.Y.: Cornell University Press, 1986.

Xenophon. *Hellenika*. Translated by Peter Kretz. Warminister, England: Aris & Phillips, 1995.

Frances Skoczylas Pownall

See also: Agesilaus II of Sparta; King's Peace.

Cosmology

In Greece, the pre-Socratic philosophers formulated theories of the cosmos, setting aside previous mythopoeic explanations and launching an empirical and scientific intellectual revolution.

Date: 600-500 B.C.E.
Category: Astronomy and cosmology; philosophy; science and technology
Locale: Greece

SUMMARY Before the sixth century B.C.E., human beings everywhere explained the world in mythological terms. These myths depicted humankind dependent on the wills of inscrutable gods who created the world and acted on their all-too-human personal whims. Nonliving and powerful natural forces were "animated," given living souls by the prelogical mentality of early people, otherwise quite sophisticated in building pyramids or irrigation canals. No other explanation was available to them, no scientific foundation on which to build a real understanding of the world and nature.

Similarly, most Greeks honored the epic poets Homer (early ninth century-late ninth century B.C.E.) and Hesiod (fl. c. 700 B.C.E.) as their teachers. Hesiod's *Theogonia* (c. 700 B.C.E.; *Theogony*, 1728) is the earliest Greek version of the origins of the cosmos. The Greek term *kosmos* means the organized world order. In Hesiod's account, the origin of all things was *chaos*, formless space or yawning watery deep, the opposite of *kosmos*. In time there emerged, either independently or by sexual union, Gaia (Earth); Tartaros (Hades); Eros (Love); Night, Day, and Aither (upper air); Sea and Ouranos (Sky); and boundless Okeanos (Ocean). A generation of powerful Titans was engendered, and finally the Olympian gods descended from Ouranos and Gaia.

About 600 B.C.E., in Ionia (western Turkey), a new way of perceiving the world was beginning. Confronted by the confusing mythologies of ancient Near Eastern peoples, their own no better, a handful of Greeks over

259

three generations attempted to explain the origins and components of the seen world without mythology. Their great discovery was that to one seeking knowledge—the philosopher—the world manifests internal order and discernible regularity. Nature can be understood. The world is a *kosmos*.

From allusions in Homer and Hesiod came hints. The sky was thought to be a metallic hemispheric bowl covering the disk of earth. The lower space immediately above the disk was *aër*, breathable air; the upper part of the bowl-space was *ouranos* or *aither*. Below its surface, the earth's deep roots reached down to Tartaros, the deepest part of Hades (the underworld realm of the dead), as far below earth as sky is above it. Okeanos, infinitely wide, encircled the disk of earth and was the source of all fresh and salt waters. Such a mixture of the empirical and the imaginative was common to most mythopoeic cosmologies.

Thales of Miletus (c. 624–c. 548 B.C.E.) was the first to rationalize the myths. He conceived the earth-disk as floating on the ocean and held the single substance of the world to be water. His reasoning, according to Aristotle, was that water can be gaseous, liquid, and solid; life requires water; Homer had surrounded the earth by Okeanos. As a unified source of all things, Thales' choice of water was a good guess, but it begged for alternatives. More important, in reducing multiple things to water, Thales had taken a first step in establishing inductive reasoning (from particular examples to general principles) as a scientific methodology.

Anaximander (c. 610–c. 547 B.C.E.), companion of Thales, was a polymath: astronomer, geographer, evolutionist, philosopher-cosmologist. It is nearly impossible to do justice to his intellectual achievement. He was the first Greek to write in prose. He said that animal life began in the sea and that humans evolved from other animals. He made the first world map, a circle showing Europe and Asia plus Africa equal in size, all surrounded by ocean. Anaximander's cosmos was a sphere with a drum-shaped Earth floating in space at its center. The Sun, stars, and Moon revolved around the Earth, seen through openings in the metallic dome of the sky.

In place of Thales' water, Anaximander offered *apeiron*, an eternal, undefined, and inexhaustible basic stuff from which everything came to be and to which everything returns. It is a sophisticated chaos. Convinced by his own logic, Anaximander imputed an ethical necessity to this process. Things coming to be and claiming their share of *apeiron* thus deprive others of existence. So, in his words, "they must render atonement each to the other according to the ordinances of Time." This eternal process operates throughout the cosmos. Using terms such as *kosmos* (order), *diké* (justice),

Xenophanes, the only ancient Greek philosopher to posit monotheism.
(Hulton Archive/Getty Images)

and *tisis* (retribution), Anaximander enunciated the exalted idea that nature itself is subject to universal moral laws.

The contributions of Anaximenes of Miletus (early sixth century-latter sixth century B.C.E.) pale before those of Anaximander. What best defines

261

Anaximenes is his empirical approach. He posited air as the primal stuff that gives rise to all things. Observing air condensing into water, he conceived a maximum condensation of air into stone. Similarly, by rarefaction, air becomes fire or soul. The Earth and other heavenly bodies, being flat, ride on air in its constant motion.

Xenophanes (c. 570-c. 478 B.C.E.), an Ionian who had moved to Italy, represents a new generation of thinkers. He interpreted the new natural explanations of the universe that had challenged the older Hesiodic mythopoeic construct as the abandonment of the old, often immoral, anthropomorphic gods, who dressed in clothes and spoke Greek. He posited a single spiritual creator god who controls the universe without effort, by pure thought. In this monotheism, he was alone among the Greeks.

Insightfully, Xenophanes said human knowledge about the universe is limited and the whole truth may never be known. He taught that natural events have natural, not divine, causes. The rainbow is only a colored cloud. The sea is the source of all waters, winds, and clouds. From sea fossils found in rocks, his cosmogony deduced a time when land was under water. Civilization was the work of men, not gods. Xenophanes was a skeptic who trusted only his own observations about the world.

Pythagoras (c. 580-c. 500 B.C.E.), an Ionian mathematician in southern Italy, had noticed that the sounds of lyre strings varied according to their length and that harmonies were mathematically related. He saw that proportion can be visually perceived in geometrical figures. From these notions he and his followers described a cosmos structured on a mathematical model. Instead of adopting Anaximander's "justice" or the Logos of Heraclitus of Ephesus (c. 540-c. 480 B.C.E.) as the dominant organizing principle, the Pythagoreans preferred numerical harmony. Pythagoras thus added a dimension to the ancient concepts of due proportion and the golden mean that pervaded Greek thought. These concepts are seen in Greek sculpture and architecture and as moral principles in lyric and dramatic poetry and historical interpretations, where *hybris* (excess) and *sophrosyné* (moderation) were fundamental principles of human behavior.

Inevitably, Greek physical philosophy began to investigate the process of knowing. Number is unchanging; ten is always ten. In a world of apparently infinite diversity and flux, numbers can be known more perfectly than other objects of experience. Though the Pythagoreans went too far in trying to explain everything by numbers, they taught that a nature based on mathematical harmony and proportion was knowable.

Heraclitus argued that change, though sometimes imperceptible, is the common element in all things. All change, he said, takes place along continuums of opposite qualities, such as the hot-cold line or dry-moist line. His contribution, however, was his idea of Logos as the hidden organizing principle of the cosmos. Logos maintains a protective balance (the golden mean again) among all the oppositional tensions in the world.

Although Parmenides (c. 515-after 436 B.C.E.) and Democritus (c. 460-c. 370 B.C.E.) fall outside the chronological scope of the sixth century B.C.E., their contributions of logic to the Greek discovery of the cosmos merit some attention. In the mid-fifth century, Democritus reasoned to a world built of the smallest thinkable indivisible particles: atoms. Parmenides—struck by the constant flux of the physical world and seeking, as Pythagoras, an unchanging object of knowledge that mind can grasp—saw existence, or Being, as the common element of things in the cosmos. He proposed the logic that while things change, Being itself cannot change, for nothing and no place exists outside the sphere of Being, so nothing could enter or leave. He is thus the most metaphysical of the philosophers, initiating ideas that would only be completed by Plato and Aristotle, the greatest of the philosophers.

SIGNIFICANCE The significance of the Ionian philosophers is that, within little more than a century after breaking with mythopoeic interpretations of the world, they had asserted its atomic makeup, conceived human evolution, discovered induction and logic, and practiced a curiosity about all natural phenomena. This was one of history's great intellectual revolutions, the origins of scientific speculation.

FURTHER READING

Gill, Mary Louise, and Pierre Pellegrin. *A Companion to Ancient Philosophy*. Malden, Mass.: Blackwell, 2005.

Kirk, G. S., and J. E. Raven. *The Presocratic Philosophers*. 2d ed. New York: Cambridge University Press, 1984.

Long, A. A. *The Cambridge Companion to Early Greek Philosophy*. New York: Cambridge University Press, 1999.

Morgan, Kathryn A. *Myth and Philosophy from the Presocratics to Plato*. New York: Cambridge University Press, 2000.

O'Grady, Patricia F. *Meet the Philosophers of Ancient Greece: Everything You Always Wanted to Know About Ancient Greek Philosophy but Didn't Know Who to Ask*. Burlington, Vt.: Ashgate, 2005.

Osborne, Catherine. *Presocratic Philosophy: A Very Short Introduction.* New York: Oxford University Press, 2004.

Popper, Karl R. *The World of Parmenides: Essays on the Presocratic Enlightenment.* Edited by Arne F. Petersen and Jørgen Mejer. New York: Routledge, 1998.

Ring, Merrill. *Beginning with the Presocratics.* 2d ed. New York: McGraw-Hill, 1999.

Roochnik, David. *Retrieving the Ancients: An Introduction to Greek Philosophy.* Malden, Mass.: Blackwell, 2004.

Waterfield, Robin, ed. *The First Philosophers: The Presocratics and the Sophists.* New York: Oxford University Press, 2000.

Daniel C. Scavone

See also: Anaximander; Anaximenes of Miletus; Democritus; Heraclitus of Ephesus; Hesiod; Mythology; Parmenides; Philosophy; Pre-Socratic Philosophers; Pythagoras; Religion and Ritual; Science; Thales of Miletus; Xenophanes.

Crates of Athens

ACTOR AND PLAYWRIGHT

Flourished: c. 449-c. 424 B.C.E.; Athens, Greece
Category: Theater and drama

LIFE   Crates (KRAYT-eez) of Athens acted and wrote comedies in Athens in the middle of the fifth century B.C.E., but nothing is known of his life outside his career. He acted in the plays of Cratinus before producing his own plays. As a playwright, he won in the dramatic competition of the Great Dionysia at least three times. The titles of seven of his plays are known: *Geitones* (*Neighbors*), *Heroes*, *Lamia* (*Goblin*), *Paidiai* (*Games*), *Theria* (*Animals*), *Samioi* (*Samians*), and *Tolmai* (*Courage*). Exact dates for the plays are not known; all were translated into English in 1931. None of his plays survives complete. About sixty fragments are known, none longer than ten lines. *Animals* has the most interesting remains. Fragments refer to a utopia in which furniture and utensils work by themselves and to talking animals who urge humans not to eat meat.

INFLUENCE   In *De poetica* (c. 335-323 B.C.E.; *Poetics*, 1705), Aristotle says Crates was the first Athenian to abandon personal abuse in his comedies and instead create plots and stories of universal interest. Crates is also said to have introduced drunken characters to the stage. In *Hippēs* (424 B.C.E.; *The Knights*, 1812), Aristophanes refers to Crates approvingly as a predecessor.

FURTHER READING
Kassel, R., and C. Austin. *Poetae Comici Graeci*. Vol. 4. Berlin: Walter de Gruyter, 1983.
Norwood, Gilbert. *Greek Comedy*. London: Methuen, 1931.
Sommerstein, Alan H. *Greek Drama and Dramatists*. New York: Routledge, 2002.

Wilfred E. Major

See also: Aristophanes; Aristotle; Cratinus; Literature; Performing Arts; Sports and Entertainment.

Cratinus

PLAYWRIGHT

Born: Date unknown; place unknown
Died: c. 420 B.C.E.; place unknown
Also known as: Kratinos
Category: Theater and drama

LIFE   Cratinus (kruh-TI-nuhs) produced comedies successfully for some thirty years, from the 450's to the 420's B.C.E. More than twenty of his plays are known and numerous fragments exist, but there are no complete plays and no fragments of more than ten complete consecutive lines. An ancient summary of the *Dionysus Alexander* reveals that the play spoofed the origin of the Trojan War. A clowning Dionysus takes the place of Paris (also known as Alexander) to kidnap Helen and consequently start the Trojan War. Another play, *Nemesis*, told a silly version of the birth of Helen. Besides the mythological travesty, these plays satirized prominent Athenians of the day, most notably Pericles. Cratinus earned a reputation as a vicious satirist, although he was capable of producing apolitical comedy such as the *Odysseuses*, which parodied the Cyclops episode from Homer's *Odyssey* (c. 725 B.C.E.; English translation, 1614). In his later years, Cratinus was mocked by Aristophanes as a washed-up drunk. Cratinus retaliated in 423 B.C.E. with *Pytine* (*The Bottle*), in which he staged his own rejection of alcoholism in favor of his allegorical wife, Comedy. He resoundingly beat Aristophanes in competition with the play, and this competition is the last known activity of Cratinus.

INFLUENCE   Cratinus was the earliest of the great triad of comedians of Old Comedy, along with Aristophanes and Eupolis. He is credited with establishing the vitality and characteristics of the genre.

FURTHER READING
Heath, Malcom. "Aristophanes and His Rivals." *Greece & Rome* 37 (October, 1990): 143-158.

Kassel, R., and C. Austin. *Poetae Comici Graeci*. Vol. 4. Berlin: Walter de Gruyter, 1983.

Norwood, Gilbert. *Greek Comedy*. London: Methuen, 1931.

Rosen, Ralph Mark. *Old Comedy and the Iambographic Tradition*. Atlanta: Scholars Press, 1988.

Rufell, Ian. "A Total Write-Off: Aristophanes, Cratinus, and the Rhetoric of Comic Competition." *Classical Quarterly* 52, no. 1 (2002): 138.

Sommerstein, Alan H. *Greek Drama and Dramatists*. New York: Routledge, 2002.

Wilfred E. Major

See also: Aristophanes; Crates of Athens; Eupolis; Homer; Performing Arts; Pericles; Sports and Entertainment; Troy.

Crete

The site of one of the earliest civilizations in Greece and of the Minoans during the Bronze Age.

Date: 3000 B.C.E.-700 C.E.
Category: Cities and civilizations
Locale: Mediterranean Sea

BACKGROUND   The island of Crete (KREET) is located southeast of mainland Greece, midway between the Greek mainland and Africa or Asia Minor, and bounded on the north by the Aegean Sea and on the south by the Mediterranean Sea. Crete is about 152 miles (250 kilometers) from east to west at its greatest width and 35 miles (57 kilometers) from north to south at its greatest length. Crete is very mountainous but also has grassy plains.

HISTORY   The earliest evidence of agriculture in Greece is found at Knossos on Crete and in Thessaly. Neolithic sites on Crete containing evidence of agriculture date back to the seventh millennium B.C.E. Later in the Neolithic period, sites show signs of trade with other peoples across the Aegean. Being an island, Crete was less susceptible to movements and invasions than mainland Greece, and contact with Anatolia, Egypt, and the Near East accelerated the development of a Bronze Age civilization around 2600 B.C.E. At about this time, it appears that settlers from Egypt or Libya came to Crete. These settlers, however, were not Egyptians or Semites but probably Indo-Europeans.

Crete was home to the Bronze Age Minoan civilization, first discovered by archaeologist Sir Arthur Evans in 1894. Evans excavated the site of Knossos in the north central area of the island from 1900 to 1941 and partially reconstructed its palace. Evans named the Bronze Age civilization that he discovered "Minoan," after legendary King Minos. One of Evans's major accomplishments was recognizing that the Mycenaean civilization had its roots in the older Minoan civilization. Evans divided the civilization's chronology into Early Minoan (c. 3400-2100 B.C.E.), Middle Minoan (c. 2100-1500 B.C.E.), and Late Minoan (c. 1500-1100 B.C.E.).

Smaller palaces with ground plans similar to the one at Knossos were built at Phaistos, Mallia, Gournia, Khania, and Kato Zakro; all are in an enclosing valley near the sea. The preferred chronology for Minoan civilization during the latter half of the twentieth century is based on the dates of the building of the palaces on Crete, their destruction by an earthquake, their rebuilding, and their eventual final destruction. This chronology is as follows: Pre-Palace period (c. 3100-1925 B.C.E.), Old Palace period

The throne located in one of the many elaborate rooms in the ruins of the Palace of Minos at Knossos. (Courtesy, Hellenic Ministry of Culture)

269

(c. 1925-1725 B.C.E.), New Palace period (c. 1725-1380 B.C.E.), and Post-Palace period (c. 1380-1000 B.C.E.).

The fall of the Minoan civilization is attributed to the eruption and implosion of the Aegean island of Thera (modern Thíra) north of Crete. Archaeological remains were first discovered there in 1866. It is theorized that the implosion of Thera (c. 1623 B.C.E.) caused a massive tsunami that destroyed the Minoan fleet, leaving the island vulnerable to Mycenaean occupation. After 1380 B.C.E., the palaces on Crete—with the exception of the palace at Knossos—were damaged by fire and sword. After the fall of the palaces, there is evidence of Mycenaean occupation on Crete. The written script switched from Linear A to Linear B, which was used on the mainland, and the art became more symmetrical, less colorful, and distinctly Mycenaean. The governance of the island changed to city-states ruled by an assembly consisting of noblemen. Minoan civilization seems to have continued, however, on the western end of the island at Khania. Around 1100 B.C.E., the palace at Knossos was destroyed by the Dorians or by the Sea Peoples, according to legend, corresponding to the fall of Mycenaean civilization on mainland Greece.

Not much is known of Crete between about 1100 and 700 B.C.E. Possibly Mycenaean refugees from the mainland and the Peloponnese settled there during this period, and during the eighth century B.C.E., Greek culture emerged on Crete, which became one of the Greek colonies. Likewise, not much of significance occurred on Crete during the Greek Classical and Roman eras. In 67 B.C.E., Rome conquered Crete and the island was integrated into the Roman province of Cyrenaica, with Gortyn as the capital. The Romans built majestic structures at Gortyn, including the Praetorium and the Odeion. The law code of Gortyn, carved in blocks, was found next to the Odeion. In 324 C.E., Crete was annexed into the Eastern Roman Empire, and Christianity was established on the island, which would become an important center for icon painting during the Middle Ages.

ARCHITECTURE AND CITY PLANNING　　The palace at Knossos was built around 1700 B.C.E. on the ruins of an earlier palace, which had been built around 2000 B.C.E. and was destroyed by an earthquake. Both palaces were asymmetrical and labyrinthine in plan, with three or more levels connected by shafts that provided the lower levels with ventilation and light. The second palace was larger than the first. Evans partially reconstructed what he called the "Palace of King Minos" at Knossos, which, including its porches and outbuildings, covers six acres (or roughly two and a half hectares) of land, and he restored many of its fresco paintings.

The unfortified palace was located about three miles (nearly five kilometers) from the sea and was the center of a thriving city of approximately eighty-two thousand people. Although the palace was unfortified, access to it was limited. Its main entrance was on the eastern end through a set of mazelike corridors. Most likely, the legend of the labyrinth originated with this entrance. The northern entrance to the palace went off into the hinterland, and the southern entrance led to a porch.

The palace was composed of distinct areas such as public areas with a throne room, living areas with such amenities as bathtubs and a toilet opening to a drain, and storage areas with giant storage jars (*pithoi*). The drainage system in the palace, with its open stone drains and clay pipes, is remarkably sophisticated. Evans's reconstruction includes red, cast-concrete, downward-sloping columns to replace the original wooden ones, and a grand staircase. The center of the palace was a large, rectangular court measuring 161 by 89 feet (49 by 27 meters). At the northwest corner of the palace is a stepped theatrical area.

LAW   In 1884 in Prinia, the site of an important Archaic sanctuary dating from the seventh century B.C.E., inscriptions were found of the law code of Gortyn (700-600 B.C.E.) dealing with family law, inheritance, slavery, and punishments for crimes. This is the oldest law code known in Europe.

LANGUAGE AND LITERATURE   No literature from ancient Crete survives, but there are numerous references to Minoan cities in Homer's *Iliad* (c. 750 B.C.E.; English translation, 1611), and Crete figures heavily in Greek mythology. In his *Geōgraphica* (c. 7 B.C.E.; *Geography*, 1917-1933), Strabo wrote that Crete was the birthplace of Zeus, who was born in a cave on Mount Ida. (Other legends relate that the cave was on Mount Dicte.) The Cretans viewed Zeus as a seasonal god who died and was reborn again the next season. His legendary tomb is located on Mount Juktas.

Legend relates that Zeus mated with the mortal Europa, who gave birth to three children: Minos, king of Crete, who is mentioned by Homer; Rhadamanthys, another king of Crete; and Sarpedon. Minos's wife, Pasiphae, aided by Daedalus, mated with a bull and gave birth to the monstrous Minotaur—a creature half man and half bull, who lived inside the laby-

Theseus at the Minotaur's labyrinth. (F. R. Niglutsch)

rinth. Every year King Minos demanded that the Athenians sacrifice seven youths and seven maidens to the minotaur until it was slain by Theseus, aided by King Minos's daughter, Ariadne. The princess fell in love with Theseus and supplied him with thread, with which he found his way out of the labyrinth.

The creator of the labyrinth was the Athenian Daedalus, who lost favor with the king and was imprisoned in a tower. He fashioned wings from feathers and wax in order to escape Crete but lost his son Icarus in the attempt. Icarus flew too close to the Sun, which melted the wax, and he fell into the sea and was drowned. Minos was also regarded as a wise king and lawgiver and was one of the judges in the underworld. Heracles fought the Cretan bull as one of his twelve labors. In his *Ethika* (after c. 100 C.E.; *Moralia*, 1603), Plutarch says the word "syncretism" (Greek *synkrētizein*) is derived from *syn* ("together") and *krēte* ("Crete") because the Cretans often quarreled among themselves but united against enemies.

RELIGION AND RITUAL   Although there is not much firm evidence about religious practices on ancient Crete, artwork yields clues. For example, a Minoan frescoed sarcophagus found in a tomb at Hagia Triada indicates a blood sacrifice associated with funerary rites. One side of the sarcophagus portrays a bull being sacrificed, with its blood draining into a rhyton (a slender, conical ceremonial vessel), as a female (priestess?) worships in front of an altar and a man plays the double flutes. The other side shows men carrying models of two bulls and a boat; men and women carrying vases and pouring a liquid into a bowl flanked by columns topped by double axes; and a shrouded man who has been interpreted as the spirit of the deceased. This indicates belief in an afterlife. In addition, small figurines made of faience (earthenware with opaque glazes), have been found in altars in the Minoan palaces. These figurines are women wearing bell-shaped skirts and bolero-style jackets, with their breasts exposed. They are called "snake goddesses" because they are handling snakes and have divine qualities, such as their tall, distinctive hats. Snakes have chthonic associations, so the figures are generally believed to represent fertility goddesses or priestesses involved in fertility rites.

SPORTS AND ENTERTAINMENT   A fresco from the palace at Knossos portrays three young people playing a "bull-leaping" game, which is theorized to have taken place in the theatrical area of the palace. Figurines in the palace also portray participants in a bull-leaping game, and other frescoes portray spectators filling the theatrical area, watching some sort of event, perhaps the bull sport.

VISUAL ARTS   Fresco paintings within the palace at Knossos primarily depicted curving vegetal and sea life, processions, double axes, and bulls. Evans's reconstruction attests to the highly decorated character of the interior spaces of the Cretan palaces. The fresco fragments found at the palace at Knossos were all in the lowest level, so the location of the frescoes in his reconstruction has been questioned. A Blue Dolphin fresco that he believed was located in the queen's apartment, for example, may actually have been located on the floor above. The most famous fresco from the palace portrays three young people playing a bull-leaping game. The boys and girls are indistinguishable, except for the darker tone of the boys' skin. Both girls and boys are portrayed in Minoan art with long wavy hair and thin, girdled waists. Men portrayed in art are beardless, in contrast to those in Mycenaean art.

Other artwork associated with the Minoans includes snake goddesses, animal idols, Kamares ware, stoneware, and octopus vases. Kamares ware is found only at the palace at Knossos and in the Kamares cave (after which it is named). Kamares ware is wheel-thrown pottery decorated with a white-on-black design, often with yellow or red accents. The painted decoration is usually organic in nature, with stylized sea life or floral motifs. Other terra-cotta vessels of the New Palace period are decorated in a marine style, with black figures on a white background, and populated with curving, organic octopuses and other sea life. In the Post-Palace period, the designs stiffen and become symmetrical. Finely carved stoneware created in Crete is usually made of serpentine. Surviving pieces include lamps, chalices, rhytons, and small seal stones incised with designs. The most famous Cretan stone pieces include the *Harvester Vase* from Hagia Triada and the *Bull's Head Rhyton* from Knossos. The Minoans also created fine bronze and gold items, including cups and jewelry.

WAR AND WEAPONS   The Minoans do not appear to have been a warring civilization. During the Bronze Age, Crete was probably a thalassocracy (maritime power), as evidenced by representations of fleets of ships in a fresco at the palace at Knossos and by its unfortified palaces. Also, the Minoan civilization's demise has been linked to the destruction of its fleet.

WOMEN'S LIFE   Women are depicted more frequently than men in Minoan frescoes, which leads to the theory that women may have had a relatively high status in Minoan society. At one time, it was theorized that Minoan Crete was matriarchal. Snake goddess figurines suggest female participation as priestesses or as divinities in Bronze Age Crete.

WRITING SYSTEMS   The first writing used on Crete was hieroglyphic, as seen on the Phaistos disk (discovered in 1908) in the archaeological museum in Iráklion (Heraklion). Two subsequent scripts dating to the Bronze Age have been discovered on Crete: Linear A, used during the New Palace period, and Linear B, found only at Knossos on Crete and on the Greek mainland. Linear A is found primarily on clay tablets that yield mainly inventories. It is largely a syllabic script consisting of seventy-five signs and a number of ideograms. It has not been deciphered. Linear B, deciphered by Michael Ventris in 1952, appears to be an early form of Greek. It consists of eighty-seven symbols and a number of ideograms and may have been derived from Linear A. The Linear B tablets discovered on Crete are mainly lists and inventories. No written records of Minoan political or social history exist.

CURRENT VIEWS   Much of Crete has not been excavated, although the palaces and royal tombs, whose artifacts reflect the wealthiest elite, have been studied. Excavations in the later twentieth century shed light on the palaces at Phaistos and Kato Zakro, a small town of Gournia, the ancient road systems of the Minoans, the cities of Mallia and Palaikastro, necropolises at Arkhanes and Armeni, and Minoan drydocks at Kommos. However, the basic outline of Minoan civilization and chronology laid out by Evans's excavations remains largely unchanged.

Excavation continues at the smaller Minoan palaces at Phaistos, Mallia, and Kato Zakro, which have not been reconstructed as was the palace at Knossos. Evans's archaeological methods and reconstructions have been much criticized, but the reconstructed palace at Knossos has also been praised as bringing Bronze Age culture to life for the modern visitor.

FURTHER READING

Biers, William R. *The Archaeology of Greece: An Introduction*. 2d ed. Ithaca, N.Y.: Cornell University Press, 1996.

Chadwick, John. *Reading the Past: Linear B and Related Scripts*. Berkeley: University of California Press, 1997.

Farnoux, Alexandre. *Knossos: Searching for the Legendary Palace of King Minos*. Translated by David J. Baker. New York: Harry N. Abrams, 1996.

Fitton, J. Lesley. *Minoans*. London: British Museum Press, 2002.

Higgins, Reynold. *Minoan and Mycenaean Art*. Rev. ed. London: Thames and Hudson, 1997.

MacGillivray, J. A. *Minotaur: Sir Arthur Evans and the Archaeology of the Minoan Myth*. New York: Hill & Wang, 2000.

MacKendrick, Paul. *The Greek Stones Speak: The Story of Archaeology in Greek Lands*. Toronto: W. W. Norton, 1983.

Metropolitan Museum of Art. *Greek Art of the Aegean Islands*. New York: The Metropolitan Museum of Art, 1979.

Sally A. Struthers

See also: Art and Architecture; Gortyn's Code; Government and Law; Linear B; Mythology; Religion and Ritual; Strabo; Thera.

Critias of Athens

STATESMAN, MILITARY LEADER, AND WRITER

Born: c. 460 B.C.E.; Athens, Greece
Died: 403 B.C.E.; Athens, Greece
Category: Military; government and politics; literature

LIFE   Critias (KRIHSH-ee-uhs) of Athens was from an aristocratic family that traced itself to Solon. The uncle of Plato, he associated with Socrates as well as the Sophists and wrote a variety of works in prose and poetry, including a treatise in praise of the Spartan constitution.

In 415 B.C.E., he was implicated in the mutilation of the herms (statues of Hermes) but was released because of information provided by Andocides. His involvement in the Four Hundred remains uncertain. While in exile for proposing a motion to recall Alcibiades of Athens, he lived in Thessaly and allegedly participated in a democratic revolution.

In 404 B.C.E., Critias returned to Athens and became the leader of the Thirty Tyrants, the pro-Spartan oligarchy. He was responsible for their reign of terror, during which fifteen hundred people were killed. According to Xenophon, he had his colleague Theramenes executed for attempting to broaden the oligarchy. In 403 B.C.E., Critias fell in battle against the democratic exiles. After his death, a monument is said to have been erected in his honor, showing a personified Oligarchy setting a torch to Democracy.

INFLUENCE   Critias appears in Plato's dialogues, one of which is named after him. He was known throughout antiquity primarily for his brutality and ruthlessness.

FURTHER READING

Curd, Patricia, and Richard D. McKirahan. *A Presocratic Reader*. Indianapolis, Ind.: Hackett, 1996.
Guthrie, W. K. C. *A History of Greek Philosophy*. 6 vols. New York: Cambridge University Press, 1978-1990.

Krentz, Peter. *The Thirty at Athens*. Ithaca, N.Y.: Cornell University Press, 1982.
Wolpert, Andrew. *Remembering Defeat: Civil War and Civic Memory in Ancient Athens*. Baltimore: Johns Hopkins University Press, 2002.

Andrew Wolpert

See also: Alcibiades of Athens; Andocides; Four Hundred, The; Plato; Socrates; Solon; Sophists; Spartan Constitution; Thirty Tyrants; Xenophon.

Croesus

KING OF LYDIA (R. C. 560-546 B.C.E.)

Born: c. 595 B.C.E.; Lydia, Asia Minor (now in Turkey)
Died: c. 546 B.C.E.; Sardis, Asia Minor (now in Turkey)
Also known as: Kroisos; Croisos
Category: Government and politics

LIFE   The fifth and final ruler of the Lydian Dynasty, Croesus (KREE-suhs) succeeded his father, Alyattes, after defeating his own half brother. He warred against the Carians, his mother's people, and conquered the Ionian Greeks while seeking peace with those on the mainland. His court at Sardis welcomed Greek intellectuals, especially Solon, the Athenian lawgiver who, however, offended Croesus by refusing to agree that the king was the happiest man on earth.

The richest man in his world, he often gave pure gold to Greek shrines, especially the oracle at Delphi, who announced equivocally that he would bring down a mighty empire if he battled Persia. In battling Cyrus the Great in 546 B.C.E., Croesus did, indeed, bring down an empire—his own.

One legend states that Cyrus ordered, then halted Croesus's execution on a flaming pyre when Croesus called out the name of Solon (the philosopher who had cautioned people about the uncertainty of life). Cyrus then turned him into a vassal. Another legend claims that Croesus was saved by Apollo, who, grateful for rich offerings at Delphi, carried him off to the land of the Hyperboreans to live in perpetual sunshine and plenty.

INFLUENCE   Croesus's interest in Greek religion and philosophy led to a greater Greek influence in western Asia Minor.

FURTHER READING

Hansmann, George Maxim Anossov. *From Croesus to Constantine: The Cities of Western Asia Minor and Their Arts.* Ann Arbor: University of Michigan Press, 1975.

Croesus
(standing) faces
Cyrus the Great.
(Hulton Archive/
Getty Images)

Pedley, John Griffiths. *Sardis in the Age of Croesus*. Norman: University of Oklahoma Press, 1968.

Ramage, Andrew, and Paul Craddock. *King Croesus' Gold: Excavations at Sardis and the History of Gold Refining*. Cambridge, Mass.: Archaeological Exploration of Sardis, Harvard University Museums, in association with the British Museum Press, 2000.

Keith Garebian

See also: Delphic Oracle; Solon.

Battle of Cunaxa

Cyrus the Younger enrolled 10,400 Greek mercenaries to help him gain the Persian throne from his brother.

Date: 401 B.C.E.
Category: Wars and battles
Locale: About 87 miles (140 kilometers) northwest of Babylon, near the Euphrates River

SUMMARY   Upon the death of Darius II, the elder of his sons, Artaxerxes II, came to the throne. Cyrus the Younger, unhappy with his prospects, revolted and tried to seize the throne. Cyrus's army numbered between 20,000 and 30,000 men, including 2,600 horsemen. Artaxerxes had about 30,000 men, 6,000 of whom were on horses. The disparity in horsemen would cost Cyrus the victory at Cunaxa (kyew-NAK-suh).

Cyrus successfully advanced through Asia Minor and Mesopotamia. He and Artaxerxes met near Babylon. Cyrus posted the Greeks, led by the Spartan Clearchus, on the right with the Paphlagonian horsemen to their right and the Euphrates River on the extreme right flank. Cyrus held the center with his 600 horsemen while Ariaeus was placed on the left with the Asiatic troops. The satrap Tissaphernes and Artaxerxes held the center, with the king surrounded by the 6,000 horsemen. In the ensuing battle, Clearchus and the Greeks crushed the Persian left, but Cyrus was slain while foolishly attacking his brother head-on. Ariaeus's forces fought well but then fled after the news of Cyrus's death had spread.

SIGNIFICANCE   The victorious Greeks refused to enroll under Artaxerxes and successfully marched home. The expedition demonstrated the vulnerability of the Persian Empire to the Greek hoplite.

The Greeks after the Battle of Cunaxa. (F. R. Niglutsch)

FURTHER READING

Bigwood, J. M. "The Ancient Accounts of the Battle of Cunaxa." *American Journal of Philology* 104 (1983): 340-357.

Cawkwell, G. *Xenophon: The Persian Expedition*. Harmondsworth, England: Penguin Books, 1972.

Hornblower, Simon. *Cambridge Ancient History*. Vol. 6. Cambridge, England: Cambridge University Press, 1994.

Prevas, John. *Xenophon's March into the Lair of the Persian Lion*. Cambridge, Mass.: Da Capo Press, 2002.

Xenophon. *The Expedition of Cyrus*. Translated by Robin Wakefield, with an introduction and notes by Tim Rood. New York: Oxford University Press, 2005.

Martin C. J. Miller

See also: Greco-Persian Wars.

Cyclades

The position of these islands and islets on sailing routes across the Aegean Sea has resulted in almost continual occupation from Neolithic times to the present day.

Date: 3000 B.C.E.-700 C.E.
Also known as: Kikládhes
Category: Cities and civilizations
Locale: Southern Aegean

SUMMARY   Geographers in antiquity were not in complete agreement on which islands should be grouped under the heading of the Cyclades (si-kluh-DEEZ); the name refers to their positioning in a circle around the holy island of Delos. All, however, include Andros (Ándros), Ceos (Kéa), Cythnos (Kíthnos), Mykonos (Míkonos), Naxos, Paros (Páros), Seriphos (Sérifos), Siphnos (Sífnos), Syros, and Tenos (Tínos). Cycladic islands tend to have limited arable land and available water but may have compensated for these scarcities in antiquity by means of sea commerce; the mining of products such as iron, marble (particularly Paros and Naxos), gold and silver (Siphnos especially); and possibly by the terracing of hill slopes to increase their food supply.

The islands were sparsely settled in the Neolithic period, but beginning in the third millennium B.C.E., an influential Bronze Age culture arose in the area. This culture is most noteworthy for having produced strikingly distinctive marble figurines of both stylized and naturalistic types. Art historians have identified several individual artists, such as the Dresden Master, from certain characteristics of these objects. Their function remains speculative, although many have come from graves, and some sort of sacred, ritualized application is likely.

From the middle of the eleventh century B.C.E., nearly all the islands appear to have been abandoned until the Geometric period of the tenth through eighth centuries B.C.E., when they were gradually recolonized by Ionians, who paid homage to the temple of Apollo on Delos. By the Archaic period, oligarchies began to form on the islands, and in some cases, tyrannies, such as that of Lygdamis of Naxos (sixth century B.C.E.), developed. The tradition of sculpture as well as various techniques of monumental architecture continued through Archaic times.

The Greco-Persian Wars saw some islands (such as Paros) contributing to the Persian naval forces. In 478 B.C.E., the Cyclades joined the Delian League. With the collapse of the Athenian Empire in 404 B.C.E., the most important islands appear to have come under the control of Spartan *harmosts*, or garrison commanders. After 394 B.C.E., these Spartan forces were driven out, and most of the Cyclades entered the Second Athenian League soon after its formation in 377 B.C.E. The Hellenistic period saw a succession of various overlords until 133 B.C.E., when Roman control was established. The popular image of the islands as desolate and poverty-stricken, an image that some scholars have recently challenged, arose during this time. A few of the islands were also used as bases by the Byzantine fleet during Late Antiquity. The islands were the site of numerous archaeological surveys and excavations in the 1980's and 1990's.

SIGNIFICANCE   Although often influenced by outside powers in historical times, these islands were the cradle of many artistic achievements in antiquity.

FURTHER READING

Barber, R. L. N. *The Cyclades in the Bronze Age*. Iowa City: University of Iowa Press, 1987.

Broodbank, Cyprian. *An Island Archaeology of the Early Cyclades*. New York: Cambridge University Press, 2000.

Cherry, J. F., J. L. Davis, and E. Mantzourani. *Landscape Archaeology as Long-Term History*. Los Angeles: University of California Press, 1991.

Reger, Gary. *Regionalism and Change in the Economy of Independent Delos*. Berkeley: University of California Press, 1994.

Renfrew, C., and M. Wagstaff, eds. *An Island Polity: The Archaeology of Exploitation on Melos*. Cambridge, England: Cambridge University Press, 1982.

Brian Rutishauser

See also: Art and Architecture; Athenian Empire; Greco-Persian Wars.

Cynicism

Diogenes' teachings and his unconventional lifestyle led to the establishment of the Cynic philosophical school.

Date: c. 350 B.C.E.
Category: Philosophy
Locale: Athens

SUMMARY Diogenes (c. 412/403-c. 324/321 B.C.E.) is considered by a number of ancient traditions as the founder of the school of philosophy called Cynicism (SIH-nuh-sih-zuhm). His thought represented a rejection of all existing philosophical systems as well as of conventional morality and social custom. Diogenes' philosophical convictions translated into public behavior that scandalized his contemporaries. Although none of Diogenes' works has survived into modern times, details of his life and aspects of his thought have been preserved by a number of classical historians and authors. Of special note is the work of Diogenes Laertius, who, in his *Peri biōn dogmatōn kai apophthegmatōn tōn en philosophia eudokimīsantōn* (third century C.E.; *The Lives and Opinions of the Philosophers*, 1853), provides information from a diverse body of sources, including Diogenes' own writings.

Diogenes was born in the city of Sinope, a Greek colony on the southern coast of the Black Sea. According to one version, his father, Hicesias, was a banker in charge of the public finances, but when it was discovered that he had debased the currency, he was forced into exile along with Diogenes. According to other versions, including Diogenes' own work *Pordalus* (now lost), it was Diogenes himself who adulterated the currency and was forced to leave his native city in disgrace.

Whatever the exact circumstances of his departure from Sinope, Diogenes was living in the city of Athens by the mid-fourth century B.C.E. On his arrival in Athens, Diogenes reportedly became a student of Antisthenes, who, in turn, had been a student of Socrates. Some ancient writers claim that Antisthenes was the first philosopher with whom the word "cynic" was associated, probably because he met with his followers at the gymnasium of Cynoserges (the white dog). Antisthenes reportedly was the first philosopher to wear a cloak and carry a staff and a knapsack, clothing and accessories that, along with the Phrygian felt cap, later became the trademarks of Cynic philosophers. Although the extent to which Antisthenes influenced Diogenes is not known, Diogenes' thought and behavior clearly represented a radical departure from all previous philosophical propositions.

Obtaining a clear biographical portrait of Diogenes is difficult because there are no contemporary historical accounts of his life. Furthermore, events in the life of the historical Diogenes are intertwined with anecdotes that are part of the literary persona that emerged in his own writings and the works of writers from the Roman period such as Lucian and Dio Chrysostom. As the founder of the Cynic school, Diogenes became a paradigmatic figure to whom many philosophical authors and biographers attributed countless acts and aphorisms. Laertius himself implicitly acknowledged the difficulty in reconstructing an accurate biographical portrait of his subject when he included several versions of important events in Diogenes' life.

Whether historical or fictional, all actions and words attributed to Diogenes conjure the image of an individual whose mission in life became to ridicule all philosophical systems and to challenge all social and moral practices. Every source mentions that Diogenes rejected material possessions. He wore a coarse cloak, went about barefoot, held his few possessions in a knapsack, carried a walking staff, and never groomed his hair or beard. Diogenes rejected the idea of work and relied on the charity of friends and strangers for his basic needs. Because he did not own a house, Diogenes slept at friends' houses, on the steps of public buildings, on the streets, and, most famously, in a bathtub.

Every story about Diogenes illustrates his disregard for rank, wealth, and power; his defiance of authority; and his desire to provoke outrage. After Philip II of Macedonia defeated Athens and its allies at the Battle of Chaeronea in 338 B.C.E., Diogenes was brought to the Macedonian king as a captive. The king asked him who he was, to which Diogenes responded, "A spy upon your insatiable greed." A few years later Philip's successor, Alexander the Great, came to meet Diogenes. When he found the cynic taking a sunbath, the young king told Diogenes that he could request anything from him, to which the philosopher replied, "Stand out of my light." Alexander is quoted as having said that if he had not been Alexander, he would have liked to have been Diogenes.

Diogenes was equally defiant toward those who presumed of intellectual authority. When Diogenes heard Plato lecturing about his theory of Ideas and using such terms as "tablehood" and "cuphood," Diogenes commented that he could see a table and a cup, but he was unable to see "tablehood" and "cuphood." During another lecture, Plato pompously defined humans as bipedal animals with no feathers. Diogenes ran outside, found a chicken, and plucked its feathers; he came back to the lecture hall and presented the bird to the crowd saying, "Here is Plato's man."

No institution was immune to the cynic's attacks. Diogenes was critical of organized religion. When he saw temple officials arresting a man who

Diogenes, the founder of Cynicism. (F. R. Niglutsch)

had stolen a bowl, he said that the great thieves were taking away the little thief. He had no use for revered social institutions. When asked what the appropriate time for marriage was, he responded that "for a young man not yet and for an old man never at all." Diogenes held no national allegiances. When asked where he was from, he responded that he was a citizen of the world. He is believed to have coined the word "cosmopolitan."

According to several sources, while traveling by sea, Diogenes was captured by pirates and subsequently sold as a slave. When asked at the auction block what kind of tasks he could perform, Diogenes replied that he could rule men. On hearing this, a Corinthian by the name of Xeniades bought Diogenes, brought him to Corinth, and entrusted him with the education of his sons. Diogenes spent the rest of his life in Corinth growing old at Xeniades' household. He died at the age of about ninety. Although he had requested that his dead body be left unburied so that the wild beasts could feed off him, Xeniades' sons buried him. One account claims that Diogenes' life ended on the same day that Alexander the Great died in Babylon.

SIGNIFICANCE   The rise of Cynicism marks the end of the Classical period in Greek philosophy and the beginning of Hellenistic thought. After the formalism of Plato and Aristotle, embodied in the rival institutions of the Academy and the Lyceum, Diogenes emerged as the philosopher of the antiestablishment.

Plato once described Diogenes as "a Socrates gone mad." The comparison to Socrates is apt because, like the martyred Athenian, Diogenes spent his life exposing the hypocrisy of society, the presumptuousness of intellectuals, and the greed of the powerful. However, unlike Socrates, whose life and thought reflect deep trust in humankind's inherent rationality and a desire to improve society through example, Diogenes, through his behavior, projected a complete lack of confidence in humankind's rational abilities and hopelessness about the future of humanity.

FURTHER READING

Branham, R. "Diogenes and the Invention of Cynicism." In *The Cynics: The Cynic Movement in Antiquity and Its Legacy*, edited by R. Branhman and M. Goulet-Caze. Berkeley: University of California Press, 1996.

Cutler, Ian. *Cynicism from Diogenes to Dilbert*. Jefferson, N.C.: McFarland, 2005.

Diogenes Laertius. *Lives of Eminent Philosophers*. Translated by R. D. Hicks. Cambridge, Mass.: Harvard University Press, 2000.

Long, A. "Diogenes, Crates and Hellenistic Ethics." In *The Cynics: The Cynic Movement in Antiquity and Its Legacy*, edited by R. Branhman and M. Goulet-Caze. Berkeley: University of California Press, 1996.

Navia, Luis E. *Diogenes the Cynic: The War Against the World*. Amherst, N.Y.: Humanity Books, 2005.

Gilmar E. Visoni

See also: Alexander the Great; Antisthenes; Diogenes; Philip II of Macedonia; Philosophy; Plato.

Battle of Cynoscephalae

The defeat of King Philip V of Macedonia in this battle effectively checked the expansion of Macedonian political influence into southern Greece while contributing markedly to the establishment of Roman power in the region.

Date: 197 B.C.E.
Category: Wars and battles
Locale: Southwest Thessaly, Greece

SUMMARY   In 200 B.C.E., Rome declared war against King Philip V after Rhodes and Pergamum appealed to the senate for aid in stopping Macedonian aggression in the eastern Mediterranean. Roman military activity in Greece through 198 B.C.E. proved largely inconclusive in slowing Philip's territorial ambitions. The following year, Roman and Macedonian armies clashed in a climactic battle at Cynoscephalae (sih-nuh-SEH-fuh-lee).

Philip V and an army of 20,000 men engaged a Roman force of equal size under the proconsul Titus Quinctius Flamininus. The battle spontaneously developed after the armies unexpectedly encountered each other in fog on Cynoscephalae ridge. Philip, advancing on the Roman formation with only the right wing of his phalanx fully assembled, drove back the Roman left, but broken ground disrupted the cohesion of the Macedonian left wing, permitting the forces of Flamininus's right to gain a complete victory in that quarter. With the defeat of Philip's left assured, a Roman tribune detached twenty maniples from the legions' right and attacked the successful portion of the phalanx in the rear. This action completely shattered the Macedonian formation. Philip's losses included 8,000 killed and 5,000 captured. Roman casualties amounted to 700 dead.

SIGNIFICANCE   Following his defeat at Cynoscephalae, Philip was forced by Rome to surrender his fleet, relinquish all claims to territorial possessions in Greece and the Aegean Sea, and pay a sizable war indemnity. Rome became the primary political arbiter in the region.

FURTHER READING

Adcock, F. E. *The Roman Art of War Under the Republic.* New York: Barnes & Noble, 1995.

Lendon, J. E. *Soldiers and Ghosts: A History of Battle in Classical Antiquity.* New Haven, Conn.: Yale University Press, 2005.

Walbank, F. W. *Philip V of Macedon.* Hamden, Conn.: Archon Books, 1967.

Donathan Taylor

See also: Hellenistic Greece; Philip V.

Cyprus

An important stop between the East and West with safe harbors and abundant agricultural products and mineral resources, particularly copper.

Date: 6000 B.C.E.-31 C.E.
Category: Historic sites
Locale: Northeastern Mediterranean Sea, fifty miles south of modern Turkey

BACKGROUND   Cyprus (SI-pruhs) is an island located in the northeastern corner of the Mediterranean Sea, fifty miles south of the coast of Cilicia, near the Levant. It is approximately 140 miles (225 kilometers) long by 60 miles (97 kilometers) wide. The island, because of its strategic location, was seen throughout history as an important possession and found itself involved in many conflicts through the ages. The island was also seen as a valuable economic resource because of its plentiful production of wheat, olives, and wine and its extensive copper deposits. The ancient writer Ammianus Marcellinus noted that Cyprus was so fertile that it could completely build and stock cargo ships solely from its own resources. According to myth, Aphrodite (Greek goddess of love, beauty, and fertility) emerged from the sea at Cyprus, and numerous temples to her can be found throughout the island, especially near Paphos.

EARLY HISTORY   Archaeological excavations on the island have uncovered evidence for a preceramic early Neolithic culture at sites such as Khirokitia and Kalavasos (Tenta), dating back to the sixth millennium B.C.E. Small, circular buildings constructed from little stones, sun-dried mud bricks, and wood characterize these small farming sites. This early phase was followed by a Late Neolithic period (c. 4500-3500 B.C.E.) characterized by square buildings, often partially underground, and the use of pottery as seen at the sites of Sotira (Teppes) and Ayios Epiktitos (Vrysi).

The daily life in those Neolithic villages was devoted to farming, hunting, and animal husbandry. The Chalcolithic period (c. 4500-2500/2300 B.C.E.) saw the first evidence of metalworking on the island with the appearance of copper implements. The copper industry on the island began to flourish, and commercial contacts were established with other regions around the eastern Mediterranean.

In the Early Bronze Age (2500/2300-1900 B.C.E.), settlers from western Anatolia began to arrive in large numbers and soon replaced the indigenous culture with their Near Eastern culture. Economic prosperity continued, and urbanization began in the coastal regions. In the Late Bronze Age (c. 1600-1050 B.C.E.), Cyprus became more commercial as trade with Egypt and the Levant increased. The increased commercial traffic resulted in the growth of large cities on the eastern and southern coasts, such as Enkomi and Maroni (Vournes). These cities were constructed from large ashlar blocks, similar to Near Eastern cities. During this period, as Cyprus became known as a rich source for copper, Mycenaean merchants first visited the island. Soon Mycenaean colonists started arriving in large numbers, and the local culture developed a significant Aegean influence.

Around the year 1250 B.C.E., the island began to suffer from the same problems that resulted in the general collapse of Bronze Age civilizations around the eastern Mediterranean. Piracy increased, resulting in decreased commercial traffic, and in 1190 B.C.E., the coastal cities were attacked and destroyed by raiders referred to in Egyptian sources as the Sea Peoples. The local culture was further changed with the arrival of new Greek colonists fleeing the collapse of the Mycenaean civilization on mainland Greece. From this point on, Greek culture, religion, and language were to be dominant on the island as the Greek colonists controlled the major Cypriot kingdoms of Kourion, Lapithos, Marion, Pahos, Salamis, Soli, and Tamassos.

PROSPERITY AND OUTSIDE RULE   As Cyprus entered the Iron Age (c. 1050-323 B.C.E.), it lost contact with Greece and strengthened its ties to the Near East. Phoenicians from Tyre settled on the island and founded a colony at Kition during the ninth century B.C.E. In the eighth century B.C.E., contact with Greece was reestablished. Cyprus became extremely prosperous, as can be seen by the wealth and splendor of items discovered during the archaeological investigation of the royal tombs at Salamis. From 709 to 663 B.C.E., the Cypriot kingdoms were part of the Assyrian Empire but were allowed to keep their local autonomy. Following the end of Assyrian rule, the Cypriot kingdoms enjoyed a brief period of independence until the Egyptian pharaoh Amasis annexed them around 560 B.C.E.

After a short period of Egyptian control (c. 560-540 B.C.E.), Cyprus became part of the Persian Empire during the reign of Cambyses II (r. 529-522 B.C.E.). Other than a few brief attempts at rebellion, such as the Ionian Revolt in 500 B.C.E. and the revolt of Evagoras I of Salamis in the late fifth/early fourth century B.C.E., Cyprus remained part of the Persian Empire until the latter's destruction by Alexander the Great. In gratitude for the assistance rendered to him by Cypriot naval forces at the siege of Tyre, Alexander granted the Cypriot kingdoms their freedom.

After Alexander the Great's untimely death in 323 B.C.E., the leading city-states of Cyprus formed an alliance with Ptolemy Soter against the advances of the Antigonids. Demetrius Poliorcetes captured the island in 306 B.C.E., only to see it recaptured by the Ptolemies in 294 B.C.E. When the Ptolemies regained control of the island, they made the city of Nea Paphos, founded by Nikokles I, their new administrative center. Continuing the economic trend begun in the Classical period, Cyprus continued to experience increased economic prosperity—a trend seen throughout the eastern Mediterranean during this period.

ROMAN RULE In the year 100 B.C.E., the Roman senate, concerned about the problem of piracy in the eastern Mediterranean and its effect on trade, passed a *senatus consultum* that encouraged all friends and allies of Rome, including Cyprus, to give no assistance or aid to pirates. This was followed by the sudden annexation of Cyprus in 58 B.C.E. A Roman tribune for that year, Publius Clodius Pulcher, was able to secure the passage of a law that reduced Cyprus to a province and confiscated the wealth of Cyprus's king. For the next ten years, Cyprus was considered part of or an addition to the province of Cilicia. In 48/47 B.C.E., Julius Caesar gave Cyprus to Egypt to be ruled by the two children of Auletes, but in actuality Cleopatra VII governed the island. Marc Antony confirmed Egypt's control over Cyprus and Cilicia in 36 B.C.E. Augustus reclaimed the island for Rome when he assumed control of Egypt after his victory at Actium over Cleopatra and Antony in 31 B.C.E. In 22 B.C.E., Augustus ceded the island to the Roman senate to become a senatorial province but a minor one governed only by a praetor. To aid in its government, the island was divided into twelve or thirteen regions, each controlled by the major city in its area. Throughout the Roman period, the island was fairly quiet, with little political or military disruption.

FURTHER READING

Hill, George Francis. *A History of Cyprus*. 4 vols. Cambridge, England: Cambridge University Press, 1940-1952.

Karageorghis, Vassos. *Ancient Cyprus: Seven Thousand Years of Art and Archaeology*. Baton Rouge: Louisiana State University Press, 1981.

_____. *Cyprus: From the Stone Age to the Romans*. New York: Thames and Hudson, 1982.

_____. *Early Cyprus: Crossroads of the Mediterranean*. Los Angeles: J. Paul Getty Museum, 2002.

Panteli, Stavros. *A New History of Cyprus, from the Earliest Times to the Present Day*. London: East-West Publications, 1984.

Steel, Louis. *Cyprus Before History: From the Earliest Settlers to the End of the Bronze Age*. London: Duckworth, 2004.

Tatton-Brown, Veronica. *Ancient Cyprus*. London: British Museum Press, 1997.

R. Scott Moore

See also: Actium, Battle of; Alexander the Great; Antigonid Dynasty; Cleopatra VII; Demetrius Poliorcetes; Mycenaean Greece; Ptolemaic Dynasty; Ptolemaic Egypt; Ptolemy Soter.

Cypselus of Corinth

TYRANT OF CORINTH (R. 657-627 B.C.E.)

Born: Early seventh century B.C.E.; Corinth
Died: 627 B.C.E.; place unknown
Also known as: Kypselos of Korinthos
Category: Government and politics

LIFE   Archaic Corinth was ruled by the Bacchiadae, a tight-knit aristo-cratic clan, of which the mother of Cypselus (SIHP-suh-luhs) was a member. Cypselus of Corinth seems to have held both military and civil office under their rule. Sensing growing hostility toward the Bacchiadae, he led an insurrection and established himself as tyrant. Although this was done primarily with the assistance of wealthy Corinthians dissatisfied with Bacchiad rule, Cypselus seems also to have enjoyed popular support. During the thirty years of his rule, he reorganized Corinthian political institutions, founded colonies in northwestern Greece, and built the Corinthian treasury at Delphi. Growing trade and external contacts brought prosperity and artistic innovation. Cypselus was succeeded by his son Periander of Corinth and then his grand-nephew Psammetichus, who was soon deposed and killed (c. 585), ending the Cypselid Dynasty.

INFLUENCE   Cypselus founded one of the earliest and longest-lasting tyrant dynasties. He would serve as a model for other Greek tyrants and as an archetype of the cruel, ruthless dictator for those who opposed tyranny—despite the fact that he almost certainly enjoyed a good reputation in his native Corinth.

FURTHER READING

Anderson, Greg. "Before Turannoi Were Tyrants: Rethinking a Chapter of Early Greek History." *Classical Antiquity* 24, no. 2 (October, 2005): 173-222.
Herodotus. *The Histories*. Translated by Robin Waterfield. New York: Oxford University Press, 1998.

McGlew, J. *Tyranny and Political Culture in Ancient Greece*. Ithaca, N.Y.: Cornell University Press, 1993.

Salmon, J. B. *Wealthy Corinth*. New York: Oxford University Press, 1984.

Shawn A. Ross

See also: Periander of Corinth.

Daily Life and Customs

Daily life in ancient Greece revolved around village life, with its farming and herding activities and its emphasis on the importance of family and tradition.

Date: 6500-31 B.C.E.
Category: Daily life

DEVELOPMENT OF VILLAGE LIFE   As early as 55,000 B.C.E., nomadic humans roamed the Greek landscape hunting wild animals and gathering cereals, nuts, and berries, as they struggled against the harsh Ice Age conditions. By 6500 B.C.E., the climate of Greece had warmed sufficiently to permit the cultivation of some of the wild plants, which allowed the people to settle in one place, to begin domesticating animals, and to construct permanent shelters. Farmers and their families lived in close-knit villages surrounded by their fields and orchards. Populations were limited by the soil fertility of the countryside, and villages typically consisted of a small number of extended families (*oikoi*) cooperating and interacting with one another. By the end of the Archaic period (c. 500 B.C.E.), many *oikoi* had merged to form larger entities known as poleis (singular polis; roughly translated as "city-states"). Still, it was village life, based around farming and herding activities, that would be the norm for the majority of the Greek population until the modern era.

FOOD AND DRINK   As elsewhere in the Mediterranean, the soil and climate of Greece supported crops of grains, olives, and grapes. Grains such as wheat, barley, and oats were ground and made into bread or into a paste or gruel. Olive trees provided fruit that could be eaten as well as pressed into oil for cooking and use in oil lamps. Before the introduction of soap, olive oil was also used as a body cleanser. Legumes, fruits, and nuts were common staples of the Greek diet. Meat and fish were eaten sparingly and typically only on special occasions such as religious festivals and family celebrations. For variety, some foods were sweetened using honey and flavored with spices. The Greeks did not use butter, nor did they drink milk. Wine mixed with water was the beverage of choice throughout ancient Greek history.

DIVISION OF LABOR   From the earliest times, gender and class determined roles within the *oikoi* and the community at large. Men were responsible for activities outside the home such as farming, herding, trade, and warfare. In addition, males participated in the community's governing councils and leadership positions. Women's roles were confined to activities within the home, including managing the household, raising children, preparing the family's food, and weaving textiles. Slavery was common in the ancient world, and most households had slaves. The wealthier the family, the more likely it was that slaves would fetch water from the well and do the marketing, which meant that wealthy women appeared in public less often than their poorer counterparts. Greek houses reflected the distinct roles of males and females, and, in all but the poorest of households, men and women had separate living quarters.

MARRIAGE, CHILDREN, AND EDUCATION   Greek girls were married at an early age, usually between twelve and fifteen, to men who were much older, often twice their age. Upon marriage, the bride became part of the husband's family. The bride's most important function was to produce male heirs to continue the husband's family lineage.

Male offspring were typically nurtured and raised by their mothers with the help of wet nurses and slaves. An exception to this was in the Greek city-state of Sparta, where boys were taken from their families at age seven to be educated by the state in preparation for joining the army. The familial attachment to daughters was not as strong as to sons. In all poleis, female offspring were not considered permanent members of the birth family because daughters joined their husbands' families after they married. In addition, daughters were often considered a liability because families had to provide substantial dowries to their husbands upon marriage. As a result, unwanted female infants would be left outside to die in a practice known as exposure. Oftentimes, prostitutes (*hetairai*) and slave traders rescued exposed infants in order to raise them in their own trades.

Children who were kept by the family appear to have had pleasant childhoods as archaeological finds of toys and small furniture attest. The family was responsible for educating children. Poor boys worked alongside their fathers learning to till the soil and herd animals. Wealthier boys might have a private tutor (*pedagogue*) to train them in such areas as philosophy, history, and the arts. A girl's education was limited to learning the household arts that would serve her father's household and her future husband's household. Again, the Spartan system served as an exception. Spartan girls were given a state sponsored education so they would be prepared to shoulder much of the running of the polis while Spartan men were engaged in military activities.

TRAVEL AND HOSPITALITY   Travel outside of one's own territory was difficult and often dangerous. Strangers were treated with suspicion and even outright hostility out of fear that a stranger, having no allegiance to the local residents, might try to steal possessions or women. When an individual did have to travel for trade, diplomacy, or a major event such as the Olympiad, a system of guest-friendship (*xenia*) developed within the Greek territories. *Xenia* involved a system of mutual reciprocity of meals, lodging, protection, and gift giving. It was understood that a stranger who accepted another's hospitality must reciprocate in kind when called upon.

THE WORLD BEYOND   Following the campaigns of Alexander the Great, Greek customs intermingled with those of the conquered territories. By the late Hellenistic period (first century B.C.E.), many Greeks occupied large urban centers in the East and profited from newly established trade. New wealth and new freedoms available in the East extended even to women, who were permitted to run businesses and to access law courts. Still, for the vast majority of persons living within Greek territories, life in their small rural villages continued much as it had for millennia.

FURTHER READING

Adkins, Lesley, and Roy A. Adkins. *Handbook to Life in Ancient Greece.* New York: Oxford University Press, 1997.

Pomeroy, Sarah B., Stanley M. Burstein, Walter Donlan, and Jennifer Tolbert Roberts. *Ancient Greece: A Political, Social, and Cultural History.* New York: Oxford University Press, 1999.

Powell, Anton, ed. *The Greek World.* New York: Routledge, 1995.

Sonia Sorrell

See also: Agriculture and Animal Husbandry; Death and Burial; Education and Training; Government and Law; Language and Dialects; Mythology; Performing Arts; Religion and Ritual; Settlements and Social Structure; Sports and Entertainment; Trade, Commerce, and Colonization; Women's Life.

Death and Burial

Death and burial practices among the ancient Greeks reflected their cultural beliefs in magic and in an afterlife that resembled a pale continuation of the person's earthly existence.

Date: c. 1200-31 B.C.E.
Category: Daily life; religion and mythology

DEATH AND MAGIC   The ancient Greeks regarded death from old age as the most natural form of death—indeed, its only natural form. The concept of "accidental" death was quite foreign to the ancient Greeks, for whom nothing occurred simply by chance or accident. Deaths caused by mishap, disease, or violence were all considered unnatural and, therefore, rendered the deceased unclean. Untimely deaths were suspected of resulting from the deceased's having displeased one of the vindictive Olympian gods, or perhaps having incurred the wrath of a witch or an amateur sorcerer who, it was believed, were fully capable of commanding demoniac powers to control the weather, ruin crops, or strike down an enemy. Instances of unnatural death obligated the surviving relatives to perform rites of expiation that were thought to diminish the offense and thereby benefit the deceased in the other world. Murder always necessitated blood vengeance.

BURIAL CUSTOMS   The ancient Greeks believed that at the moment of death the *psyche* (soul) would depart from the body. If denied a proper burial, the soul would be doomed to wander the earth as a ghost, unable to enter into the underworld, the Land of the Dead (Hades). The responsibility for burial usually fell to the children of the deceased; this was a serious obligation. Failure to bury a deceased person under one's care was not only considered an egregious breach of filial duty but also regarded as a crime punishable by execution. In one notable instance, victorious Athenian generals were put to death for neglecting their duty to recover and bury the dead bodies of soldiers under their command following the Battle of Arginusae.

Following the death of an individual, the person's body was washed by the closest family members, perfumed, and dressed in fine white garments.

Articles of jewelry were often interred with the body, as well as a coin (placed into the mouth) for Chiron, the mythical ferryman who, according to tradition, rowed newly departed souls across the River Styx to the gloomy Land of the Dead. The body was laid in a coffin and displayed to mourners in the home of the deceased. Loud displays of anguish and ostentatious grief (rending of clothes, shearing of hair) were customary.

On the second day, relatives or slaves bore the funerary coffin in a solemn procession through the city streets to a cemetery precinct set aside as a *necropolis* (literally, "city of the dead") outside the city walls. There the

In Greek mythology, destiny and death are determined by three old women known as the Fates. (F. R. Niglutsch)

301

After being sentenced to die, the philosopher Socrates drinks hemlock as his followers begin the customary displays of grief. (F. R. Niglutsch)

body was formally interred. At the gravesite, a large decorated vase, a stone statue, a *stele* (monumental stone marker), or a simple altar—the size and elaborateness of which mirrored the person's prominence in life—was erected as a memorial to the deceased. After the burial, libations were poured. Then, mourners returned to the house of the deceased, where complex purification rituals were performed. All those who had been defiled by contact with the dead were required to bathe prior to the funerary feast. Later, the entire house was washed with seawater.

Burials during the earlier Homeric Age (c. 1200-800 B.C.E.) typically involved cremation of the remains on a wooden bier, as was typical during unsettled or seminomadic cultural periods, when the tending of gravesites proved impractical. In contrast, burials during the later Archaic, Classical, and Hellenistic periods (c. 800-31 B.C.E.) reflect funerary customs more in keeping with traditional ground burial of the body and veneration of the gravesite. A cult of the dead required that special observances be held on the third, ninth, and thirtieth days following the burial, as well as upon each anniversary of the person's passing.

GRAVE STATUARY   The ancient Greeks revered the period of young adulthood when individuals reach their physical prime. It is notable, in this respect, that virtually all grave statues depict the deceased as idealized youths, irrespective of the deceased's actual age. Beginning with the Archaic period, the most notable form of memorial statue was the male kouros, an athletic striding nude, fully six feet in height, with arms held rigidly at his sides. The female counterpart, the kore, was always depicted dressed in a woolen peplos, most often in a frontal pose. The kouros and kore figures, like all ancient Greek sculpture, were originally painted at the hair, eyes, and mouth in order to achieve a more lifelike appearance. It is interesting to note that the enigmatic "archaic smile" found invariably on kouroi and other sculptural portraits probably alludes to the so-called death smile caused by the onset of muscular rigor shortly after death, thus identifying the subject of the work as a person deceased.

In addition to these statues, large vases of the krater or dipylon type were used as grave ornaments. Since the dead were believed to inhabit the underworld, these vessels had holes pierced in their bases through which offerings of wine or milk could be channeled into the grave. Both the statuary and the vase forms of memorial continued in use through the Classical period. In addition to grave monuments, it was customary to place an image or a small statue of the deceased at the home altar. These ancestral images were crowned with laurel twice each month, as well as at the appearance of the new Moon—that time each month when the Moon disappears only to be "reborn" three days later.

FURTHER READING

Baroja, Julio Caro. "Magic and Religion in the Classical World." In *Witchcraft and Sorcery*, edited by Max Marwick. Baltimore: Penguin, 1970.

Durant, Will. *The Life of Greece*. Norwalk, Conn.: Easton Press, 1992.

Flaceliere, Robert. *Daily Life in Greece at the Time of Pericles*. London: Phoenix Press/Orion House, 1996.

Stokstad, Marilyn. *Art History*. New York: Harry N. Abrams, 1995.

Larry Smolucha

See also: Art and Architecture; Daily Life and Customs; Halicarnassus Mausoleum; Mythology; Religion and Ritual.

Delphi

Delphi was the site of the temple and oracle of Apollo, the quadrennial Pythian Games, and a theater of Dionysus.

Date: c. fourteenth century B.C.E.-390 C.E.
Category: Historic sites; religion and mythology
Locale: On the slopes of Mount Parnassus in Central Greece

SUMMARY   Greek tradition suggests that Delphi (DEHL-fi) was an ancient oracular site where a holy stone called the *omphalos*, or "navel," located in the temple of Apollo, marked the center of the earth. The Homeric *Hymn to Apollo* describes how Apollo captured the oracle from the goddess Earth by defeating the monster Python. The shrine was also considered a place of purification where those inflicted with blood guilt, such as the mythical Orestes, who committed matricide, could seek physical and spiritual cleansing.

From about 1100 B.C.E., the shrine was administered by a Panhellenic association called the Amphictyonic League. Delphi's greatest oracular influence occurred as the city-states of Archaic Greece devised law codes and established colonies. Such issues were both easy to affirm and conducive to the oracle's good reputation. Two famous law codes, those of Lycurgus in Sparta and of Solon in Athens, were both closely associated with Delphi. Even Croesus of Lydia is said to have consulted the oracle.

Representatives of cities (or, less frequently, private individuals) made inquiry of the Pythia while she sat on a tripod in Apollo's temple, but only on the seventh day of each nonwinter month. Women were not permitted to consult the oracle directly. The typical response was probably not a riddle but a simple yes or no to a policy question previously deliberated by a city; moreover, replies were almost always affirmative. Those who accept as genuine some of the longer responses traditionally associated with the oracle speculate that the Pythia induced self-hypnosis or inhaled narcotic fumes emitted from a chasm in the earth, but that is unlikely.

The temple of Apollo, destroyed by fire in 548 B.C.E., was rebuilt under

Delphi.
(Library of Congress)

the direction of the great Athenian family of Alcmaeonids. The *temenos*, or sanctuary, was filled with about twenty treasuries erected by individual city-states as well as numerous commemorations of military victories and individual accomplishments. One noteworthy monument was the Portico of the Athenians, built to display plunder captured from the Persians in the Battle of Marathon (490 B.C.E.).

Pythian Games were held at Delphi in honor of Apollo from antiquity. After 582 B.C.E., the games occurred in the third year after the Olympic Games and were considered one of the four sets of Crown Games. Events included musical as well as athletic events. A stadium was located above the *temenos* on the slope of Parnassus. Apollo possessed the shrine only during the summer months. In winter, Delphi belonged to Dionysus, the Greek god of wine, and a theater dedicated to the god was located just to the north of Apollo's temple.

SIGNIFICANCE   Delphi was a major Panhellenic shrine for almost two thousand years. Despite plundering by the Persians, the Gauls, and the Romans, Delphi continued to serve as an oracular site until it was closed in 390 C.E. by the Christian emperor Theodosius the Great.

FURTHER READING

Broad, William J. *The Oracle: The Lost Secrets and Hidden Message of Ancient Delphi*. New York: Penguin Press, 2006.

Burkert, Walter. *Greek Religion*. Translated by John Raffan. Cambridge, Mass.: Harvard University Press, 1985.

Golding, William. *The Double Tongue*. New York: Farrar, Straus and Giroux, 1995.

Morgan, Catherine. *Athletes and Oracles: The Transformation of Olympia and Delphi in the Eighth Century B.C.* New York: Cambridge University Press, 1990.

Valavanis, Panos. *Games and Sanctuaries in Ancient Greece: Olympia, Delphi, Isthmia, Nemea, Athens*. Los Angeles: J. Paul Getty Museum, 2004.

Thomas J. Sienkewicz

See also: Croesus; Delphic Oracle; Homeric Hymns; Lycurgus of Sparta; Marathon, Battle of; Solon; Solon's Code; Sports and Entertainment; Theater of Dionysus.

Delphic Oracle

The oracle at Delphi provided a common meeting ground for early Greek city-states and a religious ratification for individual cities' decisions.

Date: 775 B.C.E.
Category: Religion and mythology; government and politics
Locale: Central Greece

SUMMARY   The ancient Greek cities, as they entered recorded history about 800 B.C.E., were disunited. Except for temporary, often strained alliances against foreign enemies, they developed no common political institutions. They were permanently in competition with one another and often at war. Decisions had to be made, mostly about internal matters, but also about war, colonization, and occasional joint enterprises. These decisions were fundamentally matters of individual sovereignty. Yet there was enough sense of being Hellenes—Greeks—to permit the Oracle of Apollo at Delphi to emerge as somewhat of a common center. To understand this development, it is necessary to glance at prior religious and political arrangements.

From roughly 2000 until 1250 B.C.E., the brilliant, powerful "palace societies" of Crete and Mycenae dominated the area. The political-administrative form of these societies appears to have been bureaucratic aristocracy. Palace societies were originally worshipers of the Great (Earth) Goddess, but with increasing male military influence, Poseidon, the earth-shaking lord of the sea, and then Zeus, the weather/sky god, emerged as major deities.

The period from 1200 through 800 B.C.E. is termed the Greek Dark Age. The rich archaeological and even documentary evidence of a half millennium earlier does not exist. From what is known, Dark Age Greece was rudimentary and disorganized. The classical philosopher Aristotle (384-322 B.C.E.), in his *Politica* (335-323 B.C.E.; *Politics*, 1598), held that the early Greeks lived "scattered about." Each clan was a little kingdom, ruled absolutely by an elder male who was father, master, and king. Aristotle may be overstating the extent of patriarchy, which he sees as analogous to Zeus's ascendancy as father and king of the Olympian gods. It was, however, precisely during this period that Zeus became dominant. His cult was established at Olympia in the early tenth century B.C.E.

Zeus was a deity appropriate to a period dominated by small-scale, quasi-feudal monarchy. Slowly, however, and no doubt in part because of the relative order provided by authoritarian patriarchy-monarchy, the small Greek communities began to recover and grow. The Classical Greek form of political organization, the polis, or city-state, emerged. These early political communities were not yet the powerful, populous, often democratic cities of several centuries later, but neither were they scattered rural citadels of warrior chieftains. They represented the partial reemergence in Greece of civilized urban life, and as such required a revised religious orientation.

The god most related to this development was Apollo. The terms "Apollo" and "Apollonian" convey an image of beauty and harmony. Apollo is *the* god of Greek classicism, especially as Phoibos Apollo, the Radiant Apollo. He is the god of healing, purification, and music. Yet the Greeks could never forget the connotations of his name. With his characteristic bow and arrow, Apollo the "far-darter" seemed to be "The Destroyer." Even the adjective *phoibos* was frighteningly close to the noun *phobos*, "fear" or "terror."

This moral ambiguity is present in the tales of Apollo's arrival at Delphi. Apollo was the son of Zeus, begotten on the nymph Leto. Enraged, Zeus's sister-wife Hera sent the dragon-serpent Python to pursue Leto. Apollo was born on the Aegean island of Delos, met Python on Mount Parnassus and wounded him, and pursued Python to Delphi, where he killed him. Thus Apollo was established at Delphi.

At issue in the establishment is the question of precedence. Scholars debate whether the cult of Apollo took over an earlier oracle of the Earth goddess Ge, or Gaia. Complicating things is the question of whether Ge, Gaia, and Hera are all later personifications of the original Great (Earth) Goddess. Mythic traditions, combined with some archaeological and linguistic evidence, tend to affirm both prior occupation and theological identity. The moral implication is that both Zeus and Apollo acted unjustly and that redress was required. Zeus appears to have suffered only through the growing influence of Apollo's cult. Yet Apollo is purified (on Crete, the Great Goddess's center); he shares the shrine with the Pythia, his priestess and oracle; and he further honors the memory of the slain Python with the Pythian Games, begun in 586 B.C.E.

There seems, then, to be an inner logic to the concomitant emergence of

*The Delphic Oracle
issues a decree.*
(F. R. Niglutsch)

the Oracle of Apollo at Delphi and the polis. Apollo is the new, young god. He represents a fresh beginning, a break with the obvious patriarchal order but also with the dimly remembered maternal religion lying behind it. Nevertheless, there is an evident compromise and implicit alliance of son and mother against father. Apollo is the personification of beauty and harmony but with an undercurrent of violence and injustice in his nature.

Given these characteristics, Apollo is the appropriate god for the classical Greek cities. They too represent a new principle, that of politics. Politics is the free intercourse of equal citizens, who conduct their affairs by speaking. Its authority stems not from the ancestral but from individual, often youthful excellence. Politics is also a spirited, often violent, sometimes terrible competition. It is a kind of order deeply in need of a neutral ground, and of moderation.

Delphi provided that ground and attempted to provide the moderation. Supposedly carved over the entrance of one of the several successive temples of Apollo were the sayings "Nothing in Excess" and "Know Thyself." These famous pieces of advice capture much of the permanent spirit of the oracle—a spirit communicated to cities and individuals with decreasing effectiveness as time passed. Yet they are not themselves utterances of Apollo's Pythian priestess, Phemonoe (fl. eighth century B.C.E.). To imagine the priestess "prophesying," that is, foretelling the future or uttering pithy, cryptic sayings, is to misunderstand, according to modern scholarship, normal Delphic procedure. (In this sense, Phemonoe, "prophetic mind," seems misnamed.) The oracle functioned approximately as a divine court of appeals. The "judges" were Apollo and, behind Apollo, at the omphalos stone marking the navel of the world, Earth herself.

Representatives of cities or, less frequently, private individuals initiated an inquiry. They did not, however, do so at their own convenience. The Pythia gave responses nine times each year, on the seventh of each nonwinter month. She did so seated on a tripod in the innermost sanctuary of Apollo's temple. There is scholarly agreement that the most usual form of the response was "yes" or "no" to a policy question previously deliberated by a city and, moreover, that the reply was almost always to affirm the policy. This simple, nearly automatic sort of "oracle" renders irrelevant the interesting question of the Pythia's state of mind when pronouncing. The traditional view, that she spoke under the influence of vapors emitted from a chasm in the earth, has been discarded. Those who admit as genuine some of the longer, more substantive responses reported speculate that the Pythia inhaled narcotic fumes or induced self-hypnosis.

Given that the oracle's usual response was an affirmation of policy proposals, it is understandable that Delphi's greatest influence occurred in the first few centuries of its existence. The characteristic early political problems were the devising of law codes and the establishment of colonies. These proposals were both relatively easy to affirm and conducive to good reputation because they provided both internal stability and widening Greek influence. The most famous examples of legislation, Lycurgus's at Sparta and Solon's at Athens, were noted for their balance and moderation, and closely associated with Delphi.

SIGNIFICANCE Delphi's broad political program appears to have been twofold—acquiescence in particular polis decisions while encouraging development of moderate institutions. This program implicitly acknowledged Delphi's own limitations. At best, it might provide an opportunity for policy reconsideration in a setting suggestive of both a common Greekness and a superhuman perspective. Delphic moderation tended toward passivity, and was successful insofar as its member cities tended in the same direction. Early, most did; later, some, especially Athens, did not, and Delphi declined accordingly.

FURTHER READING

Bowden, Hugh. *Classical Athens and the Delphic Oracle: Divination and Democracy.* New York: Cambridge University Press, 2005.

Broad, William J. *The Oracle: The Lost Secrets and Hidden Message of Ancient Delphi.* New York: Penguin Press, 2006.

Burkert, Walter. *Greek Religion.* Translated by John Raffan. Cambridge, Mass.: Harvard University Press, 1985.

Clay, Jenny Strauss. *The Politics of Olympus: Form and Meaning in the Major Homeric Hymns.* Princeton, N.J.: Princeton University Press, 1989.

Dempsey, T. *The Delphic Oracle: Its Early History, Influence, and Fall.* New York: B. Blom, 1972.

Fontenrose, Joseph. *The Delphic Oracle: Its Responses and Operations.* Berkeley: University of California Press, 1978.

Morgan, Catherine. *Athletics and Oracles: The Transformation of Olympia and Delphi in the Eighth Century B.C.* New York: Cambridge University Press, 1990.

Parke, H. W., and D. E. W. Wormell. *The History.* Vol. 1 in *The Delphic Oracle.* Oxford: Basil Blackwell, 1956.

John F. Wilson

See also: Delphi; Homeric Hymns; Lycurgus of Sparta; Mythology; Religion and Ritual; Solon; Solon's Code.

Demetrius Phalereus

PHILOSOPHER AND RULER OF ATHENS (R. 317-307 B.C.E.)

Born: c. 350 B.C.E.; Phaleron, near Athens, Greece
Died: 283 B.C.E.; Egypt
Also known as: Demetrius of Phalerum; Demetrius of Phaleron
Category: Government and politics; philosophy

LIFE   Demetrius Phalereus (duh-MEE-tree-us fuh-LEE-rews) was born to the Athenian deme Phaleron and reportedly educated under Aristotle and Theophrastus. In 317 B.C.E., a few years after Athens fell to Macedonia, Cassander took over Athens and put Demetrius in charge of the city. Demetrius governed Athens and largely stayed out of the wars that raged among the successors to Alexander the Great. He became best known for his legislative and social reforms, which seem broadly guided by his philosophical education. These reforms included curbing extravagances, canceling subsidies for the poor for public functions, and instituting a census. All these reforms responded to the desires of the wealthy Athenian aristocracy. In 307 B.C.E., Demetrius Poliorcetes ("Besieger of Cities") took Athens, and Demetrius Phalereus fled. He subsequently served Cassander and Ptolemy Soter. Under Ptolemy Philadelphus, he fell into disfavor and died in 283 B.C.E.

INFLUENCE   Demetrius remains an example of a successful combination of ruler and philosopher. He governed Athens during a crucial period after the loss of the democracy and as it became a cultural center for Greece. He is also credited with persuading Ptolemy Soter to build the Alexandrian library. Although almost all of his writing is now lost, he was a widely read and respected Peripatetic philosopher in antiquity.

FURTHER READING
Fortenbaugh, William W., and Eckart Schütrumpf, eds. *Demetrius of Phalerum: Text, Translation, and Discussion.* New Brunswick, N.J.: Transaction, 2000.

Green, Peter. *Alexander to Actium: The Historical Evolution of the Hellenistic Age*. Reprint. Berkeley: University of California Press, 1993.

Habicht, Christian. *Athens from Alexander to Antony*. Translated by Deborah Lucas Schneider. Cambridge, Mass.: Harvard University Press, 1999.

Wilfred E. Major

See also: Alexandrian Library; Aristotle; Athens; Cassander; Demetrius Poliorcetes; Ptolemaic Dynasty; Ptolemy Soter; Theophrastus.

Demetrius Poliorcetes

KING OF MACEDONIA (R. C. 294-C. 288 B.C.E.)

Born: 336 B.C.E.; Macedonia
Died: 283 B.C.E.; Cilicia (later in Turkey)
Category: Government and politics

LIFE   The son of Antigonus I Monophthalmos, Demetrius Poliorcetes (duh-MEE-tree-us pahl-ee-ohr-SEET-eez) served as his general against Ptolemy Soter (312 B.C.E.) and Seleucus I Nicator (311 B.C.E.) and later against Cassander (307 B.C.E.) when Demetrius took over several cities, including Athens and Corinth. His victory over the Ptolemaic fleet allowed Antigonus to claim kingship for himself and Demetrius (306 B.C.E.). His year-long unsuccessful siege of Rhodes (305-304 B.C.E.) gave Demetrius his nickname "Besieger of Cities." He reconstituted the Corinthian League (302 B.C.E.), and the isthmus remained his power base after the collapse of the Antigonid kingdom following the defeat of Antigonus and Demetrius at Ipsus (301 B.C.E.). After marrying his daughter to Seleucus, Demetrius received Cilicia in return (299-298 B.C.E.). His star rose again when he reestablished control over Athens, defeated Sparta, and seized the Macedonian throne (c. 294 B.C.E.). However, his preparations to recover the Antigonid kingdom caused Seleucus, Ptolemy, Lysimachus, and Pyrrhus to ally against him and attack Macedonia from the east and west (c. 288 B.C.E.). Despoiled of almost everything in Europe in accordance with the treaty of 287 B.C.E., Demetrius tried to contest Anatolia but had to surrender to Seleucus (286 B.C.E.). He died in captivity, indulging in drinking and other vices.

INFLUENCE   Demetrius's life reflects the tumultuous period following the death of Alexander the Great, which consisted of almost incessant wars of the Diadochi before relative stabilization in the late 280's B.C.E.

FURTHER READING

Billows, Richard A. *Antigonos the One-Eyed and the Creation of the Hellenistic State*. Berkeley: University of California Press, 1990.
Duggan, Alfred Leo. *Besieger of Cities*. New York: Pantheon, 1963.
Wehrli, C. *Antigone et Démétrios*. Geneva: Droz, 1968.

Sviatoslav Dmitriev

See also: Antigonid Dynasty; Cassander; Diadochi, Wars of the; Lysimachus; Macedonia; Ptolemy Soter; Pyrrhus; Seleucid Dynasty; Seleucus I Nicator.

Democritus

PHILOSOPHER

Born: c. 460 B.C.E.; Abdera, Thrace (now Avdira, Greece)
Died: c. 370 B.C.E.; Abdera, Thrace (now Avdira, Greece)
Also known as: Democritus of Abdera
Category: Philosophy

LIFE   Democritus (dih-MAHK-riht-uhs) was born to a wealthy family in the city of Abdera on the Greek mainland. He is believed to have traveled widely in Egypt and Asia Minor. He was a disciple of Leucippus, who is believed to have proposed the atomic hypothesis between 440 and 430 B.C.E., but about whom little is known. Democritus was a prolific author, writing more than seventy works on a wide range of subjects, including ethics, music, astronomy, and mathematics. He is thought by some to have reached the age of one hundred.

Democritus.
(Library of Congress)

INFLUENCE   Democritus elaborated the atomic theory as formulated by Leucippus. His atoms were of several different kinds and were both indestructible and indivisible. The atoms had definite shapes and properties. Because the world consisted of only atoms and empty space, there was no room for the gods or survival of the individual after death. Democritus's atomic theory was adopted by Epicurus and his disciples. Much later, its materialism made it unacceptable to the authorities of the Catholic Church, who found Aristotle's metaphysics of form and (infinitely divisible) substance more compatible with Catholic theology. Scientific acceptance of the atomic hypothesis would not come until the eighteenth century.

FURTHER READING

Bailey, Cyril. *The Greek Atomists and Epicuris.* New York: Russell and Russell, 1964.

Chitwood, Ava. *Death by Philosophy: The Biographical Tradition in the Life and Death of the Archaic Philosophers Empedocles, Heraclitus, and Democritus.* Ann Arbor: University of Michigan Press, 2004.

Lee, Mi-Kyoung. *Epistemology After Protagoras: Responses to Relativism in Plato, Aristotle, and Democritus.* New York: Oxford University Press, 2005.

McKirahan, Richard D., Jr. *Philosophy Before Socrates.* New York: Hackett, 1994.

Warren, James. *Epicurus and Democritean Ethics: An Archaeology of Ataraxia.* New York: Cambridge University Press, 2002.

Donald R. Franceschetti

See also: Epicurus; Leucippus; Philosophy; Pre-Socratic Philosophers.

Demosthenes

ORATOR

Born: 384 B.C.E.; Athens, Greece
Died: October 12, 322 B.C.E.; Calauria, Greece
Category: Oratory and rhetoric

LIFE   The Greek orator Demosthenes (dih-MAHS-thuh-neez) was born in 384 B.C.E. When he was seven, his father (who bore the same name) died. His mother, Cleobule, was left with very little money to care for him and his sister, since the executors of the estate embezzled most of it. Demosthenes was an awkward child, with little strength, and he was handicapped by a speech defect that he later overcame (although probably not by putting pebbles in his mouth, as legend has it). He received a good education of the standard sort and special instruction in rhetoric. He then went on to the

Demosthenes. (F. R. Niglutsch)

Principal Works of Demosthenes

Kat' Androtiōnos, 355 B.C.E. (*Against Androtion*, 1852)

Peri tēs Ateleias pros Leptinēn, 355 B.C.E. (*Against the Law of Leptines*, 1852)

Peri tōu summoriōn, 354 B.C.E. (*Symmories*, 1852, also known as *On the Navy Boards*)

Kata Timokratous, 352 B.C.E. (*Against Timocrates*, 1852)

Kat' Aristocratous, 352 B.C.E. (*Against Aristocrates*, 1852)

Kata Philippou A, 351 B.C.E. (*First Philippic*, 1570)

Uper tēs Rodiōn Eleutherias, 351 B.C.E. (*For the Rhodians*, 1852)

Olunthiakos A, Olunthiakos B, 349 B.C.E. (*First and Second Olynthiacs*, 1570)

Olunthiakos G, 348 B.C.E. (*Third Olynthiac*, 1570)

Peri tēs Eirēnes, 346 B.C.E. (*On the Peace*, 1744)

Kata Philippou B, 344 B.C.E. (*Second Philippic*, 1570)

Peri tēs Parapresbeias, 343 B.C.E. (*On the Embassy*, 1852)

Kata Philippou G, 341 B.C.E. (*Third Philippic*, 1570)

Peri tōu en Cherronēsōi, 341 B.C.E. (*On the Affairs of the Chersonese*, 1744)

Peri tōu Stephanou, 330 B.C.E. (*On the Crown*, 1732)

The Orations, 1852

study of law with a famous probate lawyer of the time, Isaeus.

In 360 B.C.E. Demosthenes was commander of a ship in the Athenian fleet, but his first ventures into public life were as a lawyer, and one of his important early cases was one initiated by himself in which he unsuccessfully attempted to win back some of the money that had been embezzled from his father's estate. Then, as one trained both in law and rhetoric, Demosthenes went on to the profession of writing speeches to be delivered orally in court. The experience that he acquired stood him in good stead when he began in 355 B.C.E. to attempt to influence the political life of Athens by his speeches in the general assembly.

His most famous orations were the three *Philippics*, and the most celebrated of the three was the third, *Kata Philippou G*, delivered in 341 B.C.E. In his speeches he warned the people of Athens that civic reform and a revival of civic spirit were needed if Athens was to hold its place in the world. He cited cases of corruption in public administration and demanded action. When Philip II of Macedonia seemed to have the subjugation of Athens as one of his objectives, Demosthenes warned the people of Athens that democracy could not survive if Philip were to conquer them. He urged the necessity of taxes, of military service, of a strong fleet, and of continued attention to political and military affairs. He also traveled throughout Greece, attempting to form an alliance of the various cities against Macedonia.

In 338 B.C.E. Philip scored a final victory against the allied city-states at the Battle of Chaeronea. Demosthenes then worked to secure funds from Persia, Philip's next target, in order to build up anti-Macedonian forces. When Philip died in 336 B.C.E. and Alexander became king of Macedonia, the Athenian cause was recognized as hopeless for the time being. Demosthenes restricted his campaign against Macedonia. In order to restore confidence in Demosthenes as a public leader, his friend Ctesiphon proposed that Demosthenes be given a gold wreath or crown. This act was denounced as illegal by Aeschines, whom Demosthenes had accused in 343 B.C.E. of accepting bribes, and Aeschines brought suit. In one of his most famous orations, *Peri tōu Stephanou* (330 B.C.E.; *On the Crown*, 1732), Demosthenes defended his record and won the case.

Demosthenes then concentrated on developing the internal strength of Athens, but his work was halted when he was found guilty of appropriating to himself some gold that had been in possession of a deserter from Alexander's forces who had been captured by the Athenians. Demosthenes' guilt was never actually established. He was imprisoned because he could not pay the fine, but he escaped and went into exile. When Alexander died in 323 B.C.E. Demosthenes was recalled to Athens and acclaimed. At the Battle of Crannon in 322 B.C.E. Athens was defeated by the Macedonians, and Demosthenes fled to the island of Calauria, where he took poison to avoid being captured by the soldiers of Antipater, the Macedonian leader.

INFLUENCE   Demosthenes was the greatest of the Greek orators, an Athenian patriot who used his skill at declamation to arouse the citizens of Athens to regain their civic pride and to resist the efforts of Philip II of Macedonia to conquer Greece.

FURTHER READING

Demosthenes. *Speeches 50-59*. Translated by Victor Bers. Austin: University of Texas Press, 2003.

Gibson, Craig A. *Interpreting a Classic: Demosthenes and His Ancient Commentators*. Berkeley: University of California Press, 2002.

Murphy, James J., ed. *Demosthenes, "On the Crown": A Critical Case Study of a Masterpiece of Ancient Oratory*. Davis, Calif.: Hermagoras Press, 1983.

Sealey, Raphael. *Demosthenes and His Time: A Study in Defeat*. New York: Oxford University Press, 1993.

Worman, Nancy. "Insults and Oral Excess in the Disputes Between Aeschines and Demosthenes." *American Journal of Philology* 125, no. 1 (Spring, 2004): 1-25.

Worthington, Ian, ed. *Demosthenes: Statesman and Orator*. New York: Routledge, 2001.

David H. J. Larmour

See also: Aeschines; Alexander the Great; Antipater; Athens; Chaeronea, Battle of; Oratory; Philip II of Macedonia.

Wars of the Diadochi

After the death of Alexander the Great, his successors fought for rule over his empire, resulting in the division of the Hellenistic world.

Date: 323-281 B.C.E.
Category: Wars and battles
Locale: Greece, Macedonia, Asia Minor, Syria, Palestine, the Aegean islands

SUMMARY Alexander the Great died without an adult heir in 323 B.C.E. His massive empire, stretching from the Balkans to India, quickly dissolved at the hands of rival generals, some attempting to create smaller empires, while others wanted it all. These men, former close associates of Alexander, were dubbed the Diadochi (di-uh-DOH-chee), Greek for "successors."

Although highly skilled and often commanding a remnant of Alexander's superb army, the Diadochi and the battles they fought were different from those of their former master. First, while most were competent and in a few cases imaginative, none had Alexander's touch. Nor could they rely upon dedicated armies of loyal veterans. Instead, Diadochi led mercenary armies, forces quite capable of turning coat for a few extra drachma. Indeed, guile and treachery were often more valuable talents than tactical flair.

Another difference involved new types of troops and weapons. Here the Diadochi borrowed from eastern armies or, in a few cases, became innovators. War elephants, larger war galleys, and massive siege equipment were examples. Size being a common feature, these devices represent not only an effort to gain tactical advantage but also a chance to display the power and wealth of their commanders.

The Diadochi fell out almost as soon as Alexander died. A series of maneuvers quickly eliminated Craterus (d. 321 B.C.E.), Perdiccas (365-321 B.C.E.), and Antipater (397-319 B.C.E.), and Eumenes (c. 360-316 B.C.E.) died soon afterward. A truce, in 311 B.C.E., allowed the survivors to divide

The Deaths of the Diadochi

Perdiccas	321 B.C.E., slain by mutineers who were bribed by Ptolemy
Craterus	321 B.C.E., killed by Eumenes while invading Cappadocia
Antipater	319 B.C.E., died
Eumenes	316 B.C.E., slain by own men who were bribed by Antigonus
Polysperchon	310 B.C.E.?, died
Antigonus I	301 B.C.E., killed in battle with Seleucus and Lysimachus, allies of Cassander
Cassander	297 B.C.E., died after being recognized as king of Macedonia
Demetrius Poliorcetes	283 B.C.E., died in prison
Ptolemy Soter	283/282 B.C.E., died
Lysimachus	281 B.C.E., killed in hand-to-hand combat by Seleucus at Battle of Corus
Seleucus I Nicator	281 B.C.E., murdered by Ptolemy Keraunos, disinherited son of Ptolemy

the empire while maintaining a fiction that all was being held in proxy for the underage Alexander IV. A year later, his assassination started another war. This was the work of a father-son team: Antigonus I (382-301 B.C.E.) and Demetrius Poliorcetes (d. 283 B.C.E.). They combined guile, inventiveness, and a degree of charisma far greater than that of the other Diadochi. Their plans called for reunification of Alexander's empire.

Working from a strong position, the pair dominated Asia Minor; Antigonus and Demetrius came close to success. The latter proved himself multitalented, a master of siege work, a competent general, and a great admiral. Using larger warships and innovative tactics, Demetrius scored a decisive victory over Ptolemy Soter's (367/366-283/282 B.C.E.) brother, Menelaeus, at Salamis (308 B.C.E.), off the coast of Cyprus. Although defeated by Ptolemy in the land battle of Gaza (305 B.C.E.), he conquered Athens and many other Greek cities, thus earning his nickname, Poliorcetes, the taker of cities.

The apex of this war came during the siege of Rhodes (305-304 B.C.E.), where, despite his employment of the *Helepolis*, the largest siege engine of its day, Demetrius failed to conquer. Three years later, their power having united all other Diadochi against them, Antigonus and Demetrius fought the climactic Battle of Ipsus (301 B.C.E.). One of their opponents, Seleucus I Nicator (358/354-281 B.C.E.), employed a large number of war elephants. Unless accustomed to the smell, horses will often bolt in the presence of elephants. Seleucus cleverly interposed his elephants between the main body under Antigonus and Demetrius's cavalry. This effectively split the opposition, allowing the other Diadochi to kill Antigonus. Demetrius escaped to rally what remained of their army. The victors now agreed to split Alexander's empire into Macedonian, Syrian, and Egyptian components.

Demetrius maintained a small fleet and army, plus a presence in Asia Minor and the Aegean, but seemed removed from contention until Cassander (c. 358-297 B.C.E.), king of Macedonia, died in 297 B.C.E. Taking advantage of the interregnum, Demetrius moved in and captured the kingdom in 294 B.C.E. Fearing a revival of his power, Ptolemy, Lysimachus (c. 361-281 B.C.E.), and King Pyrrhus of Epirus united to destroy Demetrius. The latter fled to Asia Minor, hoping to stir up his former comrades, but failed and was captured by Seleucus.

A final showdown now took place between Seleucus and Lysimachus. The latter was cut down in hand-to-hand combat during the Battle of Corus (281 B.C.E.), and shortly thereafter, Seleucus, the last of the Diadochi, was assassinated.

SIGNIFICANCE   The real turning point was the Battle of Ipsus, for only Antigonus had the strength and vision to re-create Alexander's empire. His failure proved that none of the Diadochi could continue that course. Instead, a general division of the Hellenistic world ensued, creating three hostile power blocks: Macedonia, Syria, and Egypt.

FURTHER READING

Anson, Edward. *Eumenes of Cardia: A Greek Among Macedonians*. Boston: Brill Academic, 2004.

Bar-Kochva, B. *The Seleucid Army*. New York: Cambridge University Press, 1979.

Billows, Richard A. *Antigonos the One-Eyed and the Creation of the Hellenistic State*. Berkeley: University of California Press, 1997.

Lund, Helen S. *Lysimachus: A Study in Early Hellenistic Kingship*. New York: Routledge, 1992.

Warry, John. *Warfare in the Classical World*. London: Salamander, 1998.

John P. Dunn

See also: Alexander the Great; Alexander the Great's Empire; Antigonid Dynasty; Antipater; Cassander; Demetrius Poliorcetes; Hellenistic Greece; Lysimachus; Macedonia; Ptolemaic Dynasty; Ptolemaic Egypt; Ptolemy Soter; Salamis, Battle of; Seleucid Dynasty; Seleucus I Nicator; Warfare Following Alexander; Weapons.

Diocles of Carystus

PHYSICIAN

Born: c. 375 B.C.E.; Carystus, Greece
Died: c. 295 B.C.E.; Athens?, Greece
Category: Medicine

LIFE Diocles of Carystus (DI-uh-kleez of kuh-RIHS-tuhs) on the island of Euboea became a famous and respected physician, sometimes ranked second only to Hippocrates. The exact dates of his life remain uncertain, but he lived after the Hippocratic school was well established and may have been a contemporary of Aristotle. No full writings of his survive, but later writers credit him with the first handbook on anatomy, along with works on physiology, aetiology, diagnoses, dietetics, and botany. He was best known for promoting the importance of practical experience in making sensible diagnoses. Diocles' insistence on practical experience may explain one fragment that calls for more complex assessments of pathological effects, rather than simply assuming a certain smell or substance always reflects the same condition in every patient. Another fragment provides detailed daily and seasonal regimens for healthy living.

INFLUENCE Careful observation allowed Diocles to distinguish for the first time among different types of diseases of the lungs and intestines. He also established that a fever was a symptom of disease, not a disease itself. Two ancient inventions also bore his name: a type of head bandage and a spoon for removing arrowheads. Later physicians such as Galen praised Diocles both for his practical knowledge and for his theoretical positions.

FURTHER READING

Eijk, Philip J. van der. *Diocles of Carystus: A Collection of the Fragments with Translation and Commentary.* Boston: Brill, 2000.

_____. *Medicine and Philosophy in Classical Antiquity: Doctors and*

Philosophers on Nature, Soul, Health, and Disease. New York: Cambridge University Press, 2005.

Lyons, A. S., and R. J. Petrucelli. *Medicine: An Illustrated History.* New York: Abrams, 1978.

Wilfred E. Major

See also: Hippocrates; Medicine and Health.

Diodorus Siculus

HISTORIAN AND SCHOLAR

Born: c. 80 B.C.E.; Agyrium, Sicily (now Agira, Sicily, Italy)
Died: c. 20 B.C.E.; place unknown
Category: Scholarship; historiography

LIFE   Diodorus Siculus (di-uh-DOR-uhs SIHK-yuh-luhs), born in Agyrium, Sicily, composed a world history called *Bibliotheca historica* (first century B.C.E.; *Diodorus of Sicily in Twelve Volumes*, 1950-1967). Of its original forty volumes, fewer than half survive; only volumes 1 through 5 and volumes 11 through 20 are still intact. He traveled to Egypt and Asia and around Europe to gather information, having learned Latin, although perhaps imperfectly. In following Apollodorus, he helped standardize the dates 1184 B.C.E. for the fall of Troy, 1104 B.C.E. for the Dorian invasion, and 776 B.C.E. for the first Olympics.

INFLUENCE   Diodorus is most valuable for his information about the era immediately following the death of Alexander the Great (323 B.C.E.), the wars of the Diadochi. He used sources lost to modern scholars, including Ptolemy, Ephorus, and Timaeus.

FURTHER READING

Hammond, N. G. L. "The Sources of Diodorus XVI." *Classical Quarterly* 31 (1937): 79-91.
_____. *Three Historians of Alexander the Great: The So-Called Vulgate Authors, Diodorus, Justin, and Curtius.* Cambridge, England: Cambridge University Press, 1983.
Smith, L. C. "The Chronology of Books XVIII-XX of Diodorus Siculus." *American Journal of Philology* 82 (1961): 283-290.
Stylianou, P. J. *A Historical Commentary on Diodorus Siculus, Book 15.* Oxford, England: Clarendon Press, 1998.

Gaius Stern

See also: Historiography; Literature.

Diogenes

PHILOSOPHER

Born: c. 412/403 B.C.E.; Sinope, Paphlygonia, Asia Minor (now in Turkey)
Died: c. 324/321 B.C.E.; probably Corinth, Greece
Also known as: Diogenes of Sinope; Diogenes the Cynic
Category: Philosophy

LIFE   Diogenes (di-AHJ-uh-neez) was a major early Cynic philosopher. Cynicism ("doggishness") predated Diogenes and may be discerned in Plato's portrait of Socrates and in the precepts espoused by Antisthenes, a notable figure in Socrates' circle, who may or may not have been Diogenes' mentor. However, Diogenes' penchant for playing like a dog, flaunting the insult of "doggishness" embodied in the name of Cynicism as though it were a compliment, linked him permanently with the philosophy. The ancient biographical tradition relates that Diogenes fled to Athens after being exiled from Sinope, a prosperous Greek Black Sea trading metropolis, where he was involved in defrauding the currency, along with his father, an alleged financier. More data regarding Diogenes' background and the details of this particular incident have not been preserved; the extant information largely consists of an assortment of aphoristic traditions contained in a treatise entitled *Peri biōn dogmatōn kai apophthegmatōn tōn en philosophia eudokimīsantōn* (third century C.E.; *The Lives and Opinions of the Philosophers*, 1853) and attributed to Diogenes Laertius, about whom exceedingly little is known.

Although all genuine early Cynic documents have been lost, it is still possible to create a profile of the ancient Cynic movement. Unlike other contemporary philosophical systems, Cynicism was more a method of social critique grounded in antiestablishment principles than a school with a doctrine that cultivated adherents. Caustic commentary on normative modes of thinking, exhibitionist acts that mocked all social trappings, and a choice of lifestyle based on simple essentials made the Cynic sage the essence of Cynicism. Metaphysical theory was regarded as useless and scientific speculation as an elitist sport. Practice and principle were fundamentally equivalent. Cynicism itself was a vocation or calling, the object of which was to challenge assumptions by accosting the public with words and deeds contrived to instigate rude awakenings.

Evidently, Diogenes viewed himself as a man who had experienced deliverance from delusion. In his view, this delusion was a state of malaise that generally characterized the plight of humanity in its endless pursuit of material gain, status, prestige, and pretensions to power. In this context, the phrase "defacing the currency," the accusation faced by Diogenes and his father, became a motto of Cynic intent. This phrase both described Diogenes' past transgression, which served as antecedent to his engagement with wisdom, and served as a summary statement of the civic role the Cynics perceived as their debt to society. Diogenes made a lasting impression in Athens by living in a great tub on charitable donations and publicly per-

Diogenes. (Hulton Archive/Getty Images)

forming bodily acts otherwise deemed indecent by custom. Numerous anecdotes yield a consistent profile. When Alexander the Great approached Diogenes and asked what he wished for, Diogenes asked the king to step out of the path of the sunlight that had been reaching him; when coming from the baths and asked if they were crowded, Diogenes said he saw many bathers but very few people. Ostentatiously hostile toward all common judgments, Diogenes proclaimed himself a "citizen of the cosmos." In the Cynic view, heritage constructs and identity claims were pompous illusions that spawned discord and conflict. They rated among the many and varied futile pursuits that sapped human agency from moral virtue. The classic Cynic outlook, in this regard, assessed human practice most negatively but looked at human potential in a positive light. Cynic eccentrics existed on earth to endorse a reordering of human priorities.

INFLUENCE   Cynicism had an effect on Greek and Roman philosophy (especially Stoic and Epicurean ethics), literature (especially parody and polemics via the Cynic diatribe and anecdotal tradition), religion, ruler ideology, Christian asceticism, and Continental European philosophy.

FURTHER READING

Branham, R. Bracht, and Marie-Odile Goulet-Caze, eds. *The Cynics: The Cynic Movement in Antiquity and Its Legacy.* Berkeley: University of California Press, 1996.

Dudley, D. R. *A History of Cynicism: From Diogenes to Sixth Century A.D.* Reprint. London: Bristol Classical Press, 1998.

Green, Peter. *Alexander to Actium: The Historical Evolution of the Hellenistic Age.* Reprint. Berkeley: University of California Press, 1993.

Navia, Louis E. *Classical Cynicism: A Critical Study.* Westport, Conn.: Greenwood Press, 1996.

Zoe A. Pappas

See also: Alexander the Great; Antisthenes; Cynicism; Philosophy; Plato; Socrates.

Dionysius the Elder

MILITARY LEADER AND TYRANT OF SYRACUSE
(R. 406-367 B.C.E.)

Born: c. 430 B.C.E.; Sicily
Died: 367 B.C.E.; Sicily
Category: Military; Government and politics

LIFE   Born into the aristocracy of the Sicilian Greek polis of Syracuse, Dionysius the Elder (di-uh-NISH-ee-uhs) brushed aside the opposition of his peers to become tyrant of the city in 406 B.C.E. Throughout his life, he fought a series of campaigns aimed at driving the Carthaginians from Sicily and constructing a Syracusan empire on the island. He also took an active interest in the affairs of the Greek mainland and eastern Aegean, forming ties with Sparta and Corinth, although he was often viewed with suspicion. In 388 or 384 B.C.E., he sent chariot teams and orators to the Olympic Games, but the teams lost, and Dionysius's poetry was ridiculed. In 368 B.C.E., in gratitude for his hostility to the Boeotians, the Athenians granted him citizenship and a crown. His play *The Ransom of Hector* (367 B.C.E.; now lost) defeated its competitors at the Lenaea festival in Athens the following year, shortly before his death.

INFLUENCE   Dionysius the Elder can be seen as the fourth century B.C.E. version of Archaic Greek tyrants such as Pisistratus and Polycrates of Samos, skilled not only in military tactics but also in diplomacy and the arts. Many ancient philosophers (that is, at Plato's Academy) and other authors (Ephorus, Polyaenus) devoted space in their works to him. Although not responsible for large-scale conquests, he occupies a position among the great military leaders of world history.

FURTHER READING
Caven, Brian. *Dionysius I: War-Lord of Sicily*. New Haven, Conn.: Yale University Press, 1990.

Sanders, Lionel J. *Dionysius I of Syracuse and Greek Tyranny*. London: Croom Helm, 1987.

Smith, Christopher, and John Serrati, eds. *Sicily from Aeneas to Augustus: New Approaches in Archaeology and History*. Edinburgh, Scotland: Edinburgh University Press, 2000.

Brian Rutishauser

See also: Carthaginian-Syracusan War; Dionysius the Younger; Syracuse.

Dionysius the Younger

Tyrant of Syracuse (r. 367-357 b.c.e. and 354-344 b.c.e.)

Born: c. 396 B.C.E.; Sicily
Died: Late fourth century B.C.E.; probably Corinth
Category: Government and politics

LIFE Son of Dionysius the Elder, the militarily successful tyrant of Syracuse, Dionysius the Younger (di-uh-NISH-ee-uhs) succeeded his father in 367 B.C.E. Not as gifted as his father, he was greatly influenced by his uncle Dion, a devoted follower of Plato, and by the historian Philistius. Dion persuaded his nephew to invite Plato to the Syracusan court, no doubt in the hope that Plato would carry out some of his political dreams there. Plato imposed a course of mathematical and philosophical studies on Dionysius, studies perhaps not suited to the young man's nature, and when Plato was rumored to be plotting to turn Syracuse over to Athens, Dionysius banished both Plato and Dion. In 357 B.C.E., Dion defeated his nephew in battle, but the Syracusan assembly, perhaps frightened at the prospect of a strong leader, removed Dion from command. After more turmoil, Dion was murdered, and Dionysius resumed his despotism, now hardened or jaded into cruelty. The Corinthian hero Timoleon organized an army of volunteers and liberated Syracuse from Dionysius, sending the deposed tyrant to Corinth, where he lived the remainder of his life teaching and begging for a living.

INFLUENCE Dionysius made his mark on history as a cautionary example of the folly of philosophers who think that they can change the world by influencing a prince and as an example of the power of a capricious fortune that could change a man from a tyrant to a beggar to a tyrant and again to a poor man.

FURTHER READING
Caven, Brian. *Dionysius I: War-Lord of Sicily.* New Haven, Conn.: Yale University Press, 1990.

Lilla, Mark. "The Lure of Syracuse." *New York Review of Books* 48, no. 14 (September 20, 2001): 81.

Smith, Christopher, and John Serrati, eds. *Sicily from Aeneas to Augustus: New Approaches in Archaeology and History*. Edinburgh, Scotland: Edinburgh University Press, 2000.

James A. Arieti

See also: Dionysius the Elder; Plato; Syracuse; Timoleon of Corinth.

Dorian Invasion of Greece

The battle for military and political dominance in southern Greece resulted in the replacement of the Mycenaean aristocracy by Dorians.

Date: c. 1120-950 B.C.E.
Category: Wars and battles
Locale: Peloponnesus (southern Greece)

SUMMARY Around 1200 B.C.E., Greece was in the late Bronze Age, a glamorous, heroic period. Many Greek tragedies and particularly Homer's *Odyssey* (c. 725 B.C.E.; English translation, 1614) and Aeschylus's *Oresteia* (458 B.C.E.; English translation, 1777) reflect not only the period's aristocratic traditions but also a threat to the established order. In Homer's epic poem, the boisterous suitors of Penelope attempt to supplant Odysseus's and Telemachus's rightful positions in Ithaca, while Aeschylus's dramatic trilogy depicts the actual usurpation of power at Mycenae by Aegisthus.

Beyond such literary representations, there is also substantial archaeological documentation for both the splendor of the late Bronze Age and the problems that it faced. In several sites in the Peloponnesus, such as Mycenae, Tiryns, and Pylos, archaeologists have found impressive palaces with substantial architecture and evidence of a writing system known as Linear B. Recorded in Linear B, along with grain, olive, wine, and livestock reports, are suggestions of an emergency mobilization against attack.

At Pylos (southwestern Peloponnesus), the Linear B archives, written on wet clay, were baked and thus preserved by a great fire that destroyed the palace. More or less the same pattern of destruction can be seen at other sites. The Linear B writing system disappeared, and for several centuries, the area's inhabitants were illiterate. The Dorians were responsible for these developments, but the precise nature of their takeover is unclear.

The literary sources that provide the principal details are relatively obscure. However, from Greek historian Diodorus Siculus's *Bibliotheca historica* (first century B.C.E.; *Diodorus of Sicily in Twelve Volumes*, 1950-1967) and Greek scholar Apollodorus of Athens's *Chronicle* (second century B.C.E.), the following account emerges: Heracles (also known as Hercules) was exiled by Eurystheus, the ruler of Tiryns in the northeastern Peloponnesus. Heracles' son Hyllus later attempted to return to his ancestral home but was killed in single combat with Echemus at the Isthmus of Corinth at the northeastern boundary of the Peloponnesus. Eventually, Hyllus's grandsons Temenus and Cresphontes and his great-grandsons Eurysthenes and Procles (sons of Aristodemus) again invaded the Peloponnesus. These invaders, called Dorians because they came from Doris in northern Greece, were more successful than Hyllus.

According to Apollodorus, the invasion route was from the northwest, as the Dorians crossed the strait at the western end of the Gulf of Corinth. Specific battles are not described, but Greek poet Pindar, in his *Isthmian Odes* (fifth century B.C.E.; *The Odes of Pindar*, 1947), assigns particular importance to the capture of Amyclae, near Sparta. In the course of the invasion, the Dorians slew Tisamenus, the son of Orestes and grandson of Agamemnon. With Tisamenus's death, the old Mycenaean royal line, dating back to Pelops (from whom the Peloponnesus derives its name) was extinguished. Finally, after conquering southern Greece, the victors divided its more fertile regions between themselves. Temenus received Argos, Cresphontes got Messenia, and Procles and Eurysthenes received Lacedaemon (the region around Sparta).

Since the early nineteenth century, scholars have generally regarded the idea of some kind of invasion from the north as the most substantial kernel of truth in the foregoing account. A different view, on the other hand, was developed in the 1970's by John Chadwick, one of the decipherers of Linear B. Working from linguistic evidence, Chadwick posits a Proto-Doric element in the population, already present in the Peloponnesus when the Linear B tablets were written. According to Chadwick's analysis, the ascendancy of Dorians over Mycenaeans resulted more from internal unrest or revolution than from outside invasion.

SIGNIFICANCE   Although the details concerning the decline of Mycenaean civilization are uncertain, it is clear that the Dorians had become dominant in southern Greece in the first millennium B.C.E. More specifically, points such as the dual kingship in Sparta are reflected in Apollodorus's work, according to which Lacedaemon was divided between two of the Dorian conquerors.

Further Reading

Chadwick, John. "Who Were the Dorians?" *Parola del Passato* 31 (1976): 103-117.

Hall, Jonathan M. *Ethnic Identity in Greek Antiquity*. Cambridge, England: Cambridge University Press, 1997.

Nixon, Ivor Gray. *The Rise of the Dorians*. New York: Frederick A. Praeger, 1968.

Edwin D. Floyd

See also: Aeschylus; Apollodorus of Athens (scholar and historian); Diodorus Siculus; Homer; Linear B; Pindar; Writing Systems.